Doing Your Own School

The Great Atlantic and Pacific School Conspiracy

Steve Arons	Walt Senterfitt
Alice Milmed	David Steinberg
Pam Senterfitt	Dorothy Stoneman

Royalties from the sale of this book will go in part for support of The Learning Place, a free junior and senior high school in San Francisco, and The Group School, a working-class high school in Cambridge, Mass.

Doing Your Own School

A Practical Guide
to Starting and Operating
a Community School

by The Great
Atlantic and Pacific
School Conspiracy

Beacon Press   Boston

Copyright © 1972 by Stephen Arons, Alice S. Milmed,
    J. Walton Senterfitt, Pamelle D. Senterfitt,
    David Steinberg, and Dorothy Stoneman

Library of Congress catalog card number: 72-491

International Standard Book Number: 0-8070-3172-0 (casebound)
                                    0-8070-3173-9 (paperback)

First published as a Beacon Paperback in 1973

Beacon Press books are published under the auspices
    of the Unitarian Universalist Association

Published simultaneously in Canada by Saunders of Toronto, Ltd.

Printed in the United States of America

The photographs in this book are by Steve Arons, who retains
    all reproduction rights to them.

9 8 7 6 5 4 3 2

Contents

v

About This Book

The six people who wrote this book came together with experiences at three schools, The Learning Place, The Group School, and The East Harlem Block Schools. The book is our attempt to collect and put in a useful form not only our own experiences but those of people working in many other new schools. While we six members of an imaginary conspiracy collectively wrote these pages, the work is really a product of the new school movement.

We started by contacting over a dozen new schools which seemed to us to represent different educational ideas and social values, run by people who are serious about their work and would be serious about their differences. You will find references to these schools throughout the book, and a brief description of each school at the end. We asked friends at each school to write or talk to us about their school, much as they would if they were trying to explain to someone how they had arrived where they are. As we read through the information we received, we noticed a number of common problems and a number of different solutions reached by each group. This became the central theme of our task—describing problems which often occur and telling of the practical solutions different people have reached.

Then began the laborious and entirely unfamiliar task of collective writing—six people trying to write one book together. There were agreements about a table of contents, drafts and redrafts of chapters, collective criticism of each other's work, egos damaged and repaired, and so much cross-editing that we are at a loss to say who really did write which section. The book was written and rewritten three times and between each draft there were very many helpful criticisms from friends and from people at new schools around the country.

Every book has a list of people who helped it to be born. Ours does, too. But in our case these people did so much of the hard, creative work involved that they might be listed as authors. Since they did not go through the head-banging drafting sessions, however, we thought it fairer to acknowledge their help without saddling them with the responsibility for the errors we may have made in putting the book together. We list everyone, including ourselves, with reference to the source of their contribution, in order to give a better idea of what went into making this book.

Mrs. Inez Andrey, former director, Martin Luther King School, San Francisco, Cal.

Judy Areen, Center for Study of Public Policy, Cambridge, Mass.

Nancy Arons, head teacher, Simmons Child Study Center, Boston, Mass.

Stephen Arons, teacher, The Group School, Cambridge, Mass.

John Cawthorne, Education Development Center, Newton, Mass.

Michaela Conger, co-founder and parent, Primary Life School, San Francisco, Cal.

Neil Didriksen, director, The Group School, Cambridge, Mass.

Jane Goldman, teacher, Primary Life School, San Francisco, Cal.

Carolyn Grace, freelance writer, Cambridge, Mass.

Judy Herrick, teacher, Berkeley Montessori School, Berkeley, Cal.

Phyllis Jarmolowich, Chairman, Parent Board, Ironbound Children's Center, Newark, N.J.

Joan Kessler, Michael Community School, Milwaukee, Wisc.

Gary Krane, Berkeley, Cal.

Charles Lawrence, director, Highland Park Free School, Roxbury, Mass.

Alice Milmed, teacher, The Learning Place, San Francisco, Cal.

Tim Parsons, Experimental Schools Project, Newark, N.J.

Tom Roderick, director, Day School, East Harlem Block Schools, New York, N.Y.

Pam Senterfitt, teacher, The Learning Place, San Francisco, Cal.

Walt Senterfitt, teacher, The Learning Place, San Francisco, Cal.

David Steinberg, freelance writer and former teacher, The Learning Place, San Francisco, Cal.

Susan Steinberg, former teacher, The Learning Place, San Francisco, Cal.

Dorothy Stoneman, former director, East Harlem Block Schools, New York, N.Y.

Derek Winens, Ironbound Children's Center, Newark, N.J.

Kathy Woodward, Center for Study of Public Policy, Cambridge, Mass.

We wish to thank the U.S. Office of Economic Opportunity. It was under grant number CG 8542 that part of the work which resulted in this book was done. The grant made it possible for everyone who helped to be fairly compensated for his/her work.

Finally, thanks to Beacon editor Ray Bentley for understanding us and this book. And thank you, Beacon Press, for publishing the Pentagon Papers.

Start at the Beginning

The purpose of this guide is to provide practical help to groups of people who want to start new schools (whether inside or outside the publicly funded system). People who are already working on new schools will also probably find this guide helpful in raising basic questions. We have assumed that our primary audience is parents and community groups, though we have at times addressed ourselves to teachers' groups, students, and even "educators." The focus of the guide is on primary schools, though there are some suggestions for high schools.

Many people begin to think about starting a school of their own because of dissatisfaction with existing public schools. Perhaps you believe your children or those of your community are not learning the basic skills they need to survive and to find a fair share of happiness. Perhaps the children are unhappy at school, or mistreated, or are not feeling confident about themselves and proud of their cultural and historical roots. Maybe you have tried to change the school and become frustrated. Or maybe you just have the feeling that things aren't going to get better soon enough to benefit your kids.

These feelings and experiences are often what are on people's minds when they draw together and utter that first "maybe we're going to have to do it ourselves." This guide was made by many people who are already doing it themselves. We have discovered that bad feelings about past schooling are often replaced by the excitement of working with kids, the strength of doing something for yourself, and the confidence of people who are building a community. The humor, seriousness, curiosity, and delight at learning, of children going to school in a healthy atmosphere cannot help but rub off on adults. The work of starting and running a new school has been energizing and meaningful and possible for many people.

There are, of course, plenty of problems waiting for you if you want to start a new school. This guide offers help on the first steps in recognizing and solving these problems, but before you begin reading you should have a sense of what is involved.

You will need to organize people around the idea of starting a school and you will have to arrive at some shared view of what you want out of the school. This means talking to friends in the community, meetings, studying other new schools, and the hard work of reaching an agreement to work together.

You will need to have a way of governing the school and arriving at decisions on which you can build. This means figuring out how much power parents, teachers, community people, and students should have.

You will need to get incorporated, file for a tax exemption, get insurance, and be sure you know all the applicable state and local regulations. This probably means finding a lawyer whom you trust.

You may want to find a director, and you will need to interview and hire teachers and other staff people. This means a lot of looking and many hard judgments about what kind of help you need and what kind of working relationships you want.

You will have to worry about money. This means understanding how to survive without much money and developing ways of increasing your resources without changing basic school values. If you are starting a school within the public system, or taking over an old one, your problem will not be money but administrative and political restrictions. We haven't discussed this subject but it could be a guide in itself.

You will need to enroll students. This means deciding how to define your community, how to be fair to all interested children and parents, and what your attitude is toward students.

You will need a building. This means looking for something that meets your own needs and then dealing with health, fire, and building inspectors.

You will need to develop a curriculum and gather materials. This means taking all your own value judgments and all the expert advice you can get and translating it into a working school.

You will need to get certified by state or local school authorities. Depending on the state you live in this process may be simple or complex. In most places you will need not only a clear sense of purpose, but plenty of political work and a firm notion of your legal rights.

You will need to deal with all the personal problems of people working together and learning together. This means tolerance, support, honesty, and a critical eye for bullshit.

When all those steps have been accomplished, you will just be starting a school. To do all this without losing the sense of what kind of school you are trying to build and what kind of education the kids need will require considerable commitment and long hours. You should be pretty sure that you want to do it before you start.

If you do want to start, this guide should help. It is designed to provide some possible answers to the common problems of starting and maintaining a school and to ask questions we have found are best brought into the open early, even if they cannot be immediately resolved.

People starting schools should be careful not to imagine that there is any *one* correct answer to questions they face. There isn't, and we have tried very hard not to suggest there is. One of the things we have learned in writing this guide, however, is that no learning or writing situation is free of value judgments. In point of fact, one of our main themes here is to encourage you to be aware of your own value judgments and not to shrink from stating them to others and then building a school around the result. You will find some of our biases in these pages but you will find nothing encouraging or condoning invidious discrimination and no instructions on how to show a profit while running a school.

The information contained in this guide was accurate to the best of our ability as of Spring, 1972; but good schools are constantly changing, and it's possible that some of the information we were given will become history next year. If you should contact any of the schools mentioned, you may find it useful to see what kinds of changes have taken place and why. We also must mention, partly for our own protection, that new schools, especially good ones, are swamped with requests for information and help. If all these requests were honored there wouldn't be time left for running the school or raising money to support it. Keep this problem in mind. Also keep in mind when asking someone for help in your project, it's fair to offer some help in exchange.

We hope this guide is helpful to you in getting your school off the ground, keeping it going, or deciding whether you want to start a school at all.

Enjoy yourself.

CHAPTER ONE

Be Clear About Your Goals

Starting a school can seem like an overwhelming task. There seem to be so many difficult issues to think about and resolve. Curriculum, staff, school governance, parental involvement, choosing students, getting accredited, finding a building. It's hard to know where to begin, especially when you're not sure you're really qualified to start a school. After all, we've been taught again and again that a school is a very special institution, an area best left to professionals who have long years of training and experience.

But when we break through the mystique of professionalism, we find the real work is not too hard or too complicated for us to do. And in many cases having these jobs done by non-professionals brings a fresh perspective and cuts through a lot of artificial complication. Many non-professional people who have started new schools have had the refreshing experience of discovering how much they can do themselves. The lesson of these new schools is that if people are ready to work hard and keep working as real difficulties arise, there's no reason why a group of "untrained" people—parents, inexperienced teachers, even students—can't start and run an excellent school. But where to begin?

Start at the beginning. Why do you want to start a school anyway? What would the ideal school be like for your situation? What do you want your school to accomplish? Broad questions like these are hard to think about concretely, but they are important. How you approach the more specific issues depends on what you're trying to do. If you're not clear on your purpose, all the rest is building on sand. When The Learning Place (a free junior high in San Francisco) was started, those of us who worked there found all sorts of new possibilities we had never even thought about when we were in school. It's so easy to limit yourself to making minor changes in familiar school models you see; but in starting a school, the sky's the limit. You may decide you want to stick fairly close to traditional models, but at least you have the choice.

Think about what a school is, down underneath all the particulars of books and class schedules. What does it mean to get an education? How does learning happen? When do people *want* to learn? How does a school help its neighborhood? How does school relate to other institutions in the community and the problems of the future? Public schools generally work off one particular notion of these issues; and you may agree or disagree with their direction. It's entirely up to you. Does a school mean desks in a row? Does it mean classes with one teacher and a bunch of kids? Does it mean classes at all?

As you begin to define your expectations, keep in mind that whatever you plan is likely to change once your school actually starts. In fact, some goals probably won't be clear until you have lived with your school for a while and seen it deal with real problems. It would be possible to set your goals so exactly and narrowly that your school would end up cramped from trying to fit reality into the framework you constructed. The best approach is to work out a clear set of expectations and to think of them flexibly, so you can refine your ideas as the school develops. Think carefully of goals before you start, but don't stop thinking about them after the school begins.

Too many schools think of goals in high-sounding general phrases that don't have much real content. Get under the rhetoric to a real sense of what you want to have happen. Don't feel your goals must be general enough for the whole world to admire; think of what makes sense to you and your community. If your sense of goals is clear, it will help to examine your school as it goes along and judge what's working and what's not.

In thinking about goals, start with the focus that brings your group together. Do you want to do a school based on a particular educational philosophy? A school for children with particular learning problems or abilities? A school focusing on the needs of a particular ethnic group or neighborhood? A school providing religious instruction, or an opportunity for parents to be actively involved in their children's education? All these types of schools have been started successfully somewhere.

Defining Goals

You may have a vague sense of what you want your school to be, but find it hard to pin down very exactly. You may find that different people involved in starting your school have different ideas about what it should be trying to do, or differing priorities among their various goals.

The people who started the Ironbound Community School (Newark, N.J.) dealt with these problems by organizing a series of seminars in which parents talked out the basic educational issues. The seminars met once a week for ten weeks, for two hours in the evening. Parents had a chance to discuss what they wanted, to have visiting experts advise on various issues, to visit other schools, see films, and evaluate new learning materials. Parents looked at the problems their children were having in school. They discussed their relationships with their children, including how their children were disciplined and how they learned. They recalled their own educational experience and how inadequate it was. They heard a speaker talk about using "open classrooms" as a specific educational technique. Out of all these discussions the parents found they gained a clearer sense of what they wanted for their children, and of how to begin moving to implement what they wanted. The goals of the school emerged directly from the seminars, and the process of meeting together over a period of time forged a cohesive group with a common sense of purpose.

Arriving at a common sense of purpose is not necessarily an easy process, and you should expect conflicts and difficulties. Discussions and meetings may not be the best way for you to arrive at your goals. Often people need to work on specific projects to understand their goals and motives clearly. Don't be afraid to begin some modest tasks as a way of understanding goals after thinking and talking and visiting have taken you as far as they can. The Group School (a working-class high school in Cambridge, Mass.) started with a wide variety of purposes and interests, not apparent to everyone. The school moved through a slow and painful process of setting up a part-time school. It required a great deal of energy, but in the process of working through these difficulties, the people produced an organization with a strong consensus around a limited set of goals. By the time the full-time school came into existence, the Group members had worked together closely enough to know themselves and the expectations of others pretty well.

The process used for defining goals by a small group of teachers may be different from the process used by a group of parents, and both may be different from a diverse group of students, teachers, and parents. Whatever process you follow for defining goals, however, you will do well to face disagreements early, rather than gloss over them with superficial language, only to have them reappear in more virulent form once your school begins. You may find the differences you uncover make it impossible to work together as a group. Michael Community School (an elementary community school in Milwaukee) found a division between parents who wanted predominantly Catholic education and parents who wanted to move away from a parochial context. Berkeley High Community School found the same division between people emphasizing political action and those emphasizing a particular educational philosophy. If such a division exists in your group, you will want to know about it early, so you can form two separate schools if necessary rather than spend all your energy fighting for control of a school that makes no one happy.

Some Goals

Some different kinds of goals of existing new schools are presented below. They reflect different issues schools have considered important. Not all will be relevant to you and your school, but some probably will be. We discuss these issues in the hope that specific examples will help you clarify your own goals.

Basic Skills. The most familiar goals for a school are those that focus on how much and what its students learn. We see this emphasized in the public schools through tests of reading levels and mathematical abilities. While many new schools seem to move away from this quantitative way of evaluating themselves, most have retained these specific learning goals for their students. The parents who formed the East Harlem Block Schools, for example, made it clear that they wanted their children to make definite progress in reading, writing, and math. The students here came primarily from Spanish-speaking families, and their parents were concerned that they become skilled in reading and writing English, while retaining their Spanish. With students who had difficulty in these areas, or who expressed little interest in these subjects, the parents expected the teachers to work extra hard to generate that interest.

Other schools also set specific learning goals, but in less traditional areas. A school focusing on the needs and interests of Black students might want to stress a Black studies curriculum or one based on the political and economic needs of the Black community. In another instance, ecology and natural sciences might be stressed, or particular job skills, or knowledge of how to use the political process. Your view of what kinds of knowledge it takes to survive in the world may determine your specific learning goals.

Some schools, less concerned about the specific knowledge or subject matter, focus on a variety of characteristics they would like to see their students develop. Berkeley Montessori School, for example, emphasizes that its students learn to use all their senses in discovering the world around them, that they learn to take care of themselves and their environment. San Francisco School wants its teachers to foster student independence, so that individual students will be able to follow their curiosity and discover what is important to them. Both these schools are concerned that students not fall into patterns of simply doing what they are told by adult authorities. They want their students to learn to define their own interests and activities, to become self-motivated learners. The East Harlem Block Schools put it this way: "This kind of sensitivity is necessary for . . . giving the children the power they will need to forge the alternatives which mean personal freedom for themselves and their people."

The goals of some schools reflect a basic concern for personal growth among students. Presidio Hill School in San Francisco works to give its students a positive sense of themselves and at the same time to have them appreciate the differences, the uniqueness, the contribution of others. Related to this is the goal of "breaking down stereotypes of all kinds: race, sex, age, ethnic, socio-economic, or whatever." The Learning Place makes its personal growth goals more specific in the following list: "Learning to make decisions for yourself,

learning to evaluate your own work, learning how to work in cooperation with others and how to work alone, finding and evaluating other
people's information as a step toward reaching your own conclusions,
coming to grips with what it means to be a man or a woman, becoming aware of your strengths and weaknesses, understanding and ex-
pressing your emotions on a variety of levels, and developing rich
relationships with other individuals."

The age of the student you intend to enroll may influence appropriate goals. As students get older you may want to help them figure
out the direction they want to move in over the next few years, and
help them to be able to set up an educational program that facilitates
this growth. This involves students assuming responsibility for their
own lives, allowing students to choose their own educational programs, and encouraging participation in the governance of the school.

The Learning Process. Schools often set goals about *how* learning
should come about, emphasizing the personal and teaching relationships in the school. These goals are particularly important to people
who have started schools in order to practice a particular educational
philosophy; but people starting schools for other reasons have also
been concerned about process and the feel of their school.

A common theme among new schools emphasizes students' learning by being free to choose their interests and to follow them through.
The concern here is that students be able to pursue their unique
interests, with the teacher helping them as they define what they want
to do. According to one school, a teacher may help students move on
their own interests and may suggest work, but may not play so active
a role as to "interfere with the child's interest in learning" or his
curiosity. A similar process concern among the East Harlem Block
schools was that their children enjoy their school, get along well with
teachers, and be treated with kindness and respect. Some of these
schools have been surprised by how well students learn even the academic subjects in this atmosphere.

Many schools seek to substitute cooperation for competition in
learning. They strive to build a feeling of community, of mutual acceptance and trust that includes both teachers and students. To accomplish this a school may use frequent school meetings, encounter
groups, rap sessions, camping trips, and learning marathons, as well as

reducing student competition in the classroom. Identities as staff people and students may be de-emphasized so people can be more like members of a learning community where each individual is respected and where people learn from each other. The New Community School (Oakland, Cal.) has a motto that "teachers teach students, students teach teachers, and students teach each other."

The Learning Place sets the goal of having its learning process include as much encounter of new and unfamiliar areas as possible. The school accepts failure as part of the process, and does not try to avoid failure. Students are encouraged to try new areas and activities, even if they're not sure they will be able to succeed. Working with students to overcome fear of failure supports this process of exploration.

How learning takes place at your school will depend on *what* your students are trying to learn. To complete the circle, the process you establish for learning will, in turn, influence what subjects or skills your students explore. Because of this close interrelationship, it's important that your skill goals and process goals harmonize well. You may think there will be a conflict between learning and process goals. For example, you may want children to learn math but also enjoy themselves and follow their own curiosity. Ironbound Community School was able to harmonize these goals because it found that when it allowed students to roam anywhere in the building and pursue interests, this natural pursuit resulted in learning even the standard subjects.

Teachers and Parents. Although students usually receive most consideration in thinking about goals, it's good to remember that teachers and parents are also important and to consider what your school will do for them. This is dealt with in more detail in sections about staff and parents, but we mention it here because you should think about teachers and parents as you formulate more general goals. The kind of work teachers feel comfortable with, the degree of support and criticism they need, and the best atmosphere for them to be comfortable should be discussed. So too with the parents. How parents relate to teachers, what roles parents want to play and should play according to the school's goals, what parents get out of being part of the school, and how much the school relies on parents for its existence are all important in defining your goals. All people in your school community will have needs to be met by participating in that community.

Community Development. Schools are often begun by people in a specific neighborhood and grow as an expression of the life and interests of that community. For these schools, goals that go beyond the traditional are often important. Perhaps your vision of a school is not simply as a learning place for children but as a community institution serving many other needs. Perhaps social and personal needs of the school's families are also going to be a part of your program. Day care, health services, family counseling, recreation may all be included. Perhaps, too, you see a community school as one which concerns itself with the social and political issues its community faces. Thus, The Group School specifically sets the goal of relating itself to issues like housing, jobs, unemployment, racism. As a community institution, The Group School is working more explicitly to establish a viable community organization controlled by and responsive to the community in which it exists. The school works to help its students become more aware of community concerns, and to develop skills and discover possibilities for returning to the community in which they have been raised.

Michael Community School (Milwaukee) sees itself fundamentally as a resource to provide varied educational facilities to its entire community. Not only does the school work with students, it also includes many other community functions—adult education, health programs, nutrition information, and community social activities.

The East Harlem Block Schools act as an advocate for the children and their families, educating parents on their health needs and rights —on how to get what they need from local hospitals, for example. A parent coordinator works with parents in welfare centers and with landlords. The school is a focus around which parents can come together and work to have their needs met by the larger society. In the school parents, students, and teachers can work to educate themselves, to bring themselves together, to take effective social action. This point is stressed in the following excerpt from an article by Tom Roderick, of East Harlem Day School:

By way of summary I shall try to distill from these experiences the feelings and thoughts which stand foremost in my mind as I work with children in East Harlem and share with them and their parents the struggle to build a school.

I begin by taking the concerns of the parents very seriously. Their anxieties about the behavior and academic progress of their children in school cannot be dismissed as retrogressive or conservative. Their children are growing up in a ghetto. Black or Puerto Rican and poor, the children have two strikes against them already in a racist society which destroys many and leaves many more virtually powerless. Their struggle is for survival; and above all they need power: personal power, which includes self-esteem, cultural pride, and basic academic skills; and collective power, the faith that through concerted action people can change the institutions which affect their lives. Only with these kinds of strengths will they be able to confront the society and forge the alternatives which mean personal freedom.

The alternative of the street is there already: for some it is a viable path; for most it is not. Our goal at the Day School is to help the children develop other alternatives, so that when they come of age, they have choices, real choices, about the kinds of lives they want to lead. As alternatives open up for them we hope that the children will not grow to reject the street and their cultural background but maintain respect for them while working for change.

This means that we are primarily concerned with developing in the children a sense of hope, of faith in their power to help shape the future. Fostering hope begins with the individual child finding and developing his strengths in the classroom; it leads right into politics: working together to effect change.

To pursue these goals, parents, teachers, and children at the East Harlem Day School are shaping a school which is unique: our school is not patterned on a particular model but represents our attempt to find the most relevant approach to the needs of our particular children and community. What we are coming to shows the influences of Leicestershire and of Schools for the Future. We believe that children learn best from involvement with materials; that the teacher's role is crucial but that children can also learn a great deal on their own and from each other; that children need to have the freedom to move around and talk and relate freely with each other; that the best learning begins with what the children bring but does not stop there; that learning should not be fractured into different subjects offered at different times in a disjointed way but that children should be encouraged to develop their interests through projects which integrate different disciplines and modes of expression; and that children should take on a great deal of the responsibility for selecting their activities.

Yet this basic framework is not in itself true freedom and independence. It is only one precondition for freedom. If the choices offered to children are boring, if the child gets no help in seeing the possibilities of the material or activity, then his "freedom" to choose is meaningless. If he chooses, for example, to work in mathematics, but only does teacher-made exercises in a mechanical way, then his freedom is severely curtailed. On the other hand, he is no further ahead if he plays with mathematics materials but gets no guidance from someone who can open up new possibilities for him. The fullest kind of freedom is to be able to learn, discover and do significant creative work on your own.

Social Action. A number of schools see themselves actively involved in a still broader process of social action going beyond the immediate school community. Some see starting a new school as a lever for changing public education in their city. Other schools deal with social conditions explicitly in their curricula or work to influence public and other private schools toward change.

New Community School defines itself as "an educational institution in the movement for social justice." It sees itself as a community taking action on specific issues in the larger community and society. This learning process helps students become aware of the needs of oppressed peoples and the issues involved in their liberation. The school encourages its students, parents, and teachers to move on these issues, to train themselves in new kinds of action, and to evaluate the effectiveness of this action as they go along.

The East Harlem Block Schools have found their community perspective has broadened from a preoccupation with the needs of the local community to an awareness of the schools' relationship with poor communities throughout the country. The schools now try to be responsive to other community groups working to establish similar

schools, and to constantly represent the needs of poor people in negotiations with day care administrations.

The more you clarify your goals, the easier it will be for you to
develop. With a clear basic direction, and a strong sense of common
purpose, you will have a good foundation for dealing with later conflicts. You will be able to refer to your purposes, and avoid the
situation of new people expecting something different from what
you're doing and then being disappointed and resentful.

Once you arrive at a clear sense of common goals, you will have
worked together as a group, gaining a sense of how that feels and the
conflicts it produces. You will have a sense of being a close-knit group
of people doing something together.

What's left is to translate your goals into the reality of a working
school.

CHAPTER TWO

Governing Your School

Who will make the decisions in a new school?
Who will decide the general direction, the educational philosophy,
   the administrative structure and procedure?
Who will make the many day-to-day practical decisions?
Who will hire and fire teachers and administrators?
Who will ultimately resolve conflicts?

The purposes of the school will influence how these questions will be answered. If your purpose is to be a parent cooperative, obviously you will want parents to have the ultimate authority, and the formal structure would reflect that. Public schools are considered to serve the interests of the entire city or district, and thus their governing boards are usually elected by vote of all registered voters, whether or not they are parents. Many established private schools have self-perpetuating governing boards, composed perhaps of parents, former parents, and non-affiliated individuals who have an interest in the school. Some new schools for junior high and high school students are governed by boards on which students are the majority and staff the minority.

Governing Board and Representation

Most schools have a governing board, frequently called a board of directors, which sets the overall direction and philosophy of the school, makes budgetary and other major financial decisions, and (usually) hires and fires at least the principal or director, and perhaps the teaching staff as well.

In deciding whether to have a board of directors or some other central governing committee, keep in mind the need to have decisions made and not simply discussed and left hanging. Especially in the first year of a new school, the number of basic decisions which must be made can be staggering. Having a process in which your entire community or school is involved may become cumbersome and too slow to really respond to the need to keep the school developing.

On the other hand, it's important to be sure the board is responsible to the community and doesn't get carried away with its own authority. This can cause great dissension, and frustrate efforts to have everyone feel he/she is contributing to the development and governance of the school. One school deals with the problem by publishing all board decisions throughout the school and allowing a majority of the school members (in this case teachers and students) to reverse a board decision at any of the periodic community meetings. This board is also very careful to discuss issues with school members before making decisions—to bring crucial issues directly to the community.

Whatever your decision you should think carefully about the balance of power between school and board. The problem of allocation of power will also arise for the director and staff (see Chapter Six). Frequently there are one or more committees making decisions in particular areas within the general policies of the governing board. For instance, often a personnel committee plays a major role in hiring and firing teachers. Other committees sometimes include budget, curriculum, building, admissions. Committees provide a way of involving more people and perhaps of getting work done faster, but cumbersome committee structures sometimes create more work than they are worth. In this instance, as with others concerning governance, be sure you are creating government needed because of actual work to be done rather than government simply for its own sake.

Who should be represented on the board? The starting point for answering this question might be parents. If you are a group of parents starting a school, you may well want the board to be entirely parents. Even if you are a group of teachers or other citizens, you may consider that parents—especially of young children—should have the ultimate authority over their children's education.

If you are planning a community school, there may be other

interests you want represented, such as outstanding community leaders who are not going to have children in your school. Or you may wish to have an all-community election of board members of your school. Some community schools have run into the problem that more experienced parents or community leaders—often those with middle-class backgrounds—tend to dominate board and committee discussions and decisions. If part of the community school's goal is to involve those parents previously most excluded from participation in their children's education, it may decide to limit the board to low-income parents or stipulate that the board and its committees must have a large majority of low-income members.

If a goal of your school is to have a racial and ethnic balance or diversity in the student body, you will want to make sure that the board reflects the same balance and diversity.

What about teachers and staff? Are they to be regarded primarily as employees and advisors or as partners in the whole educational process with some interests of their own that deserve to be represented on the board? Frequently, community or parent-cooperative schools serving low-income parents inexperienced in organizations want to make sure that professional educators do not dominate decisionmaking. They often decide that the board should be all parents, with the staff in an advisory capacity, though obviously respected and relied upon.

You may decide that the teachers have a legitimate interest in helping shape the school along with parents and students and so should be formally represented on the board. This most commonly happens when the school is started by a group of teachers or a group of parents, students, and teachers together.

The question of board membership is closely related to the way you define the school community. You must consider not only who will be on the board, but who will be allowed to vote for board nominees. You might, for example, have only parents on the board, but allow teachers to vote in elections along with parents. The subject of defining the school community is dealt with in Chapter Four.

Students and Decisionmaking—Who Is Running This Place?

Some important questions to consider include, "How much distinction is there to be between students and teachers?" "What kinds of responsibilities should students have?" "How much are the teachers willing to trust the judgment of the students?"

Existing schools involve students in school governance to widely varying degrees. Elementary and pre-schools naturally delegate little decisionmaking responsibility to the kids. Many new junior high and high schools involve students intimately in school functioning.

At both The Group School and New Community School (Oakland, Cal.), students participate in setting basic school policy. New Community School states explicitly that:

> "Students are on the Board of Directors and school committees so they will be in positions where they can lead, where their views can make a difference in how the school operates and what it does. The actuality of the school should be shaped as much by the students as by the staff."

Schools have found they can derive important benefits from involving students in this area. Taking part in decisionmaking often helps students become responsible for themselves and aware of the personal difficulty in applying group standards to people with different views. In sharing responsibility with students, adults also reduce the likelihood of misinterpreting student opinions and making decisions that breed student dissatisfaction. In addition, if adults handle all governance and policymaking, children are more likely to view them with the awe, distrust, and fear they sometimes assign to authorities.

Although it's definitely possible to structure a school to include student involvement on these levels, it's not easy for students or staff to become accustomed to this degree of sharing responsibility. For example, student say in handling finances at The Learning Place involved deciding whether money would be allotted for staff medical insurance coverage. It's necessary to consider situations like these and determine whether staff members are willing to accept the possible personal consequences. In most cases students seem to be careful in carrying out their responsibilities and making decisions for their community. In the health-plan discussion, careful consideration resulted in the community decision that it was necessary for the teachers' coverage to be paid by the school.

The fact that student decisions usually agree with those of the staff does not necessarily mean that students handle these unusual responsibilities with ease. When students are suddenly given administrative power, they often find the burden of responsibility too great and resort to trying to please the teachers by guessing what the teachers' response would be and acting accordingly.

While it seems desirable to involve students where possible, both students and adults have trouble accepting this concept. Schools have arrived at several methods of dealing with this difficulty. Each measure is only a partial answer and will be most effective when used with the others.

The Group School has tried to handle student insecurities in decisionmaking by clarifying, redefining, and limiting particular responsibilities to make them more manageable. Students can more easily accept responsibility when they do not feel the entire burden of leadership has descended on them. Along with this measure should come an understanding that more responsibilities will follow as the student community feels more comfortable and able to accept them. Progressive, gradual increase of power is also less threatening than immediate total sharing of the burden. Finally, staff support should accompany student decisionmaking from the start. Teachers must look for students' insecurities at every step and discuss them with students, stressing that these insecurities are shared by adults—because they are.

Involving and Training Parents

If you have decided you want parents to play a major role in running your school, you are going to have to help them overcome a good deal of initial reluctance, inexperience, and even fear. You will be asking parents to do something they more than likely have never done before. They, like most of us, have been conditioned to believe that only professional educators know what's the right kind of education for their children. At first many will still believe they don't know enough and can't learn enough to make wise decisions about educational and administrative matters. Besides, many parents will be new to things like boards of directors, budgets, hiring staff, and the other organizational processes and procedures in running a school. Overcoming negative conditioning and inexperience will be gradual, but here are some hints drawn from the experience of other schools; and you can probably think of more yourself:

1. Run seminars or workshops for all interested parents so they can become familiar with the educational and administrative issues and choices involved in setting up the school. As the school gets closer to actual operation, run more specific training workshops in the different skills parents will need to know. Board members may want training, for example, in conducting meetings, group process, asking questions of professionals, getting information needed for decisions. Personnel committee members may want special training in reviewing applicants' qualifications, conducting interviews, investigating previous experience. All parents should be invited to workshops in the curriculum the school adopts, so they can become familiar with what their children will be learning and how they can help them at home. In general, continuing in-service training of parents is as important as in-service training of teachers and other school staff.

2. Have the staff go out of their way to present issues to parents and make the parents decide on them before proceeding to other business. One technique is for the staff to stimulate vigorous reaction and consideration by aggressively presenting a proposal they know parents will oppose. This method is an honest one, of course, only if the staff makes it quite clear they intend to follow the parents' decision even if it is directly opposed to the staff proposal.

3. Set up one or more staff positions of parent coordinator, to be filled by a parent, with the responsibility of involving other parents in the school by home visits, small group meetings, helping board and committee members prepare for meetings so they feel good about their role in them, helping teachers make parents feel welcome in the classroom and conferences, etc.

4. Employ parents as assistant teachers, community teachers, home workers, and in whatever other positions they can fill now or be trained for. They will immediately contribute a strong parent and community perspective to the school that will help make other parents feel welcome and feel like it's their school. As they become more confident in their positions, and as they learn more about teaching, they can help explain everything about school to new parents and help them gradually feel competent to participate. Also, simply by holding positions of responsibility in the school, they serve as positive models for new parents.

5. Try to see that experienced, articulate parents and staff do not dominate meetings and discussions to the exclusion of less confident, newer parents. This can be a special problem with low-income parents who have not had much, if any, previous experience as participating members of organizations. One school moved to counteract this problem by providing that at least 75 percent of all board and committee slots had to be filled by low-income parents. Another school tried to reduce staff domination of discussions by providing that staff members not attend regular board meetings unless specifically requested to do so by the board.

Day-to-Day Decisionmaking

Once you have a process established for making broad decisions, you need to think about how they are going to be carried out and how all large and small operational decisions are going to be made. It's good to think clearly about several things:

1. Some person or group should be clearly responsible for each kind of decision necessary to run the school. One of the most frustrating things about large schools and school systems is the fuzziness in responsibility; individuals are always passing the buck and sending complainers on a runaround. This can happen also in smaller, alternative schools, either because of insufficient planning or well-meaning attempts to share authority and keep any one person or group from dominating.

2. Make sure that individuals with responsibilities in certain areas are free to make reasonable decisions on their own to carry out these responsibilities. But at the same time you don't want teachers or administrators making what are actually policy decisions in the guise of day-to-day operational decisions. For example, sometimes a problem will come up which the school has never faced before in the same way. Suppose the issue is whether or not to admit a student with special emotional and learning difficulties. Suppose that normally the director is empowered by the board to admit students within the standards approved by the board. If the director were to decide by himself in this case, it might become a precedent that would eventually significantly change the nature of the student body without any careful discussion and deliberation by the board. Perhaps the general rule should be that both staff and board should always examine day-to-day decisions for issues that have not yet been thought out and decided by the board, or other appropriate decisionmaking bodies.

A similar problem arises when the director or a staff member has a particular kind of skill or expertise that no one else possesses. Sometimes such a person makes policy decisions by himself in the process of exercising that expertise. For example, suppose a staff member is expert at writing funding proposals and negotiating with foundations or other government agencies for funding. In the process of negotiations, situations frequently arise when the agency will not agree to fund exactly what the school wants, but will give money for a different program or the original one with certain changes. Should the school agree? Obviously, in most cases the decision should lie with the board or with some other group representing the school's constituency. But many times the habit of respecting a professional's expertise will lead to letting him/her decide since only he/she understands the technical points involved and can judge what the funding agency will actually agree to.

One structural means some parent-controlled schools use in dealing with this danger is to provide that each professional educator in the school, from directors to teachers, works all the time as part of a team including parent paraprofessional staff members or board members. The East Harlem Block Schools provide that some board members can also be parent staff, so there is a link between the parent members of staff teams and board decisions. It works well in both directions; parent staff know what the board decided and what its general thinking is and can remind professional staff whenever necessary. They can also take back to the board an intimate knowledge of day-to-day work and decisions of the school.

Balancing Individual Rights with School Needs

Until the last couple of generations, individual educators had very few rights in the structure of American education. A serious, competent teacher could be fired with no recourse if some parent came to hold a personal grudge or if a school board member's daughter needed a teaching job, or if he/she expressed unpopular views. As school systems became consolidated and bureaucratized, and as teachers banded together to fight for rights and protection, the balance swung in the opposite direction. Tenure is granted teachers and administrators after a very short time and with little or no real evaluation of their competence and dedication. Afterwards, it's difficult to remove teachers even when they are clearly incompetent, uncooperative, or insensitive to the cultures and lives of their students.

New schools must wrestle with this dilemma and find some middle ground that feels right to both staff and parents (or students or the community at large). If you decide to offer tenure to teachers, you should think through what length of service and what kind of evaluation is appropriate before it is granted. Furthermore, you should think about fair procedures for challenging and removing even a tenured teacher if that should become necessary. Many schools have decided against giving tenure, and only have contracts which must be renewed at the end of each year. Some schools also provide a probationary period for new teachers at the beginning of each year, during which they could be removed with cause without receiving the remainder of their year's salary.

In cases where an individual staff member's effectiveness is questioned, it's very important to have a process for decision known in advance and accepted as fair by both parents and teachers. The real key to whether it works depends on the trust among all members of the school community—a trust built gradually and tested in a series of actual problems and crises.

The same difficulty may arise in cases of possible expulsion or transfer of students. Suspension and expulsion have been so abused by public schools that your school may wish to adopt a blanket policy that there will be no expulsions for any reason. On the other hand, instances may arise when it becomes clear that your school is simply not capable of educating a particular child. Providing the school commits itself to finding another place where the child can be happier and better educated, and providing the process for doing this seems fair and sensitive to the family involved, it may be in the school's and the family's best interest to allow the child to leave.

Size and Centralization

Most people realize that a key problem of the public school systems is sheer size, both of individual units and the entire system. If you are seriously interested in a participatory form of school governance and a non-bureaucratic form of learning, the question of size is important. In a very small school—50 or fewer students—it's not too difficult for everyone to participate. In general school meetings everyone can ask questions and make suggestions. But the larger the school, the more difficult participation becomes. It's very easy to have good formal democracy, a board elected by all the parents, for example. But if this is the only or main means of participation, most parents are going to be excluded or represented only indirectly. They still have the power of raising hell if they don't like what's going on, and with a parent board the chances are their complaints will be sympathetically heard. But this is really just a negative or veto power. Very few parents are actually involved in planning or deciding what steps to take.

One way of solving the problem is by having a decentralized structure, as the East Harlem Block Schools do. Here, the parents of each classroom elect one member to the board of directors. The "local school committee," comprising not more than three classrooms, makes much of the policy affecting those classrooms and hires and fires teachers in that local unit. One factor contributing to the success of their structure is its slow and careful development. The parents originally founded a day care center, then a kindergarten class, and have since added one elementary grade per year.

Sharing Information

Everyone knows of organizations which are open on paper, but are in fact controlled by a small group or even one person. Frequently this can be traced to the fact that this small group, or an executive director, control the flow of information. Since they know the most, they naturally have the most say in decisions. Even if someone else feels strongly about an issue, he can be neutralized by statements like, "But you don't know all the facts."

It's important to be conscious of how information is shared. Are there regular meetings to share information with different groups of people in the school? Is the board consulted and involved *before* policy alternatives or proposals are presented? Or, if not, are staff proposals presented early enough for the board to have plenty of time to investigate the issues and consider alternatives? Are all board meetings open to all parents and/or students? Are staff meetings open to parents?

We have touched on some of the main issues to think about in planning how your school will be run. The process of incorporating (see Chapter Ten) may be a good first occasion for working on these issues. Obviously, all problems cannot be prevented by having a beautiful structure and set of procedures. Often what goes on in organizations is much different, for better or worse, than what its formal structure implies. So you must also think about how these structures will actually work in practice and what extra steps you must take to make them do what you want them to do.

CHAPTER THREE

Parents

What will it mean to be a parent at your school? Possible parent roles in governing a school have already been discussed in the chapter on governance. Beyond that, what about other roles for parents, roles that are possible in new schools perhaps for the first time?

Starting from your purposes, think about how closely you want parents to be involved, and how important that involvement is to you. Do you want parents to take primary responsibility for some areas? Are there some areas in which parents would not be particularly helpful? If it comes down to a question of limited time and energy, how much time can you spend developing effective parent roles? What are the long-term consequences of not working closely with parents?

When The Learning Place (a junior high) was started, the founders assumed parents should be involved, the more the better, and this involvement would grow naturally from the informal nature of the school. As the school developed, both assumptions proved wrong. It became clear that there were many blocks to parental involvement, that school staff usually put the day-to-day work of the school ahead of working with parents. The staff also found students were opposed to having their parents so closely involved and, further, when the question was raised with parents directly, they agreed with the students.

After the school had been in operation for some time, however, it was found that the political and economic support of parents was essential to the school's survival. Support was difficult to get unless parents identified more with The Learning Place. More important, it was discovered that students had to deal with two very different sets of expectations about their school work—those reflecting the school's standards (heavily influenced by the kids) and those reflecting the standards of each child's parents. If parents and school were to avoid undermining each other, The Learning Place would have to put more energy into familiarizing parents with the school and opening roles for them in the school.

It was awareness of the relationship between school, students, and parents which enabled The Learning Place to shift its position. The lesson seems to be that whatever your decisions on parent involvement, they should be flexible and not based just on assumptions about what *ought* to be.

If you decide you want parents to be closely involved, you can begin to anticipate some of the problems other schools have had and begin looking for ways to overcome them.

Parent-School Distance

One basic problem arises because parents, traditionally, aren't involved in the day-to-day, nine-to-three activity of a school. Consequently, while students and teachers can begin working together closely as a real community, parents have trouble sharing this sense of group work and commitment. Without this shared sense, all other forms of parental involvement tend to be strained and distant. Parents feel uncomfortable relating to the ongoing work community, have only peripheral information on what is happening, and may misunderstand much of the school program. Swamped with the work of doing a school, teachers often become preoccupied with the immediate problems and neglect working with parents. This makes the separation of parents even more acute.

At Presidio Hill School (an elementary school in San Francisco), parents form a majority of the governing board, but their other involvement is limited to organizing fund-raising events and helping with field trips. Basically they are content to have the hired staff be responsible for the school's daily activities. Relations between staff and parents have been strained because of this separation between parent governance and parent involvement. Basic divisions of this sort between policymakers and those implementing policies day-to-day arise from the widely differing responsibilities of the two groups. More parent involvement might reduce tensions by helping staff and parents adopt similar perspectives on the school's problems.

The structural distance separating parents from teachers and students often stems from feelings among both parents and staff that the school should basically be left to the professionals, meaning the staff. Parents often feel they have little to offer a school because they don't have any formal educational training or experience. And staff often reinforce this with their own sense that teachers are the people who know what's best for the school.

Integral Parent Involvement

An important consideration in dealing with the problem of distance is finding ways that parental involvement becomes an *integral* part of the school operation, rather than an appendage grafted onto the school "because it would be nice to have the parents more involved." The latter kind of involvement generally fails because it isn't essential to the school and generates little energy and interest. The most successful roles for parents seem to evolve out of situations like that of the East Harlem Block Schools, where parents are not only employed as regular assistants to the teaching staff, but the staff is accountable to the parents in a very practical way. At the East Harlem Block Schools, 28 out of 50 staff are parents, and 35 parents also serve on various governing committees. Parental involvement includes teaching assistantships, day-to-day school planning, administration, and working as counsellors. Parents are constantly involved in the day-to-day process of the school. They attend all regular meetings of the professional staff. They have enough information to be an integral force in making decisions and working problems through. Their work is not a luxury to the school, it's vital. The school would close if 35 parents could not be found to accept this kind of responsibility.

It should be noted that this program was developed with great effort and energy by both staff and parents. The arrangements involve close working relationships between parents and staff, both in school and out, and a high level of trust. Staff members recognize the importance of parents being involved, and communicate their desire for involvement in their dealings with parents. The energy they put into working with parents far exceeds that of most other schools.

To build parents' confidence and parent-staff relationships, the Block Schools have used guidance groups and personal counselling for staff and parents together, run by a professional mental health consultant. They use home visits and frequent consultations with parents in groups, in addition to the day-to-day school work parents do. They have worked conscientiously in recognizing and overcoming parental feelings of being unskilled, at having little they felt was important to offer. The development of these working relationships has taken much time and work, but it seems necessary in order to have a truly functional form of parent-staff working community. Two basic factors in such a program's success are: staff must be totally committed to working with and for parents; and parents already on staff or governing committees must be totally committed to drawing in more parents.

Helping Parents Become Involved

It's important in working with parents to be sensitive to their anxieties and look for ways to openly encourage participation and build confidence. You may want to set up special meetings where parents talk about what's on their minds in a relaxed, informal atmosphere. You may want to encourage your teachers to work energetically with parents, and build the strongest possible personal relationships in order to help them feel at ease and willing to express their thoughts. You may want to run workshops for staff and parents on educational issues and techniques, so parents can become familiar with the professionals' way of working and language, and vice versa. You may want to have some of the more confident parents work directly with other parents in encouraging their help. If you simply expect parents to speak up and work their way into the school on their own, you will probably be disappointed, even if your school is initially put together by parents. As The Learning Place found, developing parent participation takes real energy. It also requires a structure that forces staff to deal with the parents' concerns, and in some cases yield to their control and direction.

Advantages for Parents

What are the advantages for parents if they become involved? At the East Harlem Block Schools parents have a better understanding of their child's development and educational requirements. There has also been a definite sense of personal satisfaction and achievement from making positive, working contributions to a school instead of being intimidated by the "professional" educators.

In some schools, the benefits are more concrete, involving adult education, family health, and day care. The more parents become integrated into these schools, the more family services develop.

At The Learning Place, a major focus of school activity is helping students become conscious of their feelings about growing up, taking responsibility for themselves, and working through difficulties of becoming men and women. The staff talks with students about their relationships with their families and this leads to working with parents directly.

Staff members have talked with parents at length about family relationships and in some cases have made real progress in helping to resolve difficult situations. Groups of parents have been brought together to talk with each other about problems they feel in their families. It's possible to go further and develop a parent counseling program on a regular basis, though it's not an easy task and should not be attempted until you have some experience working with difficult family situations.

The close relationship between teachers and students not possible in public school allows teachers to provide outside perspectives to both parents and students. Doing it is difficult—parents may be reluctant to have outsiders "meddle in family affairs." But if you can create an atmosphere of mutual trust, the results can be exciting for everyone involved, and contribute to closer parent relationships with the school in other areas as well.

It's well to remember that it's difficult for a parent to be confronted with a personal assessment of his/her child or the family situation. The problem of trust, privacy, and protectiveness, and sometimes defensiveness, should be discussed openly with groups of parents. Perhaps in such group discussion suggestions can be made about how to respect and discuss different staff and parent opinions about a child without having the situation viewed as criticism or unwanted meddling. Then private conferences can take place based on these suggested methods.

Parental Support at Home

One parent role that is of vital importance, though not related to direct involvement in the school, is providing active support for students when they are at home. In a new school, students have to adjust to new expectations of them and to a new school environment. This is particularly true if the school you start differs radically from traditional schools. The adjustment isn't easy for teachers and parents, and it's certainly not any easier for students. The first months of a new school are marked by the turmoil of this adjustment, as students and teachers together work out new forms of relationships and build a whole new structure of personal interaction.

If parents are not supportive of what is being built at the new school, the student finds himself torn between school and home. Perhaps a new set of expectations is forming at the school, but his parents' expectations are still associated with previous schools. In addition to his own uncertainties about the new situation, he must deal with parental pressure. The results can be disastrous.

It's vital, therefore, that parents actively and energetically support the experimentation their children are doing by being part of a new school. To make this possible, it's important that staff clearly explain what's happening at school, particularly the new and unfamiliar. Staff should watch for questions and misgivings that parents may be reluctant to verbalize, and work with parents to achieve a shared set of expectations for the students. In many schools, staff members are content if parents leave them alone and keep quiet about their doubts. But this is hardly sufficient for a student having trouble with new forms of learning. The difference between active parental support and passive, reluctant acceptance of something not fully understood can make the difference between success and failure of a school with a specific student, or even the success or failure of the school as a whole. The support you will generate from working for a true sense of common understanding with parents will also go beyond the immediate effect on students to help avoid parent-staff conflicts in later situations.

CHAPTER FOUR

School Membership

Defining Community of Interests
or Community of Neighbors

The usual starting point in determining the make-up of the student body is choosing between a school serving a particular geographic community (a defined neighborhood) and a school serving people with common interests (arts, ecology) or sharing certain characteristics (Spanish speaking).

Many existing schools require residence in a particular community or general area. For example, Michael Community School and New Community School serve a particular geographical area and attempt to reflect the racial and economic aspects of the community. The Group School has a different focus; it's designed mainly for students from a white working-class area. It originated to ". . . consist predominantly of students from working-class and low-income families . . . both black and white."

Other schools serve only certain kinds of children. At the East Harlem Block Schools, for example, most of the children come from poor families; district lines for the school were originally drawn to include only tenement buildings. Your school might also be based primarily on the arts or might be weighted heavily toward a science curriculum. It may have a defined curriculum method, such as Montessori, or it may be most interested in children with perceptual handicaps. The list of "specialties" is endless, but in each case the prospective student body is probably not limited to a small neighborhood.

Perhaps the most important advantage of using a geographical community base is that it allows the school to become a broadly functioning part of the community. Parent participation is facilitated when they have ordinary daily contact with one another on the block or in the neighborhood. Cooperative relationships with other institutions (clinics, service agencies, government) may be easier to establish, problems to which the school must relate (outside the classroom) are easier to identify, and the school itself may become a cohesive force in the neighborhood. Problems of governance may be different for schools not based on neighborhood. In thinking about how to define your school community you should keep these governance problems in mind, along with consideration of how you want your school to relate to its neighborhood and what skills and facilities you will need for the group you have made a commitment to.

Balances to Consider

In addition to the question of whether to serve a particular neighborhood, other factors should be examined which may further narrow your target. For instance, you may wish to maintain certain ratios or balances in your student population. The following examples, questions, and comments are intended only as a helpful starting point:

Sexual Balance. How important is a balance of boys and girls? To adolescents, who spend so much of their energy coming to terms with their sexuality, the balance is probably most crucial. To younger children, it's probably not so necessary, though it might be preferable if you're trying to avoid stereotyping sex roles. This balance should also be considered in picking staff.

Age Balance. How wide an age range is desirable? Are there certain ages which should not be mixed? How will the stage of emotional development characteristic of a particular age group affect personal interaction and the curriculum of the whole school? How does the size of your school affect the age range possible?

Even if you have already determined the general educational ideals on which the school will be based, the range of activities and needs of the students will be drastically different depending on their ages. If enough space and staff are available, different ages can coexist. In a more tightly knit group, more conflicts might arise. For example, the Primary Life School feels there are so many changes between the ages of seven and eight that the two ages should be separated if possible. Before deciding on age groupings you might discuss the emotional characteristics and mental development of different age groups with someone knowledgeable about the subject.

Teacher-Student Ratio. What is the most effective teacher-student ratio for classes and for the school in general? How can the school best balance the need for individual attention and the necessity for longer group interaction? How does the type of structure effect the ratios desired? Many schools which stress individual instruction and personal relationships favor a ratio of about 1:7 or 1:8; those with more structured environments (Montessori, for example) allow for as many as 14 or 15 students per teacher.

Racial Balance. How will the goals of the school affect its racial balance? If part of the curriculum will center on the needs and interests of a particular racial group, the school will mainly attract members of that group. If your intent is to enroll members of a minority group but your curriculum and teaching methods are irrelevant to its needs you will have difficulty attracting students of that group. For example, some minority families feel the free school approach is a luxury proposed and defended by middle-class people who have trouble in beoming integrated. If you aim at attracting children from a variety of racial and ethnic groups, you will design a program that stresses racial interaction and is relevant to all groups. (Multi-Culture Institute of Berkeley designed its program with this purpose in mind.)

Emotionally Disturbed Children. Often schools exclude children they do not want to deal with, sometimes by labelling them "emotionally disturbed" even if they're not. Nevertheless, some children do have emotional needs so strong their membership in the school would require basic restructuring of the entire school community or resources you do not have. Your school might actually be destructive to a child who needs special attention you cannot give him. In addition, other school members might become frustrated by fruitless attempts to aid the disturbed child. How much emotional imbalance can the school handle without destroying itself? How can you balance your desire to help people who might fail elsewhere with the disintegrating effects of too much emotional imbalance?

Recruitment and Selection of Students

Some schools have little trouble recruiting students, especially when they develop as split-off or replacement schools for already existing institutions. In one instance, dissatisfied parents who had already formed their own school committee and had forced the hiring of a teacher of their own choice, formed a new school with this teacher and a parent as co-directors. Similarly, Michael Community School began when St. Michael's School, a parochial school, folded for lack of financial support and was replaced by a community school. The initial enrollment was substantially that of St. Michael's Parish.

More commonly, new schools must give careful attention to recruiting. Most schools rely on word-of-mouth, coverage in news media (newspapers, magazines, and radio), and advertisements of school meetings. Preparing a brochure to be mailed to all prospective parents and students and distributing posters are common helpful methods.

You may be able to arrange speaking engagements about the school. If your school is at all innovative, college classes (especially in schools of education), church groups, and public school classes may be interested in hearing about it. Sometimes these groups will request (or at least permit) students to come along. You might also try combining recruitment with some sort of fund-raising venture or group activity, such as a garage or bake sale, potluck picnic, fair, or neighborhood campaign.

In all types of advertising, keep in mind who would be most interested in your school. Give extensive and explicit information about the school's expectations, goals, and methods. This will minimize wasted time for you and parents or students confused about what they are getting into. Your advertising and brochure should stress what you aim to do, not what you're reacting against or trying to avoid.

Many schools have successfully used conferences with prospective families to explain the school and determine whether the family feels comfortable with it. Even if the child and the school seem to fit together well, both school personnel and prospective family will have a much clearer idea of the realities after speaking with each other. Several different types of conference are possible. A few people from the school (most likely just teachers, but possibly teachers and students or teachers and parents) can meet with the child and his parents. This type of conference can be very informative; parents, teacher, and children might all come away with a clearer view. Often, however, the child lets his parents do all the talking. In this case, it would be advisable to arrange for an additional conference which parents would not attend. Perhaps a meeting could be arranged with several prospective students and staff.

Occasionally it becomes apparent from meeting with a prospective student that the school is simply not the right place for him. In the case of a free school, for example, the child or parent may decide the environment is too unstructured or that the parent wants classes to proceed in a more customary fashion.

It's important in meeting the child and parents to consider the child's relationship to his family and the attitudes of *both* parents and child to the school. The Learning Place receives applications from a considerable number of "skeptical" parents. Often their children have been through several unsuccessful experiences in other schools; the parents contact a new school as a last resort. Sometimes students are able to convince parents to try the school, even though they have strong reservations about it. Moreover, parents may show interest in a school because it's the thing to do, or they are being pressured by someone else's opinions. Upon inquiry parents may reveal that they disagree with much of what the school is all about.

If there is a substantial conflict between your views and those of a child's parents, think about whether the child will be able to handle this discrepancy—and whether you can handle it. If many parents differ with you, you'll either have to educate them or yield to their preferences. If these conflicts are not resolved, the parents may undermine the progress of the child or the school may seriously damage the relationship between child and parent.

Being on the lookout for these kinds of potential conflicts is always to the school's advantage. Pointing out conflicts to students and parents may lead them to a fuller understanding of the school and avoid parents having unwarranted expectations about your school.

You may eventually find you have more applicants from your chosen community than places in the school. At this point it's probably most equitable to rely on a first-come, first-served or lottery system of selection. There are many other ways of choosing among applicants who all meet the school's criteria and wish to attend. The presence or absence of other opportunities for the child is one. Whatever method you use, be sure it is clear to parents *before* selection and fair to all concerned.

CHAPTER FIVE

Attitudes Toward Students

Student Involvement in the Learning Process

Learning can be thought of as an interaction among teachers, environment, and students. The element which is central in setting the basic tone of your school will determine your attitude toward the students and the nature of their involvement.

Teacher-centered Learning. Most elementary school classrooms are teacher centered. According to this model, the child does not create his own learning situations. The teacher molds the situation and the student responds. He may express boredom, interest, anger, excitement, frustration, or bewilderment. He finds learning most stimulating when his reactions are taken into account by the teacher.

At Primary Life School the teachers at first presented the children with many choices at once. Students responded with confusion, and chaos ensued. This caused the teachers and parents to reevaluate the environment they had shaped. They reduced the number of choices and introduced new materials more slowly. Student response to the change was encouraging. Children were better able to make choices and focus on particular areas.

East Harlem Block Schools, Michael Community School, Multi-Culture Institute, and Martin Luther King School share this belief in giving ultimate responsibility to the teacher. Each of these schools, however, aims at creating an environment in which the student is treated as an individual. His interests and uniqueness are important indicators to the teacher. The student's responsibility involves making his individuality clear and his preferences apparent. Furthermore, it is the teacher's responsibility to encourage free responses and be sensitive to them.

Environment-centered Learning. In the Montessori-influenced schools, the environment and materials are central. Here the student encounters a carefully ordered world. Montessori materials are programmed, sequential, educational toys similar to those now popularized by toy companies such as Creative Playthings. With their help the child learns to move from the concrete to the abstract, from the known to the unknown, from perceptual to conceptual thinking. He chooses which materials to use and learns by doing. The theory behind this method is that if the child is to have free choice, the materials he uses need to be structured. At many Montessori-type schools the child wanders freely indoors and out, experiencing the world as he wishes and looking to his teachers as guides.

Student-centered Learning. In the third type of model, the student holds the major share of responsibility in deciding what he wants to learn, plays an important part in determining what materials are presented, and takes a hand in molding his own environment. In some situations, students share responsibility for teaching classes. Most schools of this sort have modified the model; responsibility is shared by students and teachers to varying degrees. Teachers may take much or little initiative in preparing materials and shaping school structure. They help students develop their own initiative by establishing an easy, continuing dialogue through which they come more in touch with each student's needs and interests.

Generally, older children are likely to assume more initiative in this way than younger children. Nevertheless, this type of learning situation has been used successfully with elementary school students. Ironbound School (in Newark), for example, believes no hierarchy of responsibility should exist, that everyone should work toward "preservation of interest in learning and the creation of an environment which will stimulate natural curiosity." Students are free to do nothing if they wish. An Ironbound student's experience with building a model airplane demonstrates one way in which learning takes place in this environment. The initial desire of the child was simply to make an airplane. In the process, however, he improved his reading sufficiently to master the instructions while also developing several manual skills.

The Learning Place started by having students take on all responsibility for their learning. Teachers were available at all times and willing to teach classes, but initiated no learning activities themselves. Everyone found this experiment highly unsuccessful. Students and teachers were bored and listless, and little creative learning resulted. After this experiment, the school felt more comfortable about asserting that there is indeed a difference between teachers and students and this difference can be used to make the school environment lively and rewarding. Teachers are aware that students are often turned off because they are afraid to take risks. As facilitators, teachers help students learn by assuring them that risks are necessary and that failure is as valuable to learning as success. Students are still free to choose what to do and not to do, but teachers try to recognize focuses of interest and encourage risk-taking in these areas. Students may ask teachers to help find outside teachers for subjects no one at the school can help them with. Some students may try to teach classes themselves. While some students may choose to do nothing, other students and teachers are also free to try to find out why and to encourage them to become involved. Both teachers and students are responsible in the learning process, and the responsibility is as much one of being honest as it is one of learning and teaching.

These three models are by no means clear-cut; each shares some elements with the others. A flexible teacher-centered environment, for example, allows for considerable student initiative in learning. You will probably find that a conscious blending of methods is most successful. But you should think carefully about the relationship between the kind of learning situations you will use and the attitude toward students you find appropriate.

Setting Limits on Student Conduct

Related to student responsibility in both governance and learning is the question of limits. Who imposes limits on conduct and what are the limits? Some schools impose virtually no limits on students. In others, there are some basic limits, and further questions are handled by teachers. In still others, students, teachers, and sometimes parents pass judgment and impose limits.

At The Group School, the question of settling limits came to a head in 1971 when an attempted robbery by some outside students led to an arrest and the temporary closing of the storefront then used by the school. The school's board of directors (four students and three teachers) responded by allowing only classes and organized activities, eliminating the "drop in" aspects of the storefront. This was then agreed to by the entire school community. Thus, the limit was set by students and teachers together. Greater control was needed to insure survival.

At Berkeley High Community School, students handle questions of individual conduct through student "tribes." New Community School has a steering committee composed of four students (appointed by department heads), one parent, and the department heads themselves (who do not vote). The committee makes most decisions governing day-to-day living in such areas as drugs, class attendance, admissions policy, and conduct.

How much responsibility is to be given to students in this area? In a one-man-one-vote community, students are easily capable of outvoting teachers. If teachers feel very strongly about certain issues, especially those involving the protection of the school or themselves, they must determine whether or not they are comfortable leaving decisions about these matters to the discretion of the entire community. It is also important to remember, however, that the presence of adults can be very powerful even if students formally hold the voting power.

Honesty and openness about the problems of limit-setting are necessary. As in the other areas discussed, delegating responsibility to students may be frustrating to them as well as to teachers. Students may want the security of basic community rules and may want to give much responsibility to teachers. The need for establishing at least some basic limits can be legitimate and important, with both younger and older children. Basic limits can provide a secure structure in which small children can move more easily toward responsibility and independence. Some restrictions on behavior might also serve to eliminate or reduce the bullying which some children find so terrifying and stifling. In addition, the student who annoys or bullies others through his frustration at lack of limits demonstrates his own discomfort at overloading of responsibility. Remember, however, that unjustifiable or arbitrary limits and rules have stifled and frustrated children more often than excessive openness has confused them.

In the case of older students who have been accustomed to rigid limits, the sudden removal of restrictions might be premature. As in questions of governance, these students often reveal their insecurities by doing only what they feel will please their teachers or exactly what they know will not please the teachers. Gradual lessening of limits will probably be more satisfactory to these children.

A community discussion on limit-setting might be advisable. Here teachers must be responsible in discussing honestly their own insecurities about authority.

CHAPTER SIX

Finding the Best Staff for Your School

In selecting and working with staff, you will want to think about:

- How to find the absolutely best staff for your school.
- How to keep the staff accountable to the particular goal and philosophy of your school.
- How to keep the staff feeling good about their work, themselves, and the school.
- How to provide the staff with opportunities to grow as teachers and as people.
- How to reserve for the school the right to fire staff members who don't work out.

How to do all of these things is quite a trick, and deserves a lot of attention. Staff can make or break a school.

Before you can find the best staff for your school, you have to know what you expect your staff to do, so you can match the people to the jobs. Assuming that you know the basic goals and outlines of your school, draw up a list of all the major functions to be performed to make the school work.

Such a list might include:

Children

- teaching and development of curriculum
- admission of new children
- finding psychological services when necessary
- health tests and problems

- finding special out-of-school resources like art programs, athletics, music, dance, science

Family

- planning and running parent programs, educational, social, home visits
- community service referral-welfare, housing, legal, health

Administrative

- business and bookkeeping
- fund raising
- getting a building
- maintenance of building
- over-all coordination
- long-range planning
- liaison with other organizations
- legal and tax work

Staff

- supervision and support for staff
- arranging and planning training programs
- visits to other schools
- arrangements for absences

Having made your *own* list, you will have to decide whether any of the functions demand specialization. That is, can all the functions be divided among a staff of teachers, or will you have to have some additional positions? Will you need a special person for maintenance, or can the whole staff share in keeping up the building? Will you need a special person to work with families, or can your teachers each work with the families of their children? Will you need a special person for bookkeeping? Or can one of the teachers take this on as his particular administrative responsibility while other teachers take on other administrative responsibilities?

The answers to this kind of question depend in part on how large your school will be, the goals you consider most important, and your funds. One school of 120 children has two people working full time on community services for families, and two more people working full time on family health programs. Obviously this reflects some ample funding, as well as a very strong commitment to the families of children in the school. The school did not develop such a family service program until its fourth year. In its first year it had only 35 students, four teachers, and one half-time maintenance man.

You might want to start with the minimum functions that must be performed and the minimum number of positions. You could add jobs and people as you feel the need.

Director

One major question suggested by a list of functions to be performed is whether you will want to have a special person responsible for administration, coordination, and staff supervision. That is, will you want a director? This is partly a question of how you divide responsibilities and whether you think there will be enough administrative or supervisory work to warrant having one person devoted to it.

But it is more than that. It is a question of how you structure the relationships between people in your school. "Director" is a loaded word. So is "administration" and "supervision." These words arouse definite feelings in people.

Your feeling may be that rank, titles, and responsibilities that give some people authority over other people go against the goals and philosophy of your school. You may want a community in which everyone takes full responsibility for the school as a whole, for each other, and for the work to be done. One new school avoids all formal authority relationships among teachers because the school doesn't want to teach the children to regard hierarchy as the natural or desirable state of things.

But perhaps your group believes the elimination of any authority relationships is unrealistic and a poor preparation for the world outside the school. Perhaps instead of continuing authority relationships that usually exist you want to demonstrate to children a new kind of authority and you want to show them that people who haven't usually had power in this society can be in positions of authority. You want the children to have models of people like themselves in charge. At the Highland Park School the head teachers in each class are community people, and the assistant teachers are professionals; in the East Harlem Block Schools the executive director is a community parent.

These two parent-controlled schools have maintained hierarchies, but have reversed the usual power relationships, for a purpose.

In deciding whether you want a director there are some other factors to take into consideration besides philosophy. One is size. The smaller your school, the easier it should be to function without a director. But if you have started small, and have evolved a style of working that doesn't need a director, perhaps you could invent ways of extending that same style to a larger school as you grow.

In addition to size and philosophy, governing structure should also influence your decision. If yours is a staff-run school, in which staff are ultimately accountable to themselves and their own philosophy, they probably do not need a director to keep them accountable to themselves, though they may want a director to help coordinate administrative work. If your school is a parent-controlled or student-controlled or parent-student-teacher controlled school that has a governing board separate from the staff, the board might need a director responsible for implementing its policies and having the authority to hold the rest of the staff accountable to the policies of the governing board. Even if the staff has representatives on the governing board, the over-all policy of the board will not necessarily be a perfect reflection of the over-all feelings of the staff. In that case, it might be helpful to have a person on staff whose job is to implement the board's policies. It may also be helpful to have a director as a bridge between groups in the school, interpreting the interests and needs of all and keeping communications open.

Without a director, a non-staff board of directors could be quite frustrated in its efforts to run a school. How would its policies get implemented? Who would the board hold accountable? How would they track down who is responsible for what? Would they always have to have joint meetings with the whole staff to determine what is going on? If one staff member was not working out, how would the board be expected to find out or take action?

It might also be easier for all the parents if your school has a director. It's helpful for parents to know who to go to with special problems that a teacher so far hasn't solved.

One further consideration is that some teachers might prefer a clear and limited commitment to the school, perhaps because they have other personal commitments. Without a director, you might want all staff members to make the kind of unlimited commitment to the school that a director usually makes. As the school grows, you might be excluding many excellent people from your staff by asking an unlimited commitment from them.

Finally, you should think carefully of how much you need a director in order to be sure that *someone* is making sure that all decisions get carried out and all work gets done. Sometimes work is overlooked or just slips through the cracks if no one is coordinating the efforts. You may wish to have a director for this monitoring purpose but not give him or her power over staff; a director's role can be limited to information, calling meetings to discuss unfinished work, etc., without giving him a position of authority over other people.

If you decide to have a director, you should consider in advance some of the problems that arise out of strong feelings people have about "directors," "administration," and "supervision."

Often both directors and staff members seem to expect that the "director" will know everything and do things beyond everybody else's abilities. This expectation is destructive to both the director and staff. It tends to make the director feel anxious and often inadequate; it tends to make the staff take less initiative, or perhaps become excessively critical of a director who does not emerge as a "leader."

Because people have excessive respect (and fear) of authority, they tend *not* to be honest, direct, relaxed, or open with people called "director," unless the director is particularly skilled at making people comfortable. So staff members often don't give the director the casual feedback and support he or she needs.

Because directors and teachers perform different functions, they may not fully sympathize with each other's problems. Directors may lose touch with what it feels like to be a teacher. They can become preoccupied with how it feels to be a director, with the pressure of their particular responsibility. Since part of their responsibility is for the performance of the teachers, they may become anxious and critical about the teachers' work instead of sympathetic and supportive.

Here are some ideas to help the staff and the director avoid alienation from each other.

- Periodically rotate roles so that the director is again responsible for doing what the teachers do—whether it is classroom teaching or setting up apprenticeship programs. Have the director experience what it is that teachers are struggling with. Of course, if yours is a school where you do not have teachers responsible for particular classrooms, it may be easier for you to arrange overlapping or rotating roles for director and teachers.

· Have a consultant or resource teacher (master teacher) take on some of the responsibilities of staff supervision. Then the resource teacher, having no role in hiring and firing, having no authority in the school, will be the person giving support and feedback to the teachers. The resource teacher is less likely in this case to be anxious and critical than is the director; and the staff is less likely to be paranoid if the person helping them is not their boss. If the director also teaches, he will be subject in his teaching role to the same pressures as the teachers and this will bring them together.

· Have the director involve staff and parents in administrative work to the extent that they are interested or willing (including resource-finding, parent communication, fund-raising, negotiations with outside agencies).

· Define the director's role as clearly as possible. Have discussions during the year of how the director is helping or hindering the staff, what discomforts he feels in his work and whether the expectations of all these people fit reality or not. Keep the problem up front.

Finding a Director

If you want a director, how will you find one? If you have had a consultant you trust he or she can help you by putting out the word with all his/her contacts. Maybe he/she will come up with the perfect person for you. But the chances are you will have to advertise for applicants, and search high and low for a director. You can:

· Put ads in newspapers.

· Notify the placement centers of all schools of education in your vicinity—even outside your vicinity. Graduates of these schools regularly check back when they are looking for work.

· Put notices in education magazines. There are many professional magazines; if you don't know the names, you might consult the librarian in a local college of education.

· Contact teachers' organizations.

As applications come in, you will need an initial screening process. It turns out to be fairly easy to eliminate the majority of applicants on the basis of either their qualifications or their attitudes and personalities. It will save your group time to have two people take responsibility for this initial screening. Short interviews will weed out the impossible applicants.

Applicants should bring you resumés, and should be prepared to supply references. After the initial screening, the next step would be to check references. The best kind of checking can be done by telephone, so you can get a feeling of who is giving you the information and can ask more about the applicant. People will give information over the telephone they would never put in writing. By checking the references you may spot some people who can impress you in an interview but who never come through; or some people who are shy at first, but who do an incredibly good job wherever they work.

Those applicants who pass the initial screening and whose references satisfy you should meet with the entire board (or governing body). You can ask them all the questions you want. You will need to frame your questions in advance to make them as revealing as possible—and to prevent a boring interview. You should also tell the applicants about your own plans and goals. This is very important, since you want to know whether you see eye to eye with your new director.

You may be lucky enough to all agree, deep in your hearts and inside your bones, that one of your applicants is the perfect person to run your school. But don't settle yet. If that person is now teaching or directing in another school, go and observe him or her there. Ask him to act as a resource person or discussion leader in one of your meetings. Or ask him to dinner. Do anything you can think of to see how he functions, to see if he grows on you. You simply can't be careful enough. If you are going to have a director, you need to have one you like and trust.

If your school is starting small, even if you eventually want a director, you might be wise to start the first year without one. You could hire an administrator and the several teachers you need; or you could divide administrative responsibility among the teachers. At the end of the year one of the teachers might emerge as someone you want to trust with more responsibility.

Teachers

Responsibilities

In dividing up functions, you have already decided whether teachers will be expected to carry out administrative responsibilities, or community organizing duties, or other jobs not usually considered part of teaching.

But you need to go further before hiring anybody. As fully as possible, you should define what is expected of teachers. You need a job description.

Strictly speaking, it would be a job description to say, "You are expected to take responsibility for the emotional and intellectual development of 30 children; and you are expected to assume all other kinds of responsibilities that the school needs in the course of developing the school, as determined by the board, the staff group, or the director."

However, such a job description reveals nothing about your goals (except that you want a highly flexible and responsible staff!) and doesn't insure that anything specific will ever be done. It doesn't tell your teachers much about what you really want them to do, and it gives you no basis for holding them accountable for what you want them to do.

It's more helpful to make your job descriptions as specific and clear as possible. It should not be seen as authoritarian to define what is expected of staff. Include in the description:

- your basic goals, especially your views about work with parents, the use of authority and structure in the classroom, and the kind of evaluation you will expect
- the methods you expect teachers to use in reaching those goals
- the role you expect teachers to take in re-defining goals as you go along
- the methods you do *not* want teachers to use
- the miscellaneous work needed from teachers (fund raising, record keeping, administrative jobs, etc.)

If you are sure of your goals but not of your methods, you can tell teachers their responsibilities are to find the best possible ways to achieve those goals. But if you are sure of some of your methods, ask the teachers to use these methods.

For example, a school might say that it expects teachers to maintain good relationships with parents, and leave the method of doing this up to the teacher. But the school might specify in the job description that for the purpose of maintaining good relationships with parents it expects teachers to make two home visits a year, have one parent conference, provide three progress reports, telephone parents about any accident or problem, and learn to speak the family's language.

Suppose you know that you want the children to learn to read, and to enjoy school. You may not know exactly *how* you want your children to learn reading, though you may know you don't want it forced down their throats. In that case, there is nothing wrong with specifying to teachers that they *must* teach reading, that they may choose *whatever method* they consider most suitable, *as long as* it doesn't result in the children disliking the learning process.

In this way, you have stated your goals, you have put some limits on the teachers and defined the area of their freedom. They are not free to ignore reading, and they are not free to make children unhappy, but they are free to use all their skill and ingenuity in attaining two of your school's goals.

If you give teachers this kind of guide, you will avoid a lot of misunderstanding.

Of course, you need not know everything before you start. As you go along you will learn more about what methods will achieve what goals. A good staff will do much of the work in finding out how to attain the school's goals, and they will probably have a role in developing further goals as you go along.

One more word about limits: the question of limits is as important as that of responsibilities. You may know that you do not ever want teachers to hit children, suspend children, curse at children, ridicule children, say critical things about a child's parents in his presence, or insult a child's intelligence. Again, make this very clear to the teachers. Don't assume that the teachers already know—even if they do, the pressures of teaching are very great and teachers sometimes do things they don't believe in. It will help prevent this to let the teachers know from the beginning what you do not want them to do.

Qualifications

Once you have worked out your goals and the specific responsibilities you will give teachers in implementing and elaborating these goals, you are ready to define what qualifications your teachers should have.

Many groups start out feeling that "qualified teachers" means college graduates who have majored in education and are certified by the city or state. That is the state's definition of "qualified teachers." Unless the state law requires it (and you should get some legal advice on this; see Chapter Eleven), you do not need to use anyone else's definition of "qualified." You may have a very different idea of what it takes to be a teacher in your school.

In thinking about qualifications, consider:

- what personal characteristics a teacher will need to be comfortable in the school community you are planning
- what special skills a person will need to contribute something unique and important to the intellectual development of the children
- what special characteristics or skills a teacher will need to support the healthy emotional and social development of the children
- what attitudes the teacher should have
- what kinds of prior experience would be useful
- what kinds of prior training would be helpful
- what kind of people and what *variety* of people you want children to have as adult models in the school

You may not find people who have everything you want. Finding a qualified staff is a matter of balancing what you would like and consider most important with what you can get. But it is helpful to start out with an idea of the perfect people you would like to find.

Balancing your total staff may be important. Some schools end up with a group of highly committed and very nice people who have no experience in teaching or running schools. Try to get a variety of strengths and experience and special abilities among your staff. If you take people with a common weakness you should plan to make up for these common weaknesses yourself by providing adequate training.

Teaching Teams

Many schools have made teaching teams the core of their staffing patterns. Team teaching is a way of making more adults—often with different abilities and styles—available to the children, and a way of having adults share responsibility for a group of children. It makes teaching less lonely, and often brings out the best in all the teachers.

Some schools have teaching teams which include community people or parents along with a "professional" teacher. The reasons: to involve parents deeply in the school process and in their children's education; to create a community in which parents are models for the children; to keep "professional" teachers tuned in and accountable to the viewpoint and experience of parents; to create a total school community which is richer than otherwise possible; to provide parents exciting and satisfying professions; to make a school where children are at home, proud of their own culture, able to speak their own language freely, able to feel continuity between their own childhood and their future as adults.

In deciding how to structure a classroom team, it might be helpful to know that different schools have tried various definitions of the classroom team relationship.

Ironbound Community School has made the team co-equals, to avoid any authority relationship among them and to place equal value on what each will contribute. At Highland Park School a community person is head teacher and a professional is the assistant, specifically to emphasize the contribution of the community person. At East Harlem Block Schools the parent board has put professional teachers in charge of classrooms and parents are assistant teachers. The board wants parents to be head teachers, but it has generally put a strong value on training and educational background of teachers, so the board is providing a high school equivalency course for parent assistants and also paying their way to college.

Relationships between two or three adults working together in a classroom are sensitive and sometimes difficult no matter what the formal relationship is. Different racial or class backgrounds may make it slightly more complex. No matter how you organize, you'll have to pay attention to the team relationships. Since there's no way to avoid some problems, there's no reason not to experiment with what you believe in!

Other Staff

Resource Teacher or Master Teacher. This person is an experienced teacher whose role is to provide support and concrete assistance to other teachers. He or she may have special curriculum knowledge or may just be a very skilled classroom teacher whose personality makes it easy for her to share what she knows in a helpful way with other teachers. The way she gets involved in each class would be defined by her relationship with the teachers in that class and by the needs of the teachers and the class. She may also have other responsibilities, depending on the school's needs.

Parent Coordinator or Family Worker. This person is a particularly trusted and respected parent or community resident whose role is to assist parents and families in any way she can, as well as to draw families into deeper involvement in the school. Involvement with the school is a way to help families—first through the pleasure of involvement—then often leading to employment, training opportunities, concrete help with all kinds of problems. The parent coordinator's knowledge of the family often helps the school understand the child; she is often the person who can bring parents and teachers together for a full discussion of a child's problems.

Personal Counselor. This person may run group counseling sessions or work individually with students whose personal needs require special help.

Consultants. Consultants can be anybody you want in any area you need: curriculum; health; mental health; group dynamics; classroom environment; anything. They can be permanently attached to the school, working perhaps a day or so a week; or they can be called in as needed. Consultants tend to be more expensive than other staff, unless you can find expert volunteers.

Vocational Counselor. This person may be helping high school age kids find jobs, plan to acquire needed skills, and understand the problems of work.

Recruitment and Selection of Staff

You can roughly follow the same procedure for hiring most staff that we described in selecting a director:

- recruiting through advertising, word-of-mouth, schools, appropriate organizations
- preliminary screening through initial interviews and checking of references
- full interview with the hiring committee
- whatever further measures you decide would be helpful: observations, invitations to participate in some of your work, invitations to some social situation, another interview, a meeting with whatever staff you've already hired

Of course, you fully inform applicants of what you believe and what you expect, including the worst! (If you expect not to have any funds for the first three months, warn them!) Let them see the job description and any other statements of goals. Perhaps the applicants don't agree with you, and you might as well find out from the beginning.

If you're hiring the rest of your staff after you've hired the director, of course the director should have a role in the recruiting and selection process. Later on, you might trust your director to do a lot, if not all, of the initial recruiting and screening. But at this point it would be best to work along with the director, sharing the whole process so you can learn as much about each other and from each other as possible. You might make a simple rule that the committee *and* the director will have to agree on new staff members. Schools which consider the relationships among staff members to be crucial might want to somehow involve all staff in the selection.

How to Keep Your Staff Happy

This is all fairly obvious:

- Hire people you like so you'll be nice to them.
- Hire people who will get along with each other.

- Hire people you have reason to believe will be successful. There's nothing like success to make people feel good.
- Give them all the support you can. Don't pull out after they're hired.
- Pay attention to what the staff says they need. Try to give it to them.
- Make sure the school provides ways and times for people to get to know each other, and to enjoy each other.
- Don't work them to death—they need a little private life, too.
- Pay them.
- Give them opportunities to grow.
- Don't keep people too long who don't work out—they drag everybody down.

How to Provide Staff with Opportunities to Grow

Staff Training

Training is essential to the continued growth of the school and its personnel. The type of training is generally the result of the governing body's concern that staff be trained to carry out the stated goals of the school. Thus, for example, the school might require that all teachers share the same training in curriculum methods, group dynamics skills, language, or cultural history. Training may also be arranged after hiring to provide skills the staff has agreed are lacking or to remedy an individual's weaknesses, develop his strengths, or pursue his important interests.

There are many training methods and resources: pre-service training, outside consultants, regular staff seminars, staff teaching each other, outside workshops, college courses, etc. When school and staff or individual agree on the importance of particular training, the school should bear the cost, if possible. And training should be separated from the evaluation process so that growth is not mixed with threat.

Staff Supervision as a Part of Training

Supervision, provided by a sensitive and skilled supervisor or group and accepted by a responsive teacher, is the best kind of training. It relates directly to the specific strengths and weaknesses of each teacher, within his own teaching situation. It should help him solve his specific problems and deepen and strengthen whatever he is already doing well. It should improve his understanding of himself, and of the students he is working with.

The school has an obligation to provide staff with the best possible supervision. Bad supervision is worse than no supervision. Nothing will drive teachers crazy faster than a supervisor who is over-critical, insensitive, and interested in imposing his own concerns on a teacher who is struggling with different issues. On the other hand, nothing will contribute more to good staff morale than a supervisor who is tuned in to the teachers, has real insights and skills to offer, knows how and when to offer them, and who essentially sympathizes with the teachers and likes them.

The following are some mechanisms for supervision:

- The director might regularly observe the work of each staff member; then meet to discuss the observations, make suggestions, respond to the needs of the staff member.

- Periodically the director and staff member might have a comprehensive discussion of the staff member's strong and weak areas with help on how to work on the weak ones.

- Instead of the director providing continual feedback, the school might have a master teacher do it—someone who has little or no involvement in hiring and firing, but whose entire role is giving support and feedback to teachers.

- A school might have a system of mutual support and supervision, wherein teachers regularly observe each other, and meet in groups or pairs to help each other.

- A consultant might also provide individual supervision on a regular basis. The consultant has the advantage of bringing special knowledge to bear on problems teachers are having, with no particular power over teachers. This combination makes it sometimes easier for teachers to accept a consultant's supervision.

As the school gets under way, staff members should have a part in defining what kind of supervision they consider most helpful.

Keeping Staff Accountable to Your Goals and Philosophy

Accountability is essentially an issue of governance. But it bears strongly on the quality of staff work and on staff attitudes. We all know schools in which teachers are held accountable by principals for maintaining law and order and doing paper work. We know schools in which teachers are not held accountable by anybody for what children learn or how they feel.

How will your staff be held accountable, for what will they be accountable, and to whom? Let's start with *to whom?* Theoretically, staff could be accountable to: parents, students, the community, themselves and each other, the government, the director, the people who provide the funds, or some trainers who represent the model teachers are following.

The design of your school will determine to whom the staff is primarily accountable. Obviously, whoever is governing your school is the main group to whom teachers are accountable. Yet you might have a situation in which parents, or students, or teachers were left out of the governing body. And you might want to develop a way teachers could be partly accountable to one of these groups, even though they were not formally represented on the governing board.

Consider a junior high school formally governed by parents, where parents decided that students were old enough to have a role in teacher evaluation. They might:

- put some students on the personnel committee
- ask students for anonymous evaluations of their teachers, to be made available to the teachers and the personnel committee
- set up evaluation classes, in which students are invited to give their honest compliments and criticisms to teachers directly
- give the student body the right to overrule certain decisions of the personnel committee if three-quarters of the students agreed the committee was wrong

• create a student evaluating committee to work separately from the personnel committee but present its thoughts to the teachers and the personnel committee for consideration

When any of these mechanisms are added to the school's structure, the staff becomes more aware of their accountability to students. This would have an important effect on teachers and on the school, especially since in junior high the interests and attitudes of students are beginning to diverge from those of their parents. It would also have an important effect on parents; they would have to give continuous formal recognition to the attitudes of their children.

The point is that formal mechanisms of accountability influence people's attitudes. People tend to take more seriously the feelings, interests, ideas, and needs of people to whom they are accountable. So, make your staff accountable to the people you think the staff should take most seriously. And if there are several groups of people the staff should take seriously, find ways to include them all in mechanisms of accountability.

Once having created an over-all structure of accountability, you have to work out its day-to-day implementation. You'll want both informal and formal mechanisms.

Informal Feedback. If you structure your school as a community of people who like and help each other, there will be many opportunities to get to know each other, develop interest in each other's work, have parties, picnics, workshops, open houses, home visits, shared responsibilities.

Planned Evaluations. Teachers also need some regular and comprehensive evaluation of their work as others see it. Teachers can count on evaluation at regular intervals, know it will be thoughtful and detailed, and will have an opportunity to discuss it and respond.

Firing

Assuming you have provided training, good supervision, and regular planned evaluations for your staff, firing should not be a complicated issue. Staff members who don't work out, despite all the help and support you have given them—who don't make changes requested of them—may be fired.

The firing procedure you follow after supervision, training, and evaluations have failed should include:

- informing the person that firing is a strong possibility and why
- explaining to him how, by whom, and on what basis the final decision will be made
- giving him an opportunity if he chooses to talk with the people making the final decision
- perhaps giving him a final probationary period if there is some new reason to believe he can or will make the necessary changes

Be sure your procedures are clear to all teachers before any issue of firing arises. That way you will avoid much unnecessary anxiety.

Salaries

Your basic range of salaries depends on how much money you expect to have and how much you will have to pay to get the kind of person you want for your school.

Will everyone on your staff get the same pay? Or will you pay more according to need? According to responsibilities? Experience? Training? Think about it before you start. Many groups begin on a conventional salary scale that emphasizes education and responsibility and then find it's difficult to change because they might have to lower some staff salaries.

Some groups have found ways to balance all the factors they value, by starting with a basic pay and adding certain amounts for training, responsibility, need, and experience. Be sure to discuss the possibility of inadequate funds so people are prepared to miss a few checks in an emergency.

CHAPTER SEVEN

Curriculum: Approaches and Models

Many articles and books have been written about curriculum, often confusing and contradictory. One reason for this confusion is that curriculum is often the last area new schools deal with seriously. The struggle for survival of the school itself, and questions of relationship and interaction among the members of the school, are more immediate and sometimes seem to absorb all available energy. Another reason for the confusion is that each school's curriculum is unique, because each community, each faculty, and each group of students is unique.

This section will not provide detailed blueprints for curriculum. A detailed, concrete statement of even one school's curriculum or one type of curriculum would require a whole book by itself. Even if we could do that here, it would be a mistake. You have to make your own curriculum as you go, in accordance with the particular goals of your school, the unique abilities of your staff, and the individual needs of your students. We can give you some starting points and guideposts for your thinking. But remember that at best these are skeletons; you must make the flesh and blood.

Curriculum basically means what you are going to teach and how you are going to teach it. But while you are considering those questions, and maybe even before you start, you must think about what lies underneath. What are the *preconditions* for learning? The most exciting material and teaching methods in the world won't work if the students are hungry, or physically uncomfortable, or afraid of the teachers, or afraid of asking questions, or fighting with each other all the time. Many new schools, in fact, consider eliminating blocks to learning and creating the right preconditions as their most important goal. Thus, the emphasis in preceding sections on freedom and respect for children, involving parents deeply in the educational process, and encouraging warm interaction among staff members and between staff and parents and students. Sometimes these aspects of education are considered under the topic "motivation."

Essential as the preconditions for learning are, it is also essential that a school not stop there. Your job is not done when all the blocks have been removed, and a student is ready to learn. If at that point he is presented with the same boring material or traditional education in the same uninteresting manner, he will quickly turn off again. So you also have to think hard about what is important to teach and how you can most effectively teach each skill, or attitude, or subject area. As we said before, there is no educational cookbook or supermarket or expert to whom you can turn for a ready solution, though you can get help. You must think it out for yourselves, and examine the ideas and experiences of others that seem helpful.

One starting point is to look at a few more or less well-defined curriculum models. Each is based on a set of assumptions about children, how they learn, and what is important for them to learn. Each includes a general approach, and sometimes a specific methodology and set of materials that have been used in many different schools with various modifications. The descriptions which follow are brief and designed to introduce the most important assumptions and characteristics of each model. You'll notice each one includes information about the preconditions for learning as well as points on what and how to teach. If you're interested in pursuing a particular model further, see the bibliography and resources section at the end of this guide.

Curriculum Models

The Open Classroom

The open education approach to primary education is based on a profound and sweeping revolution in English primary schools involving new ways of thinking about how young children learn and about classroom organization, the curriculum, and the role of the teacher.

These new schools are known variously as Leicestershire schools, open structure schools, integrated curriculum schools, or British infant schools. Many innovative community schools in this country have adopted some form of this approach.

Teaching in these schools is based on a definite body of theory stressing individual learning and learning in what has been called the concrete mode—messing around with stuff. The child learns by his own activity; abstract thought is built from layer after layer of direct experience. The theory holds that each child develops at a separate pace and in different ways and that this ought to be reflected in the patterns of teaching. It insists that knowledge does not fall into neatly separate compartments and that work and play are not opposite but complementary.

The theory describes a new role for the teacher as a catalyst and stage manager who provides children with the kinds of experiences which will help them along in their thinking and in learning basic skills like reading and math. The role of the teacher is to create an environment rich in diverse materials for the child to manipulate, then to intervene as a facilitator or guide only to increase the boundaries of the child's exploration of the materials, not to tell him the answers. Teachers work to help the child pursue whatever interests him because these schools have found the child will naturally, happily, and successfully learn the skills he needs. The role of the teacher is to step in and redirect the child when he needs help, not to dominate the child's total time and attention.

Following is a description of the Westfield Infant School for children from five through seven in a working-class neighborhood in Leicestershire, England. Though this example is from England, it resembles classrooms you might find in Morgan Community School in Washington, D.C.; the Underwood School in Newton, Massachusetts; or the East Harlem Block School in New York City.

If you arrive at the school early, you'll find a number of children already inside—reading, writing, painting, playing music, tending pets. Teachers sift in slowly and begin working with students. It's hard to say just when school actually begins because there is very little organized activity for the whole class. You may see a small group of children working on mathematics or reading, but mostly children are on their own. Moving about and talking freely, the children learn a great deal from each other. The teacher also moves about the room, advising on projects, listening to children read, asking questions, giving words, talking, sometimes prodding.

Some open classroom schools have adopted "family" or "vertical" grouping—children of different ages (say five through seven) are mixed together. This further promotes the idea of children teaching children. Family grouping seems particularly successful in the early years, when newcomers are easily absorbed, and older children help teach young ones to clean up and take the first steps in reading. The older children also learn a good deal from playing the role of teacher.

The physical layout of open classrooms is markedly different from most traditional schools. There are no individual desks and no assigned places. Around the room there are different tables for different activities: art, water and sand play, number work. The number tables have all kinds of number lines—strips of paper with numbers marked on them in sequence—on which children learn to count and reason mathematically. There are beads, buttons, odd things to count; weights and balances; dry and liquid measures; and a rich variety of apparatus (both homemade and commercial) for learning basic mathematical concepts.

Every class has a library alcove with books of all kinds available whenever they are wanted. There is a play corner with dolls and furniture for playing house, and often a dress-up corner or a puppet theater.

The teacher leaves much of the day's routine open to the children. The ground rules are that children must clean up when they finish and they must not bother others. There is no special time for separate subjects in the curriculum, and no real difference between work and play. In fact, these schools are based in part on the notion that what adults call play is the principal means of learning in childhood, a notion that seems plausible when you consider how much children learn informally before they come to school.

Generally, teachers start the morning by listing available activities. A child might spend the day on his first choice or he might not. Although there is a commitment to letting the children choose freely, in practice many teachers give work when they think it's needed. But to a very great extent the children really have a choice and go purposefully about their own work.

The classrooms are fairly noisy because the children can move and talk freely, and sometimes the teacher has to ask for quiet. However, when children work independently, discipline becomes less a problem than it is in a more formal classroom. When the class is taught as a unit, and every child is supposed to pay attention as the teacher talks, discipline can be a very serious matter. Quick children get restless; slow children are bored. In an open classroom, most children are usually absorbed, and those who are restless may go outdoors or play in the hallways.

The way children learn to read is an example of the kind of individual learning and teaching that goes on in an open classroom. At first it's hard to see just how children do learn, since there are no separate subjects. But after a while it becomes clear that, to a great extent, the children learn to read from each other. They hang around the library corners long before they can read, handling the books, looking at pictures, trying to find words they know, listening and watching as the teacher listens to other children reading.

There is an attempt to break down the mental barriers between the spoken, written, and printed word. Each child is given his own notebook for free writing. He may draw a picture in it, discuss the picture with the teacher, and dictate a caption to her which she writes down for him. He copies it just underneath. In this way he learns to memorize the look and sound of his dictated words and phrases until he reaches a point where, with help, he can write sentences.

In much the same way, children make their own dictionaries. Gradually the child amasses a reading and writing vocabulary and becomes fluent; you can see six-year-olds writing stories, free-verse poems, accounts of things done in class, all for an audience that includes other children as well as the teacher.

As a rule, teachers don't pay much attention to accuracy or neatness until a child is well along in his writing. Grammar, spelling, and punctuation are introduced after a time, not as separate subjects or ends in themselves, but as living ways to get meaning across.

The way math is taught further illustrates how classroom practice fuses with the ideas on child development that have shaped these new schools. Among the most important of these ideas is that primary school children learn basic mathematical concepts much more slowly than adults realize, and patterns of abstract thought used in mathematics must be built up from layer after layer of direct experience—seeing, hearing, feeling, smelling. A child learns how to sort and classify things—all sorts of everyday things—into sets, comparing the sizes of sets, the number of objects in each one. He learns how to count and to measure. He learns simple fractions, and aspects of addition, multiplication, and division as these arise from real situations in the classroom. He learns about shape and size and proportion by handling all sorts of concrete materials. What is important is not how much the children learn, but how much they understand. Rote learning and memorizing have been abandoned, partly because they bore children and teachers, but basically because they are poor ways to learn. Children are given an opportunity to watch children and talk to them about what puzzles or intrigues them. In this way, open schools are producing classes where mathematics is a pleasure and where, each year, there are fewer and fewer mathematical illiterates.

A word more ought to be said about the role of the teacher in an open structure school. Formal classroom teaching—the instructor standing up front talking to a group—has disappeared because it imposes a single pattern of learning on a whole group of children, and because it ignores the extent to which children teach each other. But even though the British infant schools stress cooperation and the children are encouraged to teach each other, there is no abdication of adult authority and no belief that this would be desirable. The role of the teacher remains crucial. A Leicestershire classroom in which the teacher is merely managing the room well enough, but not responding to individual children, is a very different place from one in which the teacher knows when to intervene, change the pace, ask a question or make a suggestion for the greatest learning advantage. These schools accept the real and legitimate authority of a teacher as an adult responsible for providing the kinds of experiences that will help children grow.

Most teachers working with children in an open structure setting are generally not preoccupied with the issue of freedom versus structure. The idea of giving children choices is a considered judgment about how they best learn. Freeing children is part of the point; encouraging them to make significant choices is desirable because often the choices reflect their needs, and in any case, this is how they learn to develop initiative, think for themselves and learn basic skills most effectively. But freedom by itself is seen as an empty educational aim. These schools are intent on teaching children to think. It is this deep pedagogical seriousness, the attention paid to learning in the classroom, which makes these schools different from many others that are superficially similar.

There are some problems associated with the open classroom. It is important that parents recognize and consider them before opting for this model.

- Most teachers are not trained to teach this way and the time needed for them to change, to adjust, will vary considerably. This means there will probably be a period of disorientation and disorganization on the part of both adults and children.

- The classrooms are not like those most parents are familiar with. They seem chaotic. They are noisy. It's often difficult for an observer to tell what's going on. Unless parents and administrators are willing to ask what is happening in the classroom and how a particular experience is important and at the same time help the teacher feel at ease, the open education approach will not work well.

- Teachers have historically not had to explain what they were doing or why. Again, the open approach will not work well unless they recognize that they must constantly question what they are doing *and* always be prepared to justify it to parents, administrators, *and* children.

- The classrooms often look messy—because so much is going on in so many places. In environments where streets and alleys are always filled with junk, this may turn off many parents. Staff must be quite sensitive to parents' feelings and prepared to work out a satisfactory approach with them.

- Improvement on standardized tests is often slower, although results even out over a period of years. It is nevertheless often difficult for parents to wait that long to see "progress."

An excellent description of how one teacher adopted this method in her classroom is found in the pamphlet, "An Interview with Pat Hourihan," published by the Education Development Center (see Chapter Twelve).

Montessori

In Rome, at the turn of the century, a young physician named Maria Montessori became interested in the education of young children, and in the course of her career developed a method of teaching which has had a profound effect on modern ideas about education generally and still serves as the basis for Montessori schools in Europe, Latin America, and the United States.

Dr. Montessori began to develop her methods while working with mentally retarded children, teaching them to take care of themselves, to be graceful and coordinated in movement, and eventually to read and write. Her graduates then entered regular schools and achieved as well as "normal" children. Her success with retarded children prompted her to try her methods with the working-class children who overran the poor districts of Rome and Milan largely unattended and unschooled, since their parents had to work and the government provided no schools or day care facilities. Her success in transforming these children into independent, purposeful youngsters who could read, write, and do numbers by the age of seven and were eager and joyful in their learning was a matter of tremendous interest to educators throughout the world. After a decline of interest for many years, her influence is once again widely felt, especially as the general public has come to believe in the importance of preschool education.

The Montessori method is a way of teaching that begins with very careful observations of what children of various ages are ready and eager to do. It assumes that children have a spontaneous interest in learning, in encountering their environment, in accepting challenges. Children are presented with a great variety of educational materials especially designed for each particular stage of mental and physical development, and they use these materials in sequence to teach themselves the various skills they want and need to learn at each stage. The role of the teacher is supportive. She may suggest an exercise to a child, offer help when a child requests it, or step in when a child becomes frustrated and can't figure a way out by himself, but the basic focus is on the child teaching himself and children teaching each other (hence the usual practice of having children of different ages in the same classroom).

The method is based on the belief that children can take responsibility for their own education, each proceeding at his own pace and in his own unique manner. The role of the adult is to provide a *prepared environment* that gives the child the means and assistance to educate himself and sets necessary limits so the child is not overwhelmed by too many choices or too much stimulation or left the prisoner of his impulses. Other fundamental beliefs are: all of a child's senses are interconnected and learning takes place through all of them; learning should be orderly and sequential; and children learn abstract ideas through experience with tangible, concrete things.

The first characteristic of a Montessori classroom environment is a warm, colorful, spacious room, immediately attractive to children and adults alike. Everything about it is child-sized: furniture, shelves and cabinets, washing and cleaning-up facilities, coathooks. There are plants and often animals and, wherever possible, an outdoor garden and play area. It is also orderly. There is a place for everything and one of the ground rules is that children return a game or toy to its place and clean up any mess before going on to another activity. However, as with most skills, this is taught by example of the teacher and older students rather than as a rigid rule by itself.

Children generally work either alone or in small groups at tables or on rugs. The children are free to move around, but encouraged to do so deliberately, with a purpose. In fact, they are encouraged to make deliberate choices about everything they do during the school day. A child may work with one set of learning materials as long as he wants and may return to it as often as he wants.

Maria Montessori developed materials in four basic areas for the 3- to 7-year-old child. These materials or modifications of them are still the basic ones for a Montessori classroom. The first is *practical life exercises,* through which children learn how to take care of their environment, take care of themselves, and be courteous to each other. Equipment here includes a child-sized but real kitchen and dining area where children can prepare, serve, and eat simple dishes. It also includes real brooms, mops, sponges, and other cleaning materials for the kitchen and classroom; gardening tools; irons and clothing to iron; practice boards to learn how to fasten buttons and snaps, tie shoelaces, tie bows, and manipulate zippers.

The second area is *sensorial materials,* to help the child develop each of his senses as finely as he can. It includes materials for developing discrimination of dimension, color, and form; of weight and sorting. Developing the senses keenly, and the coordination of the fine muscles of the hand, is regarded essential preparation for learning writing, reading, and mathematics later. An example of these materials are sets of ten cubes decreasing gradually in size from ten centimeters on a side to one centimeter on a side. The child learns to stack these on top of each other in the proper order by experimentation. There are often sets of ten items, increasing or decreasing in size or some dimension. This is in order to gradually prepare the children for arithmetic, and understanding our number system based on ten. Another characteristic of all Montessori materials is what's called the *isolation of difficulty*. Each item in a set of materials differs from another in only one respect, so as to teach the child that particular quality without confusing him. In other words, if the purpose is to teach the concept of thickness, all the items will be the same length, width, and color but each one in the series will be somewhat thicker than the other.

The final two areas are the actual materials for teaching mathematics and language, after the sensorial materials have laid the groundwork. Math materials include number rods, beads, counting boxes, sandpaper numerals. Language materials include sandpaper letters, word and picture cards, labels and labelling games, and various books and word games.

One of the more striking facts about Montessori schools is that children who attend them learn to read, write, and do arithmetic much sooner than children in conventional schools. In general, children in Montessori schools are writing by the time they are four and some learn when they are three-and-a-half. Children read somewhat later, but usually by the time they are five and most can do addition, subtraction, multiplication, and division of even very large numbers by the time they are six. The exercises by which children learn arithmetic exemplify the Montessori method: they are highly structured and sequential; they move from concrete objects to symbols and abstract ideas; they focus on the individual child working alone although some depend on the cooperation of several children; and they are designed so the child can measure his own progress and perfect his work.

The preparation for arithmetic begins with the sensorial materials. All blocks, cylinders, and many other toys are in sets of ten, increasing in size from one centimeter to ten centimeters in some dimension. So the child is gradually prepared for the first math exercise, which is teaching the numbers and symbols one to ten. The first exercise is a set of number rods, increasing in length from one centimeter to ten centimeters. As with all materials, the child takes up this exercise when he is ready, indicated by when he asks the teacher to show it to him or when the teacher asks him if he would like to do it and he responds positively. The teacher then takes the number rods over to a table or rug where the child wants to work. She demonstrates one way to do the exercise, for instance by naming each rod ("this is one") and then placing the rods on top of each other so as to form a staircase. Then she may conduct what Montessori calls the "three-period lesson." First she goes through each item, or maybe a few at a time, and names it: "this is one," "this is two," etc. Then she asks the child to point each one out as she says: "show me one," "show me two," etc. Finally, she puts them in front of the child one at a time, asking "what is this?" If a child makes a mistake in naming an item, the teacher does not correct him by saying "no" or "you're wrong," but instead backs up and repeats the lesson until the child grasps it. Then the teacher puts away the material (unless the child wants to use it by himself) and the child takes it out by himself whenever and as often as he wants to after that. The teacher never intervenes unless the child seems really frustrated or upset. The children are encouraged to use it however they want to, since the material itself is self-correcting. (For example, the staircase made out of number rods will look out of line if the child has placed some rods in the wrong order.) Once a child has mastered the material, he usually plays with it in all sorts of ways, making up his own unique games or getting other children to join him.

At the same time, the children are exposed to the sandpaper numerals, a series of hardboard cards with one numeral cut from sandpaper pasted to each one. The children learn the names of the numerals while tracing the sandpaper and feeling their shapes (so that they are learning to write the numerals at the same time). As soon as they have mastered both the number rods (concrete) and the sandpaper numerals (symbols, or abstract) they put the two together, matching up each rod with the corresponding numeral.

Then the child takes up the spindle box, which has a compartment for each number from zero to nine (this is the first time that the number zero is introduced) and a bunch of spindles. The set has the exact number of spindles required to count out the right number for each compartment.

Teachers often make up games for groups of children to play together which reinforce the concepts taught by the basic materials.

Next the children start learning the decimal system with materials known as the "Golden Beads." There are single beads, strings of ten beads, squares of one hundred beads, and cubes of one thousand beads. There are several exercises using the beads, so that children soon learn place value in numbers. There is one game called "The Crisis of Nine" in which the children learn that one more bead or number added to nine makes ten, which requires moving over to the next column or place. The children seem excited by the fact that they deal with large numbers, in the thousands, almost immediately. Once again, as soon as they have mastered the concrete numbers with the beads, they learn to match them up with the abstract symbols through number boards and overlapping cards.

Then they start adding, first with the beads again but translating each answer into numerals. They learn addition in a group at first, with each child responsible for picking out the right combination of beads for his number, placing it in a column with other children's numbers, and then all of them together counting up the total and selecting another set of beads to represent that. They learn subtraction in the same manner.

The game of skip counting lays the groundwork for multiplication. They lay out chains of beads made up of links of a given number of beads. For instance, they might start by counting by fives, connecting links of five beads each and tagging them at intervals indicating the cumulative total. Soon, they have learned the multiplication tables in this manner, having a great time stringing together long chains of beads numbering in the thousands and stretching all across the classroom. Once they have mastered multiplication and division concretely, they switch again to the abstract level and use big multiplication boards with movable numerals and then learn to use the abacus. They have long since begun writing the numerals themselves and therefore can transfer problems back and forth between the apparatus and their own paper.

Basic arithmetic skills have been mastered by children by the time they are six or seven. This leads to an important point to remember in considering the Montessori model as a possible curriculum baseline for your school: Maria Montessori's original work was done with three-to-seven-year-olds and even today the materials and methods of the Montessori school are most distinctive at that age level. Although Montessori herself later worked with older children and many modern Montessori schools go up through elementary school, classrooms for older children are less unique and often resemble, for instance, an open classroom of the Leicestershire or British infant school model. Furthermore, the basic Montessori method encompasses just the four areas mentioned above (practical life, sensorial development, language, and mathematics) and doesn't include music, science, social studies, or art. However, using the principles of the Montessori method like the isolation of difficulty, the three-period lesson, and moving from the concrete to the abstract and the known to the unknown, most Montessori teachers and schools have developed curricula in these areas as well.

A big problem for many considering starting a Montessori school is the cost of acquiring the basic materials and equipment. No firm in the United States manufactures them. They must be imported and are fairly expensive. However, much of the equipment can be made by parents and teachers themselves if they have the time and patience. And some U.S. manufacturers (such as Creative Playthings) make items very similar to certain of the Montessori materials. The best bet in considering this problem would be to find and consult a nearby, friendly Montessori school that is innovative in spirit and not determined to do everything exactly as it was done in the original Montessori schools.

That brings up another problem with Montessori education that has turned many Americans off: the tendency of official descendents of Maria Montessori's schools and training programs to develop a kind of religious orthodoxy and jealously guard all details of the original method. They seem to say that if you don't do it exactly the way Montessori herself did it, you're not truly following the Montessori method and cannot be recognized as a Montessori school. But this tends to preserve the letter rather than the spirit of Montessori's work. She regarded herself as a scientist and experimenter. The heart of her method was careful observation of young children and responding to what the children needed and wanted. She was constantly inventing new materials, equipment, and exercises as she gained new insights and perceptions of particular children. A true practitioner of her method would continually be experimenting and changing in tune with emerging perceptions of the particular children in a school and the particular community in which they reside.

Some critics have charged that the Montessori method's emphasis on children working with materials by themselves tends to neglect the children's emotional development and their ability to interact creatively and sensitively with other children. It is certainly true that Montessori herself was primarily interested in the development of the child's intellect, grace, and independence. However, creative Montessori teachers incorporate all sorts of opportunities for enhancing emotional growth and group interaction, for example, in discussions about stories the teacher reads to children or they write or read themselves and in outdoor classrooms and playgrounds. The emphasis, however, is on paying attention to the children's natural and spontaneous interest in these activities and discussions, rather than planning them in a particular way and according to a particular schedule. At one hour a Montessori classroom may be noisy and bustling with activity, at another time quiet as a library with everyone working on his own. Both are considered natural and valuable atmospheres.

The basic Montessori methods and materials are fairly easy to teach. Training programs for teachers last as a rule only one year. Much harder to teach is the central underlying skill of careful observation of children and the accompanying ability to respond to the endless varieties of their almost universal plea: "help me to do it myself." Montessori herself knew no way to teach this except practice and experience in working with children. As J. McV. Hunt said in his helpful introduction to the 1964 edition of *The Montessori Method:*

If a teacher can discern what a child is trying to do in his . . . interaction with the environment, and if that teacher can have on hand materials relevant to that intention, if he can impose a relevant challenge with which the child can cope, supply a relevant model for imitation, or pose a relevant question that the child can answer, the teacher can call forth the kind of . . . change that constitutes psychological development or growth. This sort of thing was apparently the genius of Maria Montessori.

Caleb Gattegno: Educational Solutions, Inc.

Caleb Gattegno is becoming widely known as the inventor-developer of some increasingly popular educational materials, especially the Cuisinaire Rods for teaching mathematics and the Words in Color reading program. It is unfortunately not widely known that he and his colleagues have developed a clear, comprehensive approach to education, with practical applications to most of the basic curricular areas.

The basic business of traditional education is the transmission of knowledge (produced by gifted people over the ages) by teachers, and the acquisition of this knowledge by students through the power of memory. The trouble with this view, according to Gattegno, is that memory is one of the weaker powers of the mind. Schools seem to tacitly acknowledge this by providing all sorts of props for students—presentation, classroom exercises, homework, review, tests, more exercises, more homework, more review, more tests, and so on, year after year. Furthermore, schools expect that children don't know very much when they begin their schooling, especially so-called disadvantaged or culturally deprived children.

Gattegno is instead quite impressed with the tremendous powers of mind and interest in learning all children have before they even start school. They have taught themselves thousands of things already, often working hour after hour, day after day, to learn a new skill, such as sitting up or walking. In particular, they have learned a language, probably the most difficult learning task anyone ever undertakes—and this usually by the time the child is two years old! Gattegno is quite impressed with the powers of mind demonstrated by children in such learning, and he spent many years studying these powers in detail. His methods of education are built on making use of and developing the powers of mind children already have when they come to school.

For example, he points out that reading and writing are simply somewhat different forms of the language children already know how to speak. He believes teachers need only teach children the code used in written language to represent spoken language, and then point out that otherwise it's the same thing they already know (rather than some strange, large new body of "knowledge"). Furthermore, children can learn this code quickly from materials that are basically games. He believes and has demonstrated that anyone can learn to read in two or three months.

Similarly, he believes the basic principles of algebra and logic (such as understanding abstraction, transformation of meaning from one situation to another, substitution of symbols) are already possessed by young children, again having been learned in the process of learning language. So he would have teachers open the world of mathematics to children on the basis of these powers of mind they already have, rather than by rote processes. One teacher who used these methods in teaching math to second graders found that "my second graders, who knew very little math when we began, explored addition, subtraction, multiplication, division, powers and roots, and different bases, with depth of understanding far beyond my previous classes. I could see that my students were beginning to free their minds from reliance on rote processes. They were beginning to use their minds to think creatively in mathematics and derive their own original ways to solve problems. They were beginning to see that the answer was not so important as the thinking that went into it. . . . With no apologies or attempts to make the material 'relevant' we moved the children into some quite abstract processes; and they loved it. They loved it because the thinking was fun; and because what they learned and the thinking they did made them feel so smart and powerful."

Gattegno's approach has been extended into the teaching of foreign languages, social studies, science, literature, art, music, and physical education. There are several books by Gattegno and his colleagues describing the approach and the specific curricula in various areas. The best way to learn about it in detail, however, is through the inexpensive workshops held in various parts of the country by the organization of which Gattegno is director, Educational Solutions, Inc. (See Chapter Twelve for more details).

Making Your Own Curriculum

You may choose to select one of these models as the basic organizing focus for your curriculum or you may select aspects from several models and merge them according to your own needs. If you wish to base your school on a particular model already in existence, explore the method carefully to be sure your goals and the results of that method are compatible. Remember any method can be changed and adapted to your situation. And remember to test your method and use your own judgment about whether it works. Don't be afraid to change your methods as you go along. Lots of experimenting is in order.

The following are some examples of schools which have made their own curriculum from scratch or adapted a model to the particular circumstances of their students or community.

East Harlem Block Schools

There will be forces operating within each school and community which will influence the content and structure of the curriculum. One of the most basic of these influences is the needs of your particular neighborhood, its unique people and problems and styles.

The East Harlem Day School, the elementary school unit of the parent-controlled East Harlem Block Schools, has about 110 children from one of the poorest neighborhoods in New York City. Most of the children are Puerto Rican, though a substantial minority are black and a few are white. It has grown out of the nursery school, one grade at a time, and now has five grades.

Each classroom has a teaching team comprised of a professional teacher and an assistant teacher who is a parent. Most of the administrative staff, including the executive director, are also parents. The continually evolving curriculum is created largely by the professional teachers, but under the guidance and ultimate control of the parents. The parents want the curriculum to give the children the personal power necessary to survive in a racist society and a faith in their collective power to change or replace the institutions which affect their lives.

During the first year, the curriculum and structure were that of a free school. The parents later rejected this model because the children were not making sufficient progress in learning the basic skills of reading and arithmetic. The parents felt then and continue to feel now that basic academic skills are the first requirement of a curriculum for every child.

During the second year the teachers concentrated on developing a strong reading and mathematics curriculum that continues to be basic to the school. In mathematics, they use the approach of Caleb Gattegno and Madeleine Goutard based on the Cuisenaire Rods and the assumption that children can learn a lot of abstract math very quickly. The children liked this approach because it was fun and because it made each of them feel intelligent. They liked to think mathematically and abstractly. The teachers made no attempt initially to relate mathematics to practical problems and applications. The children do this later on their own.

The reading curriculum is more eclectic. The first-grade teacher starts with the organic approach of Sylvia Ashton-Warner. Children learn to sight-read and then to write words that are powerful for them personally. They trade words with each other. After a few months, once they have perceived the basic notion that reading is merely another form of the spoken language they already know, the teachers start phonics and other decoding skills. Teachers use phonics materials from several sources, including Gattegno's Words in Color program and the Sullivan Reading Materials.

The parents and staff also consider it important that children begin to learn about science and scientific thinking. The heart of the Day School's science curriculum is the series of units and materials developed by the Educational Development Center (EDC) known as the Elementary Science Series. Most of these are presented as experiments in which children record their observations in a notebook and build and compare their discoveries. Individual teachers have developed units on the human body, animal behavior, and various kinds of nature study. Older children go together on a ten-day trip to a farm each spring during which they do intensive study of natural science.

Social studies is the current focus of the curriculum-building process. The content has come from things on the kids' minds and from parents' concern for developing cultural pride and solidarity. One of the most successful units dealt with the use of drugs in the community. The kids see junkies every day and are both fascinated by and afraid of drugs. The unit combined the personal experiences of parents and several ex-addicts with scientific and medical facts compiled by the professional teacher. Another successful series was one dealing with sex education. This year, the fourth-grade class is doing an extensive study of Puerto Rican history.

In classroom organization and the structure of the day, the Day School has been influenced strongly by the open classroom or British infant school model. However, each teaching team is free to structure its classroom as it wishes, so long as the students are learning the basic skills and are happy and engaged during the day. Teachers often modify the degree of structure several times during the school year.

Some classes alternate throughout the day between periods of structured lessons or group activity (usually in small groups) and periods of free exploration and interaction with the various materials around the classroom. Other teachers concentrate the structured activity in the morning and leave the afternoon free for individual activity or field trips. Still another teacher may follow the open format for the entire day, but will work in a carefully planned way to draw individual children or groups of children into different kinds of work challenging to them. Even during an entirely open day, each child will typically have several assignments, such as a requirement to write a page or two in his notebook.

Nearly every class has two or three discussions each day involving the entire group. This is a way for teachers and children to share responsibility for the classroom and for planning in particular. It is also a time for discussing interpersonal problems in the classroom, on the playground, on the street, or at home. These discussions also contribute a great deal to forging a genuine unity in the class.

A common principle in all classrooms is to have frequent discussions of students' work on an individual basis in subjects such as art or math. A key purpose of such discussions is to highlight the discoveries of individual children and make them available to the whole group.

Each class also has a quiet period every day, lasting from twenty to forty-five minutes depending on age. The only rule is that no one can talk to anyone else. Most children read or write or do some other quiet activity. Parents and teachers consider this especially important to these children whose lives at school and home are otherwise quite crowded and noisy.

The Learning Place

The Learning Place, a junior-senior high school in San Francisco, is an example of a school for older children which has adapted some of the open structure and Summerhillian ideas used by others for younger children. The Learning Place, though, has recognized the limitations of that philosophy in an urban setting. Children do need lots of freedom to be themselves and move at their own pace in learning. But they also must learn how to deal with this freedom in a constructive manner, and with the complicated and often hostile environment of our cities. A "free" school in a large city is very different from a boarding school in the country.

The students at The Learning Place come from lower and middle class homes. There is diversity, including some students with emotional problems, some with strong aversion to academic pursuits, some who are extremely bright, others who are angry and have many problems relating to their parents.

The curriculum is hard to capture because it's constantly evolving and changing to meet the needs of the students and the school community. One month may see a heavily scheduled academic course, the next month will be camping trips and working on building their space. The types of activities are greatly varied. There may be a classroom situation with a teacher and students pursuing a specific discipline: math, spelling, biology. Or the students may be having direct experiences in the community: setting up a breakfast program for elementary children, visiting a court session, planning and executing a trip to Grand Canyon, working out school-community problems. Or the students may become involved with teachers or other adults on a personal, tutorial basis, learning through apprenticeships, conversations, intellectual explorations, activities.

The primary principle is that the learning needs and patterns of each student are different. There should be a variety of settings and opportunities to meet these needs and patterns. Another principle is that the child will learn a wide range of skills and facts when he is not afraid of failure and when his natural desire to know has not been crushed. The staff believe that as long as the child is told what to learn under very rigid conditions, with rote learning being the primary method, he will never explore for himself what he can do best; he will be a slave to what others say he should do and think and learn.

At this point in the development of the curriculum at The Learning Place, students and staff are beginning to ask for more discipline and depth in academic areas. After two years of lots of playing and some good work, they are moving toward seriously pursuing interests in art, carpentry, sciences, general skills of reading, writing, spelling, and math, and, most important, emotional and social development.

The students' request for disciplined academic work comes from real excitement about learning. No one is forcing them to spend hours understanding genetics or algebra—they *want* to learn and the teachers enjoy teaching them. As a result, the time required to learn a course is drastically reduced. Moreover, while it might be that a "required" curriculum would not differ from what students study at The Learning Place, the difference in motivation between "required" and desired is critical.

Highland Park Free School

Highland Park Free School is a parent-controlled school with about 200 students drawn from the predominantly poor Black community of Highland Park in Boston. Each classroom is run by a community teacher with the assistance of a professional teacher. The ages of students are equivalent to kindergarten through eighth grade.

Since the start of the school there has been tension between educational experimentation and the feelings of some parents that learning basic skills requires a highly structured classroom like that of the public schools the parents remember. In spite of this tension there are substantial differences among the many classrooms in the school, since each teacher team is in charge of its own class. Increasingly, however, the school has been moving toward sharing certain parts of the curriculum throughout the school. This effort is a result of an increasing awareness by parents and teachers of the mutual needs of the students, the Highland Park community, and the Black community generally.

The classrooms are less rigidly structured than most public schools, but more structured than the British infant school or Montessori classrooms. A typical day for six- and seven-year-olds would include:

> Breakfast: this period stresses responsibilities for the students in serving, cleaning, setting up the classroom, feeding animals, etc. The purpose is to teach that the class belongs to the students in the sense that it cannot function without their help.

Yoruba Songs and Recitation of *Ngozo Saba*: the seven principles, followed by small group discussion of one of these guiding principles or of some issue brought up by students or teachers.

Reading hour: the class will typically be divided into four groups of 5 or 6 students, each working on a separate project. One group may be using phonics flash cards, one practicing letter formation, one reading out loud, and one writing stories about pictures. Teachers move from group to group providing help and encouragement where needed.

Mathematics: another hour devoted to number skills and organized in the same small group fashion with students working at their own pace.

Science or social studies project: this may be, for example, drawing a map of the neighborhood or of a country being studied.

In each of these morning sessions there are specific tasks students are encouraged to complete. Recesses are spread throughout.

Lunch

Afternoon: This time is generally less structured and resembles models like the British infant school. There are many materials available and students pick any project they want to work on. Student interest is the center of the curriculum at this point, although this interest is sometimes organized into trips or projects done by the entire class (an urban studies project once made a map of how different land was used in the neighborhood). Some activities are outside the school, such as dance, music, and art work offered at the Elma Lewis Center in Roxbury.

The vehicle for providing some curriculum common to all the classes has been the *Ngozo Saba,* seven principles adapted from Nyrere's principles of African Socialism. These were first introduced after the director returned from a visit to Africa during which he became convinced of the importance of rituals which could provide an implicit, symbolic organization for the school and replace the irrelevant rituals of public schools (e.g., flag salute). The principles are: unity;

self-determination; collective work and responsibility; cooperative economics; purpose; creativity; and faith. These were adopted by the parents and staff readily as an expression of values important to their community. In addition to using them in morning ritual and discussion, the school attempts to relate these principles to most discussions in the classroom (e.g., what did we do today to make ourselves more unified as a class or how does this historical movement reflect antagonism to cooperative economics?), and to discussion in teacher's meetings of classroom situations. As time goes on the meaning of these principles to the community has become obvious in concrete situations, and the principles have thereby become the beginning of a curriculum common to all the classes in the school.

The *Ngozo Saba* describe some of the values the school feels are needed in order to help develop strong individuals with self-respect and a commitment to the Black community. The structured situation in the class, especially mornings, reflects the need to provide unity between home and school. It has been found by the school that too much tension between the often highly structured home and a wide-open classroom makes it difficult for students to function well. It's not a matter of discipline, but of creating enough structure for a child to feel comfortable and confident about making his or her own decisions.

There has also been an increase in the school's analysis of the technical skills the community will need in the future. Skills are stressed which students do not bring to school with them. For example, standard English is taught, but almost as if it were a second language. The message is that street language is adequate and important, but that standard English must also be learned in order to get along in the technocratic white culture. It is like learning to speak French when going to France. No putdown of the mother tongue is implied, only a recognition of a skill needed to get along in another world.

Math and science are also stressed since it has become increasingly apparent to the school that there are not enough people with technical skills in the Black community. The school feels that if students can get excited about math and science at a young age, it will lead them naturally into technical expertise later.

Throughout the school there is an attempt to select or make materials relevant to the urban, Black experience, and related to the *Ngozo Saba*. The community is often a resource, providing useful materials and a reason to be concerned with what is being learned.

Staff and parent curriculum committees have increasingly focused on getting teachers and parents to reflect on community goals so that curriculum and materials can be made with the needs of the community in mind.

The Group School

The Group School is a student- and staff-run high school for working-class youth in Cambridge, Massachusetts. Its curriculum and entire program are a response to the needs of working-class youth and the social and economic pressures of a working-class neighborhood. The Group School accepts the ideas of its students about what education is—learning from experience—and tries to help every student become a self-motivated learner.

The curriculum is constantly evolving, but its core includes basic skills, employment, working-class history and culture, and personal growth. The basic skills program responds to the need of these 14-to-21-year-olds to sharpen those skills not adequately developed in public schools. No student is required to take basic skills, but most do in fact involve themselves in one of the many different reading and math programs available. There are courses in remedial reading and math as well as in higher levels of these skills needed for college entrance examinations, high school equivalency examinations, or creative writing.

The employment program aims to meet the needs of these students to have gainful employment to support themselves and their families, and to eliminate the need for any student to choose between work and study in order to preserve his or her self-esteem. The program places students in jobs and provides personal counseling and seminars dealing with the problems of work, the structure of working situations, and future work plans. The Group School is also developing plans for vocational counseling and eventually vocational training.

Working-class history and culture, embodied in the entire attitude of the school but focused on in a course called "Hard Times," provides an opportunity for students to understand the labor history of which their parents and grandparents were a part and to relate these experiences to a political and economic analysis of the present world of work. It is a history of America viewed through the eyes of the working class. Here, as elsewhere in the school, much teaching is done through role playing, projects, and examination of the real issues facing the students. A women's history class focuses on contributions and problems of women in a male-dominated society.

The Group School also pays considerable attention to the emotional growth and needs of students, especially because this concern has been passed over or repressed by the public schools from which they came. There are encounter groups, including one women's group, and considerable personal counseling aimed at helping everyone recognize and express his or her own feelings. To some the school has taken on the aspect of a family—open and not so judgmental as to discourage personal expression.

The school also provides opportunities for students to pursue whatever their personal goals may involve. There are craft workshops; music, drama, science, law, and politics classes; and sports. And the school has a large group of volunteer teachers who provide instruction in any subject students show an interest in.

Personal services, often through referrals to cooperating agencies, are also a basic part of the school's effort to provide all the assistance students need in getting a sound education. Physical and mental health, legal, employment, and family problems are among those the school helps students deal with. Any problem preventing a student from gaining full value from his education is treated as a personal concern by the school and no issue involving a member of the school community is considered irrelevant or beyond the scope of the school's purpose.

CHAPTER EIGHT

Curriculum: Important Questions

In this chapter we will discuss several problems commonly faced by people building a curriculum for a new school.

Basic Skills

Controversies have often centered on the manner in which basic academic skills are taught and the general emphasis such teaching is given. You can eliminate much of this potential conflict by thinking carefully and clearly about basic skills as you build your curriculum.

What fundamental skills are necessary, in your view, for later learning and ultimately for survival in the world? Few groups would disagree that reading, writing, and basic arithmetic are essential skills. Most communities will add others to the list of basic skills, such as fluency in two languages. How soon must basic skills be learned? How are you going to teach these basic skills? Or how are you going to provide for children to learn them on their own?

Sometimes, people starting new schools, especially if they aren't parents themselves and aren't in close touch with parents, slide over these questions quickly. They might say, for example, "Learning skills is not as important as being in a loving, healthy environment where the child can develop freely. Anyway, in a rich and caring environment, children will want to learn most skills on their own." That may be a valid approach, but unless it is very well thought out and accepted by everyone in the school, there will be a lot of anxiety and maybe even hard feelings later when some children are *not* in fact learning to read and write. You must be sure that your judgment about the importance of basic skills reflects the needs of the students and not a fanciful idea of the kind of world they are going to have to cope with.

On the other hand, in some schools parents' valid concerns about learning basic skills have led to very rigid priorities for teaching them. In the worst settings, like many public schools, teaching skills is regarded as the only important thing and everything else is considered a "frill." But even in new schools, where parents and teachers understand that children learn most and best in an environment where they're happy and respected, parent (and teacher) anxiety may create a lot of pressure on the teachers and children and may force adoption of a rigid timetable. This can be as harmful as ignoring basic skills.

Look at the experience of other schools which have experimented with different approaches to teaching skills, in more free and open contexts. Results have generally been good when parents trusted teachers who were serious about teaching and really cared about the kids, even though parents were initially skeptical of their methods. Some new schools have been pleasantly surprised themselves at how well their graduates have done when they entered traditional public high schools.

Here are some guideposts:

· Think carefully about what skills you consider important.

· Think carefully about how you propose to teach them.

· Don't be afraid to try very different and unusual methods if they make sense to you.

· Make sure all your parents understand very thoroughly the school's approach to the learning of skills.

· Make sure the staff is regularly accountable to parents on children's progress.

Structure

Parents starting a school may be disturbed at the seeming lack of structure in some other new schools they visit or have heard about. When they don't see kids sitting in desks or all working quietly at tables (in other words, when they do not see the only classroom structure they have personally experienced), they are afraid kids can do anything they want, and consequently will not learn.

In fact, there are many different ways of structuring a classroom that don't much resemble a traditional school. It's important to go beyond the initial fears of chaos and no-learning and look beneath the surface for the structure. At first glance, for instance, an open classroom along the lines of the Leicestershire model may seem noisy and disorganized. Closer inspection would show, however, that the environment provides a lot of structure—there are a limited number of materials around and planned activities from which children choose. These materials are carefully selected and activities are carefully planned not only to allow children to express their own feelings and ideas and progress at their own rate, but also to insure that each activity of a child's day contributes to his learning and growing in areas parents and staff consider essential. Furthermore, the teacher is quietly moving among individual children and groups of children, helping those who are frustrated, suggesting new possibilities to some children, and mediating conflicts among children who would otherwise become destructive. He or she is a basic part of the structure. There are, in addition, certain rules about how children treat one another and how they care for materials. Even if these rules are few and simple, they provide another element of structuring the activity in the classroom.

Finally, the examples presented by the adults' behavior are a part of the structure. Very little about this seemingly chaotic situation has not been carefully planned and structured, and the results are often very impressive. Sometimes you will find adults in fact *have* tried to avoid creating and imposing structure, even one as open as in a Leicestershire classroom. They have usually done so because they believe any structure imposed by adults (other than that naturally flowing from their personalities) is artificial and limits the natural creativity and curiosity of children. However, in such cases, the vacuum does not last long. The kids themselves create a structure. They establish rules and patterns of behavior they enforce or attempt to enforce with each other. If you choose to let the students create their own structure, you should watch this evolving structure closely to see whether it's actually helping the kids learn and grow happily.

The students in elementary school haven't much experience in making social structures work. Even though they may be free of many of the hangups and bad habits of their elders, they are still young and some of them may have been hurt and distorted by unhealthy structures and insensitive treatment before. Therefore, sometimes the kids evolve structures that are not helpful to learning and yet don't change them because they don't know what is making them unhappy. If adults don't intervene, or wait too long to do so, these patterns may destroy the school and/or cause a lot of pain and unhappiness to the kids. Shire School in San Francisco, for example, functioned fairly well for a number of years with loving teachers who imposed very little structure. Then one fall and winter, for reasons which are not clear, the student body began to split into generally hostile and unco-operative factions. More and more the school was consumed by fighting, bickering, and stealing. For a while the staff stood back, expecting this to be a phase the kids had to pass through in learning to live and work together. As the situation became more and more painful, they tried to intervene, but by then the children were unresponsive to anything the staff thought of and finally the staff and some of the parents decided they had no choice but to close the school.

If the structure of your curriculum is designed to provide freedom for students to make choices for their own learning (and learn to take responsibility for their own learning by living with the results of those choices—learning from mistakes as well as successes), you need to look at it carefully from time to time to make sure it's actually doing that. Sometimes, having too many choices limits rather than broadens freedom—a student may easily become bewildered and confused and then either withdraw and do very little or become angry and interfere with the learning of others.

There are some schools which purport to offer unlimited choice, where each student is encouraged to decide what he wants to learn. Even here there are often hidden pressures, expectations, or structures which limit choice. It is better to have these things clear than to presume there are no bounds to the freedom in the school. Unlimited choice is aimed for. It may work very well among older students who are self-motivated already and have some clear notions of what they want to do. But for younger students, and others who have previously been almost totally dependent upon external authority for directing their education, a situation of unlimited choice may limit their freedom severely. Insurmountable confusion is not freedom.

Fortunately, these situations of too much choice or unclear restrictions on choice can be changed fairly easily if you are closely and frequently observing what's happening. You can limit the number of choices for a while, if students seem to be getting generally frustrated. On the other hand, you can open up the structure—creating more choices and encouraging individuals to develop their own activities—when there seems to be a lot of "champing at the bit" or boredom. You can examine what pressures students feel and see if these are the desired product of your structure or lack of it. As students grow older and more experienced in handling freedom creatively, you will want to modify your structure accordingly.

In summary, we want to emphasize that the question of structure need not be an emotionally charged issue in which the choice is between structure and no structure. There are plenty of different kinds of structure, if you will take the time to look for them. There is really no such thing as an unstructured school. The real question is whether your structure (whether you designed it or it just happened) is working for you; whether it is promoting the kind of learning and interaction and happiness among the kids that you want. If not, it can be adjusted from time to time with small and moderate changes, so long as you observe closely what's going on and don't allow destructive situations to persist.

Politics and Curriculum

A third question commonly discussed and sometimes avoided, concerns the political impact of the curriculum. If we think of politics as the power relationships between people or groups, then every school is both an expression of a political situation and a teacher of politics. Textbooks or teachers may totally avoid advocating political positions but the school will still have political implications, and it's best to admit this and examine your reactions to it.

Every school has a political structure. The general governing method represents the power of varying people—staff, parents, kids, other community members—over decisions made at the school. This will serve as a model from which students will draw certain conclusions about what should or should not be the relationships of these people and of people generally. If you discover differences between the values you hold and the values your school structure represents, you will no doubt want to make some change.

Just as with student selection and governance, there are choices in teaching methods which have political implications and effects. The relationship among teachers and the relationship between teachers and director or teachers and students expresses values about the relative allocation of power over different kinds of decisions. At the Ironbound Community School considerable thought has been given to this problem in the context of a white working-class neighborhood with traditionally strong views about authority. The parents have decided after examining the development of their own childhood, that the teachers, assistant teachers, and parent volunteers should be in a relation of absolute equality as regards power in the classroom, and their relationship to the kids. To do otherwise, they believe, would be to foster undesirable notions of hierarchy among people.

The same kinds of implications stem from the degree of cooperativeness or competition fostered among children—how much rules and regulations take the place of personal relationships, the effect of grading, tracking, or other differentiating among students, etc. It is easy to believe in political neutrality, but the reality seems to be that basic values about power and human organization are taught by subtler examples than textbook instruction.

You may well find conflict in yourself between the ideals you hold and what you perceive as the most practical or efficient method of getting your school to do what you want it to do. We may teach the importance of democracy, but run our schools as an autocracy in order to get things done. We may ask children to get along with one another, but only regard them in competitive struggles. The political effects of your methods should not be ignored when it comes to figuring out whether you are reaching your goals. These effects are as real and perhaps as important as whether reading is learned.

What Process of Curriculum Decision Will You Use?

The experience of many new schools involves slow, trial-and-error development. This is especially true of curriculum, which, for the majority of schools, seems to be the last area to receive careful, well-organized attention. This is not entirely surprising, since the struggle for survival often takes much of the energy people would like to apply to the pursuit of excellence. The process of curriculum decision is fragmentary until people suddenly see it as a neglected area and treat it with special energy.

The chief exception to trial-and-error development is found in those schools adhering to a specific curriculum theory developed by people outside the school. The programmed, sequential use of materials characteristic of the Montessori method is a good example. Though minor modifications are often made, those who use the method find most of the decisions about what to teach and how to teach have already been made.

If your school grows out of some organizing principle other than a curriculum model, there will be much greater need for a process of planning curriculum with which you are comfortable. The parameters of this process may be set by decisions you have already made about your school. For example, a school which places a high degree of importance on parent participation will adopt a process by which parents can influence or control the basic aspects of curriculum.

In setting up a method of making curriculum decisions, provide for the following:

1. *Formulation of curriculum plans in advance.* This will involve a process of translating the general goals into a teaching plan (for example, that reading and math skills should be taught in both English and Spanish, but that no child should be pressured to learn English before age 9 if his natural inclination is to work with art materials or work in Spanish). This planning process must take adequate account of the interests of parents and teachers alike so that everyone will be able to support the decisions once they are made. Since few people are aware of the many different kinds of curricula, the group you set up to make these decisions may want to do some studying on its own, for example through a set of seminars, or through requesting staff to present a number of alternative plans. If you have a curriculum committee, there should be some way for it to relate its work back to the entire parent or community body.

2. *Reactions of teachers, students, parents.* When the curriculum is in operation, there will be reactions about its usefulness. You should pay attention to the teachers', parents', and students' evaluation. It may be that the curriculum is not comfortable

for teachers, is beyond their skills or is turning the kids off. Some system of discussing these reactions should be set up, for example, monthly discussions among teachers and parents on how a program is working out. Such evaluation should probably not be left until the end of the year, because many modifications can be made during the year. Being responsive is something a small school can do well. Remember it's just as important that teachers feel productive and parents feel supportive as that students learn, because all these are tied together. Testing may be part of this process, but it will not answer many important questions about emotional development.

3. *Making changes.* In some situations, the group monitoring reactions to the curriculum may not be the same as the group that set up the curriculum in the first place. The involvement of teachers and students may be heavier. In any case, it should not be a giant struggle for the monitoring group to get action on its perceptions. Don't set up a structure that separates planning and action so completely that you cannot move back and forth between them easily. This may amount to nothing more than maintaining some intimacy among all the people involved in curriculum decisions. *Don't bureaucratize.*

4. *Getting new information from outside.* Knowing about other schools' experiences is often the most neglected area of curriculum decisions. Undoubtedly, a number of schools have similar goals and students. They can probably be located through the New Schools Directory. There are also groups which make it their business to develop curriculum materials and ideas and help schools and parents get acquainted with different approaches. If you want to improve your curriculum, you should probably keep in touch with these groups and schools (see Chapter Twelve, *Resources*). Some way of introducing this kind of information should be built into your curriculum decision process, for it is easy to overlook.

Some schools have seminars for parents or for the curriculum committee(s) during the year. Others hold such sessions during planning time or during summer. Sometimes outside help is sought in response to a particular problem; for example, parents may be interested in textbooks, but really have little experience in evaluating them.

Whatever the process, it's a matter of maintaining education for teachers and parents as well as students. This is one of the big benefits of a small school with heavy involvement of all segments of its community. The education of parents and teachers about what is going on in the school and how it can be improved, the spreading of educational "expertise" throughout the community, is not just a luxury. Many schools which have inaugurated new teaching methods without the involvement of parents have experienced serious confrontations about how the school is run. It is an inevitable collision unless the process of curriculum decision involves parents and staff together and unless attention is paid to educating parents and staff as well as students.

The relative influence of students, teachers, directors, parents, experts, and the community at large varies tremendously from school to school:

- One school leaves curriculum planning totally up to the individual teacher in the individual classroom. The teacher may or may not involve other people in his decisions.

- Another school has four parent curriculum committees developing curriculum ideas for teachers to carry out in communications, social science, natural science, and math.

- Still another has a parent curriculum committee which doesn't plan, but listens to parent complaints and seeks adjustments to satisfy them. It also runs curriculum workshops for parents to increase parent planning of curriculum.

- The school director had considerable influence on curriculum matters but the school later moved to group decisions by the teaching staff because people felt more self-respect working this plan.

- One school has an elaborate curriculum decision process in which authority rests with parents, but the entire staff and the educational director are involved. There are daily meetings of teachers and assistant teachers to evaluate the day and plan the next day; weekly meetings with the teachers and education director to discuss curriculum problems and student and staff reactions; monthly meetings of the entire staff and parents, to talk about curriculum practice and philosophy; voluntary workshops by experts on new curriculum materials or methods; and two-week workshops in September on curriculum planning.

· Another school makes curriculum by hiring staff with particular interests.

· Another school's curriculum is based largely on the expressed interests of students working on projects.

· One school spent ten weeks in parent seminars discussing everything from the psychology of young children to their own experiences in school before deciding on the kind of curriculum they wanted. They then simply hired teachers who shared their philosophy and created personal relationships among parents and teachers sufficient to exchange reactions and change plans when needed.

Perhaps the most important factor in making a curriculum decision process satisfactory is that the school be small enough to allow direct participation of everyone who wants to be involved. A predominance of curriculum experts or curriculum administrators seems to be a reaction to a school so large that it's impractical for parents, teachers, and students to participate fully in these vital decisions.

CHAPTER NINE

Evaluation Questions

Student Growth and Progress. Will the school give grades to students? Will it otherwise comparatively rank them or their progress?

Will the school have testing? Diagnostic testing? Standardized testing similar to that of the public schools? Experimental, e.g., "culture-free," testing trying to measure ability and/or achievement in different ways? Tests within the classrooms or instructional program?

Should there be regular evaluative conferences between teachers and students? Teachers and parents? All three together? Will the teachers write regular written reports on the progress of children? How will students evaluate their own progress?

School Self-Evaluation. Does the school wish to adopt some regular, conscious procedures for evaluating its progress or success?

Do you want to specify goals such that later on you can concretely evaluate to what extent you have reached them?

How often do you want to evaluate? Weekly? Monthly? Annually? Different times for different aspects?

Do you want to evaluate in informal, but perhaps regular, meetings?

Do you want to engage a consultant or volunteer not directly associated with the school to advise you on evaluation, and perhaps to gather some data to feed back to parents, staff, students?

Outside Independent Evaluations. Do you wish to arrange for some sort of outside evaluation by an independent person or group? For what reasons? Under what conditions? How closely do you want to work with them?

If a community school, how about some sort of community evaluating team or process (analogous to teams of visiting professional educators that evaluate schools for the regional accrediting associations)?

What stance are you going to take toward outside agencies—state or local school district—or colleges that may approach you wanting to evaluate the school for purposes of their own?

Evaluation by Prospective Parents. How do you want prospective parents to evaluate your school? In other words how should a parent decide whether or not to send his/her child to your school?

Do you wish your self-evaluation to be oriented in this way? Do you want to have an outside evaluation designed for this purpose? Do you want testing and achievement scores and data available to prospective parents?

Have you considered making up a checklist of things a prospective parent should do in considering and evaluating your school?—talking to one or two other parents already in the school, visiting a classroom for at least half a day, talking with one or more teachers, looking over some of the instructional materials, carefully reading the school's statement of goals, comparing your school with at least one other school, stating clearly his or her expectations of your school so that you can discuss honestly with the parent whether or not you believe the school will meet those expectations and what problems might arise.

CHAPTER TEN

Fund Raising

It would be great if we could offer an optimistic report on the possibilities of raising money to support community schools. But the truth of the matter is that it is a long, hard road and many people spend more energy on fund raising than on education. Good hustling, hard work, and a little luck can keep your school afloat for a time, but eventually we all face the problem of finding some reliable, stable source of income. It is this goal which you should keep in mind and toward which your other funding strategies should build.

It is important to understand the political and economic context into which community schools are born. To receive public tax money a school must be part of a system which is administered by a locally elected school board. Unless you are setting up a community school within the public system through the exercise of your own political power or the benevolence of that system, you are beginning *outside* the definition of schools which will be supported by tax monies. You may get some of the crumbs from the tax table, but basically you will either have to depend on private support or struggle to change the way school money is distributed. Most of this section deals with getting private support or tax table crumbs, but these sources cannot sustain a community school for very long. Most community schools must sooner or later face the issue of getting public funds.

Those who elect to set up their own schools by taking over a piece of the public system, elect to confront the issue of getting resources first. Those who begin outside the system may be able to build a good school and they may be able to build internal strength and political support by deferring the confrontation, but sooner or later they will probably either face this problem or dissolve. We note with some anger that our economic system and the present method of funding education allows the rich to avoid the issue of getting public funds for the education of their choice while the poor and the working class must constantly struggle with that issue.

Tuition

Many schools examine the idea of having a tuition at some time in their history. Often this is not practical because parents simply cannot afford tuition. Other schools feel that tuition violates their beliefs even if some parents could afford to pay. And schools with tuition often supplement their income from other sources.

If you are considering imposing some kind of tuition, it is not difficult to construct a system of graduated tuitions based on the ability of each family to pay. Strict income-tuition figures are usually not useful because the decision of what a family can "afford" is so personal and so much a reflection of other expenses they may have. Setting up some general guidelines, such as a maximum tuition and an average tuition for broad categories of income, is best. These can be used as the basis of discussion between the school and the parents about what can be afforded. These negotiations should be private. Keeping tuition amounts confidential may help avoid embarrassment and pressure.

Private Aid

Private assistance may come from local individuals and businesses, from local foundations, or from national foundations. You want to develop your own funding strategy based on where you think you can be most effective; but a few schools have discovered some general rules of thumb about the private assistance route.

First, most national foundations will want to know whether you have attempted to raise money locally. Being able to enumerate local attempts, successful or not, may help you to be taken more seriously. Local individuals, especially ones whose positions or numbers might impress other people with money, can be very helpful. You are trying to break into a world in which a relatively small group of people respect the opinions of each other or people "like them." Once a few of these people give you money, you have begun to acquire the "respectability" which can be used to convince still more people of the merits of your request.

In approaching businesses, remember that while you may feel they owe something to the community in which they make their profits they often do not see it this way. Such an argument needs considerable political pressure to be effective. If you are approaching a businessman simply on the basis of a good idea which deserves his support and is important to his community's health, remember that most contributors like to be more involved than Santa Claus when they are giving their money away.

This does not mean that they wish to control your school, but simply that they want to be respected for their judgment (their business judgment is probably pretty good) as well as the size of their corporate purse. Simple things like asking advice and keeping contributors informed about your school may go a long way toward helping you get contributions from them in the future and from their business associates. We know of at least one case in which a local businessman gave a course in management to a school director who solicited him for funds. The course proved very helpful to the director and the school. If you pick people carefully you may be able to build some real community support.

Much of the work of raising private money involves connections—people who know people who know people who can help. You need the patience to follow up leads. Take time talking to many people, keep in touch with those who have helped, constantly try to stay on the scent. It can be a colossal drag. More things turn to ashes than to money. But if this is how you have decided to raise money, keep cool and keep hustling.

Local foundations and charities are usually small and sometimes are joined together into associations of foundations or charities. They may share one executive officer to do initial screening of proposals. If they are not joined, you may have to pick through the separate ones yourself. Before approaching these people try to find out as much as you can about how much they usually give and for what, what times of year they consider applications, what kind of supporting information they like to have. The library may have a foundation directory which will start you on this road; conversations with knowledgeable people around town (go out and look for them) will also help.

With local foundations, as with any fund raising activity, do not restrict yourself to a single description of your school as just a school. People's definitions of school are flexible; and what you are doing may be a lot more than a school. Maybe you provide social services to kids and families—you may be a multi-service center. Maybe you have a health program which can be funded separately, or a counseling program which can be attractive to those interested in community mental health, or an arts program which emphasizes "humanistic" teaching. Look at your goals and programs for things which can be funded separately. Remember that a lot of this is the art of "packaging"—making your school look unique and attractive to people whose interests you know something about. It is a little cynical, but it works.

When you get to the point of approaching large national foundations (Ford, Rockefeller, etc.), try to find out about their thinking before you make a proposal. They usually have policies about what they are currently interested in, and though you can break through this sometimes, it is best to know about them. Currently alternative schools are not terribly popular. There are hundreds and thousands of proposals from alternative schools. Foundations seem to be worried about them as endless drains which will never become self-supporting and therefore will always be asking for funds. If you can convince foundations you have a reasonable chance of becoming self-sufficient or getting public money, they will be much more interested in sustaining you while you start.

Foundations are also worried about the fact that money going to alternative schools does not affect the majority of kids who stay in public schools. If you can make a case that you are working to have an effect on the public schools, you will be in better shape. The old argument that private schools serve as models which public schools emulate because of their effectiveness is useless—largely because it simply isn't true. (You need some leverage and some aggressive tactics to change the direction of the public school juggernaut.)

Again, think freely about how to describe what you are doing. Alternative schools may be out, but "innovative curriculum development" may be in.

Be careful about being led on. Most people will tell you if you have a very slim chance, but some people wait a long time before letting the other shoe drop. Don't be afraid to ask whether you're getting serious consideration and what your chances are. Otherwise you can drain a lot of time and energy on an uncertain enterprise.

Just about every city has a few people who are experienced in raising runds from foundations and private individuals and corporations. The notes in this section are no substitute for talking with these people to find out what your best course of action is.

Self-support—Business, Contracts, Services

When you solicit funds from a foundation or an individual or a business corporation, you are essentially asking them to hand over a part of their profits to a worthy cause. This raises all the problems of having to ask for what you may feel you should be entitled to (public schools do not solicit money this way) and of justifying your values to someone else (as a matter of survival) merely because they happen to have made some money or controlled some capital. This is not entirely pleasant and raises a number of difficult political-economic questions.

It may be possible to eliminate some of this and at the same time to move toward a stable independent source of funds. To do this you may want to think about going into business yourself. We do not mean by this that schools can be run for profit (we doubt that this can be done without either exploiting the staff or cheating the students). But if your school is operating and fairly stable, you may be able to hire additional staff who would do work, at least part time, which would yield the school a profit. As an example, researchers from universities or from government agencies sometimes ask community schools to provide information about the school—to give of their experiences and the fruits of their work. Many community schools have started charging for this information. It is a very small business (which must be kept under control so you will have time left for the school) based on the fact that researchers get paid to gather this information.

The kinds of self-support you might consider could include at least:

1. *Contracts: doing work for city or state agencies.* This work would be done by people hired by you and the rate of payment would have to be high enough so that money was left over from the actual expense of doing the work to support the school. It is much better if the work itself also benefits the goals of the school. An example is The Group School, which has a contract with the local Youth Resources Bureau to run two counseling groups. One of these is for adolescents referred by the YRB (kids who are near to being in trouble with the courts) and one is run for students within The Group School. These students would want this kind of program anyway, so there is no diversion of the purposes of the school. The contract supports staff doing work the school wants done and also provides a little extra cash since the salaries of the people doing this work are higher than the amounts they actually need to get along on.

Contracts can be based on any expertise which you have or which you can acquire by hiring people who wish to be part of the community.

2. *Businesses.* It has been suggested that community schools could also go into business using the profits from the business as a means of supporting the school. We have not found any notable successes (or failures) in this area, but there have been a number of people talking about it. A number of good suggestions in this area can be found in Jonathan Kozol's book *Free Schools* in the chapter "Warehouse Bookstore: Rehab Housing: Franchise Operations." You might also look into the ideas of Charles Hampden-Turner, who has written on uses of Community Development Corporations. He can be contacted at Cambridge Institute, 1878 Massachusetts Avenue, Cambridge, Mass.

The crux of this tactic is that you become the business which you were formerly asking for money. The prospects are untested and the administrative and business expertise required to really make such an operation run successfully might prove a great obstacle. At least it should be considered. If you do get into it, be sure to get not only expert business advice, but also legal advice as to how to do this without jeopardizing your tax status with the Internal Revenue Service.

3. *Services.* This really amounts to a kind of income sharing be-

tween people who have services they can sell and the school. The school becomes a community institution with many different kinds of people associated with it. Some of these people contribute part of their pay for services they render outside the community. In exchange the community provides a certain amount of economic security by insuring at least a minimum adequate income to these people in hard times. One example is this book. It was written by some people at two community schools and the royalties will go to the support of these two schools.

The main trouble with businesses and with services is that they rely on people being willing to take less profit from their work than they can get. They are a contradiction of the entire profit motive. Yet we have seen people moving in these directions because they are committed to their schools and communities more than to their personal physical comfort and because they have come to recognize some of the social and economic drawbacks of operating on the profit motive. Many of these people believe that it would be better to change the entire economic system or at least the means of financing education, but in the meantime this is viewed as a relatively non-exploitive way to survive in the world as it is.

State Programs

It may be a considerable amount of work but it is generally worth inquiring into the state programs which might prove a source of aid to your school. You should not expect to find general school aid, but you may be able to get some money for specific purposes. Most attempts at providing general aid have foundered on the federal or state constitutional prohibitions against state support for religion. There are continued efforts to provide generalized support in accordance with constitutional requirements, most notably tax credits and tuition vouchers, but none have been successful yet.

There may be state laws in your area providing transportation or textbook loans or supplemental services (for example, health checkups) for nonpublic schools. These should be checked into.

Most states have surplus property programs, usually available through the state department of education. You are probably eligible for this program in which government surplus, from desks to dental equipment, is available for a modest handling charge (almost free). When inquiring into this, check with your lawyer if you are told you are not eligible.

Most states also administer a federal program providing free or low-cost lunches, breakfasts, and surplus foods for schools which have a large number of students from poor families. Check through your state department of education and double check any resistance you encounter with your lawyer to be sure it is legitimate.

Many states also have programs for providing supportive services for young people who have been in trouble with the courts or are near to being in such trouble. If you are careful and can find a cooperative person in such a state program you may be able to get some support if your program is helping these kids.

Once you get past these basic programs—transportation, text-books, food, surplus property, and youth resources programs—the search becomes more difficult. Still it may be worth it. Many available programs may not be specifically for schools, but may nevertheless help you. In Massachusetts for example, a state law makes it possible for nonprofit corporations in existence for over two years to hold raffles or lotteries and keep the proceeds. There may be a welfare provision for new career training which could be used by parents learning to become teachers. Social or medical services may be available on a referral basis at local clinics or agencies and these might be useful to you. Start looking and keep looking.

Federal Programs

This is the real haystack. And there may not even be a needle in it. The same problems in aiding private schools (separation of church and state required by the Constitution) apply to federal aid as to state aid.

In addition, Congress has not seen fit to aid nonreligious private schools. This is partly because for a long time nonpublic schools were either religious (largely Catholic) or were elitist prep schools which didn't need any federal money. Perhaps if community schools become more numerous they will command enough attention to get some aid even if religious schools cannot constitutionally receive support.

It can be a hassle to apply for federal funds. Most programs have not only governing laws but administration regulations and guidelines as well. The task of fitting within these regulations can take a lot of time and things may still not work out. It also happens that the conditions of the grant can be burdensome. It is still possible, however, to get some help from the federal government. You must decide whether you really need what is offered and how much energy is going to be required to pull it off. For this reason it is advisable to work with someone who can tell you exactly what the federal program requires and then help you figure out how or whether to fit into it. A local legal service lawyer can help with this. So can some of the federal bureaucrats themselves. It is part of their job to explain to you what is required and what is available.

The following federal programs should be looked into:

Elementary and Secondary Education Act (20 U.S.C.A. 241, P.L. 89-10). ESEA is really the only large federal program of aid to education besides aid provided to "impacted areas." The funding usually goes at about the 1.5 billion dollar level, almost all of it going to public schools.

Title I. This title is for *"educationally deprived" children,* which in effect means poor children. Eligibility depends upon showing of significant numbers of children whose families earn less than $2,000/year or are on AFDC. Because of the church-state problem, private schools can participate only in "services" provided by the public school. That is, no money is actually granted to a private school, but is given to the public school in a Title I target area which then makes services available. The act states that such services are to be "special educational services and arrangements, e.g., dual enrollments, educational radio and TV, and mobile educational services." This has been known to include remedial teaching, having students as tutors, psychological testing and counseling, and special equipment. The regulations then go into considerable detail about the fact that equipment must be owned by the public schools and loaned to the private schools. Teachers (e.g., remedial reading) must be on the public payroll and visit the private school (see regs. Title 45, part 116.19a-g). The regulations can be obtained by writing to the Office of Education in Washington, or contacting the Law and Education Center at Harvard University.

The regulations (116.19b) also provide that in any program to be administered by a local education agency (public school board), there must be consultation with representatives of private schools to determine the needs of such schools and how they can participate. This usually results in consulting parochial schools but not community schools, perhaps because they are less numerous and visible. In any case, you are entitled to consultation and, if you qualify, you may get participation. Whether that participation is helpful and non-burdensome to you will depend upon the arrangement you make with the local school authorities.

It is a good idea to get some legal assistance in approaching the local school authorities for participation. You do have some rights in this matter and it is important to know both what you can demand and what depends on cooperative arrangements with school authorities so that you do not jeopardize your negotiating position. It might be possible for a group of community schools with substantial numbers of poor children enrolled to band together and have Title I pay for equipment and supplemental teachers who would be busy all the time with the community schools.

The structure of the law's administration makes the local school authorities responsible for preparing an application for Title I funds each year, with added applications for summer programs. These applications are received and processed by the State Department of Education, which at present requires that they be in at least six weeks before the program is to begin. Deadlines tend to change, though, and it is important to find out what they are. Once the state approves the local applications, the federal money is disbursed without much further ado.

There is, of course, very little reason for the Title I guidelines to be as strict as they are for nonreligious schools. There is no church-state problem involved with them. For the meantime, however, they must be lived with. We suggest that you get a copy of the latest Title I application from your local school board (you are entitled to it according to the regulations) and see whether there are any programs which you might want to participate in or whether you can think of new ones to suggest. Keep an eye open for whether community schools have been consulted as they are required to be. Check with your brother schools. If enough schools with poor children in them got it together it would probably be possible to get Title I help on good terms.

Finally, every community which has a Title I program is required by state and federal guidelines to have an advisory board elected locally. Parents and community groups are represented. You may find a sympathetic ear at the advisory board. They are probably interested in the same kinds of changes in education that you are even though their present leverage is inside the system.

Title II. This section of the act provides aid to, among others, private schools, in improving their *libraries.* The money does not depend upon the income of the families of your students, but in most states it does vary with the tax base of the area in which you are located. Library grants come in two types, the regular library improvement program and the special purpose grant. Guidelines for this program can be obtained from the Library Extension Bureau of State Department of Education.

The regular grants depend in their amount on the number of students in the private school and the present condition of the library. Per pupil the amounts are small, but there is a minimum grant of $200 so that it may be worth it even for a very small school.

You will have to show that you are a publicly certified school (see State Requirements), are willing to sign a compliance form for Title VI of the 1964 Civil Rights Act (no discrimination in use of federal funds), and are not interested in receiving books of a religious nature. Ask about the regular program and about the special purpose grants.

Title III. This section provides for innovative and experimental educational programs. Provision for participation of nonpublic schools is indicated, but we have not heard of any community school receiving substantial assistance.

Food. For the operation of federal programs providing lunch, breakfast, milk, surplus commodities, and kitchen equipment, administered by the state, see *state aid.*

Teacher Training (and Salaries?). The Manpower Development and Training Act (P.L. 87-415) may be a source of funds for training teacher aid. In a cooperative arrangement a contract would be written between the Department of Labor, which administers the act, and a community school or other institution which was willing to make teaching at the school a part of the training. As far as we have been able to find out, the chances of drawing such a contract depend almost entirely upon the particular Labor Department Field Representative you are dealing with.

Outside Chances. Another potential source of assistance in paying teacher salaries is the Career Opportunity Program of the Education Professions Development Act. If it works, the C.O.P. program will pay low-income persons including veterans to prepare for teaching jobs. Where it has been successful with community schools (very rare) the government has used the program to pay tuition at a local school of education and a stipend while the eligible persons "practice teach" at the community schools. As with most federal programs run out of the Office of Education there is need to justify the program in terms of impact on public schools. The programs are cooperative arrangements between the federal government, a local college or university, and a school.

Slightly more possible, but equally difficult to arrange, is assistance from VISTA or from the Teacher Corps. Both of these programs have uncertain futures, but might be a source of teachers or subsistence salaries for your teachers.

Finally, you might make some inquiries about the *Follow Through* program. This is a continuation of the Headstart program attempting to keep track of and help Headstart kids once they get into the first few grades of elementary school. There is one occasion in which this program was operated through a community school in Massachusetts, but the arrangement involved several other local and state agencies to such a great degree that it seems unlikely that it would happen again. Nevertheless, it may be worth inquiring into if you have some contacts with a model cities program, a state education agency, or some university.

Advice. As with all government programs, the trick is to know enough about the guidelines to be able to write your proposal so that it fits in. The other basic requirement is the proper size, shape, and number of forms and copies. Save yourself some grief if you are applying, find out all the requirements before you sit down and start writing proposals. Good luck, and remember, the government ain't likely to support alternatives to the government.

CHAPTER ELEVEN

Technical Problems: Incorporation, State Regulations, Bookkeeping, Taxation, and Insurance

Incorporation

Most alternative schools will find it advantageous to incorporate as nonprofit, educational, or charitable corporations. Forming a corporation serves two legal purposes: (1) incorporation limits the liability of the individuals involved in the school for purposes of debt collection and other damage actions; (2) more importantly, incorporation helps the school to qualify for federal tax exemption by the Internal Revenue Service as a nonprofit agency.

Incorporation also serves several nonlegal purposes. Being incorporated is one of those things which assures skeptics of the stability and acceptability of your school. If you are applying for funds someplace, trying to get a lease, or trying to get certified, it will help to be incorporated. For your own purposes, you will find that the most interesting and useful part of incorporation is in working out a form of governance for your school, and making one of many attempts to define your goals. The bylaws can be viewed as writing the first constitution of the school. There will probably be plenty of changes to be made as you go along, but at least this helps you focus initially on the question of governance and the relationship between what you need to survive in the world and the ways that you want to relate to each other inside the school.

Nonprofit corporations are chartered by the state in which they operate, and generally require both articles of incorporation and bylaws. You should check into the particular requirements in your state. In general, bylaws cover the following matters:

- name and location of office
- definition of membership and procedure for terminating membership if desired
- meetings—regular, annual, special notice requirements for meetings and quorum requirements
- board of directors—membership, election, powers, and duties and meetings of the board of directors
- committees—if necessary
- officers—titles, functions, duties, terms of office, and election and removal procedures (corporate officers usually include president, vice-president, secretary, and treasurer)
- provisions for parliamentary procedures and the corporate seal
- amendments—provisions for amending the bylaws

Bylaws may present a problem for some alternative schools. Corporate law is based on the delegation of authority to the officers and board of directors of the corporation. This may be inconsistent with a desire for a more democratic way of operating a school. Furthermore, most state corporate laws do not recognize anyone under the age of 21. This also may create a conflict between the way the state wants a corporation operated and the way you want decisions made in your school. You can avoid this by having an unofficial set of bylaws for your own use, or by setting up a responsive board of directors which can simply meet a few times a year to ratify what has been done by a more informal procedure affording greater participatory democracy. In this way, the board of directors is the official body of the corporation but the policies are really being set by the parents, teachers, and students at their own meeting. In any case, you should check your plans against the legal requirements by consulting a lawyer.

You may feel that bylaws should not be allowed to be used as a tool by anyone upset with the products of a more democratic procedure. If so, do not give either the board of directors or officers excessive power, make their removal easy, make their terms short (they can always be reelected if they are cooperative), and make it easy to loosen the bylaws through simple amendment procedures.

You can make the bylaws and corporate form respond to your needs and goals. But remember that there is always the outside chance that someone, sometime, will question whether you have a real corporation. This is especially important in applying for federal tax exemption. If you do not maintain the integrity of the corporation, individuals may be liable for something the corporation would ordinarily be liable for. Or it may jeopardize your tax exemption or make it hard for you to gain the confidence of those with whom you deal. Because of this possibility it is essential that you talk the whole matter over with a lawyer who is sympathetic to your goals. Many things can be done by you which might become evidence that your corporation does not exist (for legal purposes). You should be aware of this and always keep yourself covered.

The section on governance made reference to several issues which you will face in determining how you are to manage the affairs of your school community and its relations with others. The resolution of these questions should be expressed in the bylaws as far as possible. In drawing bylaws remember two additional things: one, there may be changes in your attitude toward the governing structure of the school or corporation and the ease of changing the bylaws should reflect how much energy you want to have to generate in order to make basic changes; two, every change you make in the bylaws should be scanned by a lawyer to be sure that it does not jeopardize the corporation or its tax exemption.

One of the most important technical aspects of getting incorporated as a nonprofit organization is making sure that your charter and bylaws are written so that it will be possible for you to get a tax exemption under section 501(c)3 of the Internal Revenue Code. This exemption is for charitable, educational, scientific and certain other nonprofit organizations. It allows contributors to your school to deduct their contributions from their income or corporate income tax and it makes it unnecessary for you to pay income tax as a corporation. Many states also follow the IRS determination in granting you tax-exempt status so you will not have to pay state sales tax on corporate purchases.

The major requirements of section 501(c)3 are that you be nonprofit and that you not engage in any political activity (as a corporation). You should be sure to have a lawyer familiar with the tax code go over your corporate papers before you file them so that he can advise you about whether you have written anything which might make it difficult to get the IRS exemption.

You should also remember when drawing up your corporate charter, which is essentially a description of your purposes and powers, that you may want to operate more than just a school. If your notion of school includes health services or parent seminars or community organizing, you should be sure that your charter uses broad enough language to enable you to do these things. The Group School, for example, is the main but not the only activity of The Group, Inc., which also runs community programs (such as counseling and training). Again, when setting up your corporation to do more than run a school as most people would think of it, be sure to have a lawyer look over the papers. Free legal help is available to those who qualify under poverty guidelines. Consult a local legal services office or OEO Office for this.

State Requirements

The regulation of private schools in most states leaves considerable discretion to state or local authorities. While the statutes may appear to make it fairly easy to establish a nonpublic school, the absence of firm rights for nonpublic schools and the unpredictability of the enforcement of the laws could at any time generate considerable insecurity for nonpublic schools. Discretionary authority can be the mother of flexibility or repression, depending on the political atmosphere.

A substantial increase in the number of nonpublic schools will probably lead to increased investigation and regulation. Doing your political groundwork, therefore, will probably be as important as knowing the legal requirements which affect you. In reading through this section keep in mind that it is your own educational standards which are most important. The basic decisions described in earlier sections should be reached before you concern yourself in detail with the legal requirements.

You should keep in mind also that while the state may make reasonable requirements designed to secure a basic minimum education to all students required to attend school, it may not compel anyone to attend public schools or so regulate private schools as to make them identical to public schools. (For support of this notion, see the Supreme Court case *Pierce v. Society of Sisters,* 268 US 510.)

State requirements for nonpublic schools come in many sizes and colors. It is a subject which you can learn about by consulting other community schools in your area and by asking a lawyer for a rundown of the requirements and the way they are enforced. The basic requirement is that a nonpublic school be certified or approved as a legal alternative to the public schools. Until this is done, students of compulsory school age who attend your school instead of a public school or another certified school, will be considered truant and they or their parents may be subject to legal action, fines, etc. The school may also get into trouble for encouraging truancy if the state has a law covering this. You should check into this in detail before enrolling any students.

The power to approve or certify a school for children of compulsory school age rests either with the state (usually the department of education) or with the local school authorities. Some states have statutes which set out specifically what the requirements are and what process has been established to insure that applicants get a fair decision. But many states are still operating under vague laws and many have no procedures at all. Some do not even have standards. This vagueness can mean that getting certified is essentially a political matter. You should check into the requirements and also the reality of how the system works.

Certification or approval is not the same as accreditation in most places. There are private associations which examine schools and then give them a stamp of approval. This quality judgment (at least according to someone's definition of quality) is called accreditation and almost never has any legal significance. There are those who claim that it helps when school graduates are applying to college and that this form of private regulation forestalls more rigorous examination by state governments. We leave it to someone else to determine whether this is so. In general these associations can be found by getting in touch with the National Association of Independent Schools in Boston.

The requirements which the *state* imposes as a condition of getting certified usually include something on each of the following subjects:

- curriculum requirements—certain courses may be required to be offered or taught
- teacher qualifications—some states require that teachers in non-public schools be certified
- records—most states require that attendance records and other information about students be kept by the school
- testing—some states have begun to require that all students take standardized tests in basic skills
- hours and days—the state may require a certain number of hours per day or days per year of school
- purposes and programs—some states require that you submit a description of your educational goals and your program

In administering these educational requirements the state may have the power to come and inspect the school from time to time.

In addition to educational requirements, you will have to meet building codes and fire, health, and safety requirements. Each of these is complex and difficult to understand. Some parts are plainly for the protection of the students and staff. Others seem more remote. The way that the code is administered varies tremendously from state to state. There are also local codes which have to be met in most places. In general, it is a good idea to try to establish some kind of friendly relationship with the inspectors and to ask them about the requirements for any particular building which you may be thinking of using. Some schools have gotten stuck with enormous renovation bills because they did not discover that their building had code violations until after they had moved in.

Often it is hard to get any building approved as a school. For this reason you may want to consider the possibility of using some building which has already been approved (such as an abandoned Catholic school). In any case, getting by the codes can become an extremely political matter in some places. Be sure that you understand the way the system works before you begin dealing with it. The best source of information is probably other community schools and the inspectors themselves.

Some state departments of education have compilations of the requirements which are made of nonpublic schools. For a fairly detailed example of all state regulations (for Massachusetts) write to the Center for Law and Education, 38 Kirkland Street, Cambridge, 02138 and ask for a free copy of "Alternative Schools: A Practical Manual."

Bookkeeping

No matter how little or how much money you have, it is absolutely essential to keep careful records of what comes in and what goes out. In addition, there are some state and federal forms which you must fill out periodically. All of this is essential to retain your tax-exempt status, to prevent anyone from questioning the validity of your corporation, and to protect you from charges of misuse of any funds you receive.

Forms

1. *SS-4.* This is the application for a federal Employer Identification Number. It is necessary for withholding taxes and to attain tax-exempt status.
2. *W-4.* This is the form which employees fill out stating the number of exemptions they claim. It is the basis for calculating the withholding tax from their salaries.
3. *941.* This is the quarterly tax report. As a tax-exempt organization you will not pay any taxes to the United States, but you do have to report salaries paid, and the withholding from those salaries is then paid to the IRS on a quarterly basis. If your withholding reaches a certain level, or if you otherwise desire, you make monthly withholding "deposits" instead of quarterly payments. This is taken care of with form *501* monthly and *941* quarterly. Your bank will be involved in this process.
4. *W-2.* This is the year-end report of withholding which you must file with the IRS and the individual staff person.
5. If you are interested in Social Security, ask the IRS for form *SS-15* and *SS-15a*. This comes to about 9% tax, half from the school, half from the employee's paycheck.
6. Your state government will also have tax and other forms. Check into it.

Accounts

Bookkeeping need only be understandable and accurate. As long as the system you use tells you exactly how much you take in and from whom, when and on what money is spent, and maintains receipts, you will probably be in good shape. Make sure the system has some permanence and is kept up to date. An accountant's book is helpful and not terribly expensive. At the end of each accounting year, have your books audited. It's for your protection.

Remember that anything you show as being received (or which you give a donor evidence of having received) must be accounted for. All money for which you give receipts must be accounted for as expenditures or as money still in the bank. If a donor asks for a receipt (for example, to prove his contribution is tax deductible on his own return), give him one and be sure to record the donation in your books. The dates and purposes and amounts of all expenditures (rent, supplies, utilities, transportation, etc.) should be recorded.

The books should record all payments to staff under the staff person's name, and the receipt of tuition if there is any. If you should receive either a federal, state, or private grant or contract, keep separate books for this so that you will be able to show them what you did with the money.

If your books are confusing or aren't working, get some professional help. Don't bumble along; accounting help can probably be gotten free someplace. Look around.

Some banks give charge-free checking accounts to nonprofit organizations. Make some calls and you'll find one that does.

Federal Tax Exemption

Soon after you have incorporated you will want to file with the federal government for tax-exempt status. This will eliminate the necessity for the school to pay taxes and it will make contributions to you tax deductible for donors. Employees will still have to pay income tax.

To gain your exemption, file form 1023 with the Internal Revenue Service. You can get it from your district IRS Office along with Circular E which provides some help in filling out the form. To qualify you must satisfy the IRS that you are an educational or charitable nonprofit institution which does not engage in political activity designed to influence legislation or election campaigns. The form requires considerably detailed information about your organization and its operation and finances as well as copies of articles of incorporation, bylaws, books, etc. You should be sure that this form is answered by a lawyer since there are some pitfalls and the application process can be drawn out considerably if you need to make changes.

Since your incorporation and early activities will influence your ability to get tax-exempt status, you should discuss these matters early and avoid mistakes. Once you have filed it will take several months for the IRS to send you a letter confirming your exemption. When you have received this letter it usually will help you in getting tax-exempt status on the state level, since most states accept the federal determination for purposes of state tax exemptions.

Insurance

As individuals or as a nonprofit corporation running a school you will want to protect yourselves against lawsuits and your students against medical expenses arising out of accidents occurring in connection with school activities. You should have some form of agreement or permission slip signed by parents of students indicating that they approve of their children's attendance there. In addition, there are several types of insurance which can be arranged at a relatively low cost. Some of these plans include:

1. liability insurance for the building in which the school is located, covering bodily injury and property damage.
2. group accident insurance covering medical expenses up to $1000 and life insurance to $10,000. This is a benefit to the school greater than just protection from suits, since many people would have to pay higher rates for such coverage individually.
3. automobile insurance specifically covering student passengers. The laws in your state covering "school buses" and transportation of students should be checked carefully. Insurance may be expensive but necessary.
4. workman's compensation plans may be available to you de-

pending on your circumstances and whether staff get paid.

5. comprehensive general liability insurance will protect both the premises and other named or unnamed places you use as part of the school program.

There are other policies, including fire and theft insurance, and the ones which are needed or available depend on the specific circumstances of your school.

Permission Slips. In addition to whatever insurance arrangements you make, you should contact a lawyer with regard to the wording of permission slips and other agreements of parents regarding attendance at your school.

It is advisable and in some places absolutely necessary that you obtain medical release forms for all students as a protective measure. These should be kept on file and be available on field trips in case of accident.

CHAPTER TWELVE

Resources: People and Things

Goals and Purposes

Summerhill, A Radical Approach to Child Rearing. A.S. Neill, Hart, $2.45. The granddaddy of all "free school" books. It might seem unnecessary to mention this book, as it has become so widely known, but for many of us, *Summerhill* has been the strongest written influence on the shaping of our educational ideas.

De-Schooling Society, Ivan Illich, Harper & Row, $5.95. This book expounds the author's theory that "for most men the right to learn is curtailed by the obligation to attend school." Illich attempts to establish some criteria for what sorts of institutions actually foster learning.

Teacher, Sylvia Ashton-Warner, Bantam, $1.25. An exciting and well-written account of one teacher's experience teaching reading, and a description of the method she devised. Sylvia Ashton-Warner was teaching Maori children in New Zealand, but her experiences and method are entirely relevant to more familiar elementary school situations.

The Lives of Children, George Dennison, Vintage, $1.95. This is an interesting journal of the highlights of a year in a community school. A number of poeple have had their thinking straightened out by this insightful description of a school without bureaucracy. There is a chapter containing practical suggestions learned by those involved in the First Street School.

Schools Where Children Learn, Joseph Featherstone, Liveright, $2.45. An eye-witness report on how several American schools have adopted and modified the British infant school model.

The Student as Nigger, Jerry Farber, Pocket Books, $.95. A brief and excellent analysis of the values that underlie traditional classroom structures and of how these structures socialize students into docile, obedient, dependent individuals. One of the more famous writings to come from the campus educational reform movement, it is equally relevant to high school and elementary school situations.

How Children Fail, John Holt, Dell, $.95. This is about how public schools keep kids from thinking, with good suggestions of ways to reverse this trend in traditional classroom structures.

The Montessori Method, Maria Montessori, Schocken, $1.95. A good general description and background to the Montessori approach. Clear descriptions of materials, and lots of practical advice on how to use them. She also explains much of the thinking that led to various aspects of her approach.

The Language and Thought of the Child, Jean Piaget, Meridian, $1.45. Piaget is a pretty significant man in the general field of child development, and this is probably the best book of his with regard to schools. It discusses the significance of different language patterns in children between the ages of 4 and 11, and how these relate to the development of the child.

Toward a Theory of Instruction, Jerome Bruner, Harvard University Press, $4.50. *The Process of Education,* Jerome Bruner, Vintage, $1.35. These two books have been recommended to us as good examples of Bruner's thought. His theory is that with the right kind of teaching, and given time, anybody can learn anything (almost). He argues that intelligence is not what determines how much a person can learn.

Experience and Education, John Dewey, Collier, $.95. This is a lecture series in which Dewey summarizes his views on teaching methods, basically in response to critics. He was a pioneer in progressive education, one of the first to talk about "learning by doing."

Day School E.P.A., Recipe for Building a School, Facts About the Nairobi School, available from Nairobi Day School, P.O. Box 10777, Palo Alto, California 94303. These are three good pamphlets put out by the Nairobi Schools, whose special emphasis is on the needs of people of color. *Day School E.P.A.* is a graphic account of the events that led to the decision to start the Nairobi Schools, and what followed from that. *Recipe for Building a School* is just that. *Facts*

About the Nairobi School is a description of what the schools are trying to do.

The Pedagogy of the Oppressed, Paolo Friere, Herder and Herder, $5.95. This book is really dense and hard to read, but Friere has developed some interesting ways of working with people, so you may find it worth wading through. His general focus is on getting people to name for themselves the most important themes in their lives, rather than having outsiders tell them what is important. From this concept, specific curricula can be developed. People who find Friere interesting may be interested in contacting Michael Sherwin (5933 Pulaski Avenue, Germantown, Pa.) who has worked to apply Friere's method to his own learning and that of people around him.

Teaching as a Subversive Activity, Postman & Weingarten, Delacorte, $2.25. This is based on the idea that "our present educational system is not viable and is certainly not capable of generating enough energy to lead its own revitalization." The authors give practical suggestions on how to educate for change.

Free Schools, Jonathan Kozol, Houghton-Mifflin, $4.95. An articulate book for those whose idea of free school is that it is not relevant to the urban poor. It might straighten you out if you think freedom and escape are identical. It contains some practical information and has a good resource listing.

Parents

How to Change the Schools, A Parents' Action Handbook on How to Fight the System, Ellen Lurie, Random House, $2.95. Written by the mother of five children, this is a catalog of what she's learned in 15 years of trying to make the public schools good enough for her kids. It contains an extensive bibliography especially relevant to New York City.

Afram Associates, 68 East 131 Street, New York, N.Y. 10037; telephone: (212) 690-7010. Afram Associates maintain both library services and consulting teams. Their emphasis is on the Black community, and education is only one of their concerns. Their Action Library disseminates information on action and position statements that cover a broad variety of issues. This subscription service includes articles, bibliographies, fact sheets, films, and tapes. Educational inquiries should go to Preston Wilcox, the executive director; library inquiries to Annette Ramsey.

East Harlem Block Schools, 94 East 111 Street, New York, N. Y. 10029. These folks see part of their task as helping other groups of parents learn from the East Harlem experience. They're happy to have visitors and run a kind of informal consulting service.

Nairobi Day School, P.O. Box 10777, Palo Alto, California 94313; telephone: (415) 325-4049. Nairobi Day School has organized a consulting team to work with other people starting new schools. Nairobi is a predominantly black elementary school that is working carefully to develop programs that address the particular needs of people of color. The school is in close association with Nairobi High School and Nairobi College. Together the schools' consulting teams help people who are developing similar programs. The schools use this service as a source of income. Special financial arrangements may be possible for community groups.

Curriculum

Reading in the Elementary School, Jeannette Veatch, Ronald, $7.00. A traditional text, but a good one, that covers many different techniques for individualized teaching of reading. It is especially useful for the teaching of beginning reading.

Citation Press Series: British Infant Schools, Citation Press, 50 West 44 Street, New York, N.Y.; telephone: (212) 867-7700. This is a series of 13 paperbound books, ranging in price from $.95 to $2.95. In the series, a number of authors examine various aspects of open education as practiced in British elementary schools. Publication was begun in late 1971, and by Spring of '72 a total of 23 titles and a cumulative volume will be available.

Teacher, Sylvia Ashton-Warner, Bantam, $1.25. See the annotation under Goals and Purposes.

Big Rock Candy Mountain, Portola Institute, 1115 Merrill Street, Menlo Park, California. This quarterly deals with education in general; each particular edition has its own theme. Especially useful is the Education and Classroom Materials issue, complete with articles on materials, list of suppliers, and a letter from John Holt discussing some good recent books on education. BRCM is like a Whole Earth Catalog on education, if that makes anything clearer.

What We Owe Children, The Subordination of Teaching to Learning, Dr. Caleb Gattegno, Avon, $1.65. Gattegno was impressed by the intellectual powers implied by a child's learning a language by the age of two or so. This book discusses how we can help children learn by linking new knowledge to what they already know.

Educational Solutions, Inc., Box 190, Cooper Station, New York, N. Y. 10003, Dr. Caleb Gattegno, director. Formerly called Schools for the Future, this consulting service runs workshops for teachers and parents. The East Harlem Block Schools found them to provide "the most clearcut, disciplined insight into how kids can be challenged. The stuff can demonstrate what it feels like to be incredibly smart and learn new skills very rapidly." They run practical workshops on how to teach reading, math, and foreign languages. The western branch is at 77 Mark Drive, Northgate Industrial Park, San Rafael, California 94903.

SRA Kits, Science Research Associates, 259 E. Erie Street, Chicago, Illinois 60611. Elaborate and "scientifically developed," these color-coded gadgetted kits can be useful in working with kids in such areas as spelling, math, and science. They are very famous. Our experience with them has been some good and some bad, depending on how interested the kids are in things like spelling, math, and elaborate color-coded kits.

The Montessori Method, Maria Montessori, Schocken, $1.95. See annotation under Goals and Purposes.

Montessori's Own Handbook, Maria Montessori, Schocken, $1.75. A concise handbook particularly designed for parents. It illustrates many of the materials and their uses. Less theory than *The Montessori Method.*

Far West Laboratory for Educational Research and Development, 1 Garden Circle, Hotel Claremont, Berkeley, California 94705; telephone: (415) 841-9710. Far West Labs is a public nonprofit laboratory that deals with the inventing, designing, developing, and testing of educational products. It tries to promote the use of these products in the classroom and in teacher training. Five primary areas of concern are: early childhood education; teacher education; multi-ethnic education; utilization and information; and communications. Visitors are welcome. For further information contact Margaret Jones at the above address.

Children Come First, Casey and Liza Murrow, American Heritage. This is an excellent description of life in the British primary schools. Very concrete and yet perceptive.

Educational Development Center, 55 Chapel Street, Newton, Massachusetts 02160. EDC offers a wide variety of workshops for teachers and is often an excellent inexpensive source of materials for use both in and out of the classroom. Materials also include films and pamphlets on learning, curricula, and innovative schools.

Nairobi Day School, P.O. Box 10777, Palo Alto, California 94303; telephone: (415) 325-4049. Nairobi Day School has developed an elaborate curriculum that focuses on the particular interest of people of color, and there don't seem to be very many such curricular models around. They are marketing their curriculum as a way of supporting their school. It's available from them exclusively.

Deganawidah-Quetzalcoatl University(!), P.O. Box 409, Davis, California 95616; telephone: (916) 758-0470. This is a university that started in July, 1971, with emphasis on the culture and traditions of Chicano and Native American people. It is an accredited university and is anxious to help other schools develop similar programs. The executive director there is José de la Isla.

Schools Without Failure, William Glasser, M.D., Harper & Row, $4.95. This book analyzes the elements of the educational system which build in failure for many students. Glasser offers many practical suggestions on how to make a school more relevant, and thus more exciting, for everyone.

Montessori—A Modern Approach, Paula Polk Lillard, Schocken Books, New York. A good overview and introduction to the Montessori method. Ties together the origin and history of Montessori with its modern practice.

Understanding Children's Play, Ruth Hartley, Lawrence Frank; Columbia University Press. A classic, about 300 pages, lots of good theory and anecdotes, basic for early childhood.

Behavior and Misbehavior, James L. Hymes, Jr., Prentice-Hall, Englewood Cliffs, New Jersey, $1.95. Easy, fast reading, fun, to the point, very helpful when you've given up.

The Logic of Action, Francis Pockman Hawkins, Elementary Science Advisory Center, University of Colorado, $1.95. Interesting anecdotal description of a year's work in an open activity program with deaf children; good comments on teacher's role and lots of detail on materials used. Probably have to write to the University of Colorado to get it. 150 pages.

The Magic Years, Selma Fraiberg, Scribner, $2.45. Useful for parents and teachers. Basic and human description of child development from birth through age six.

Water, Sand, and Mud as Play Materials, pamphlet from National Association for Nursery Education, 155 East Ohio Street, Chicago, Illinois, $.50. Short, sweet, a very good way to validate the joys of mess and the learning opportunities of mess!

The Balance Book, E.S.S., Educational Services Inc. The address given in the book is Box 415, Watertown, Mass. 02172, 147 pages. A full, detailed, concrete guide to all the possibilities for using and studying the principle of balance, with many different materials. For young children—nursery through early primary.

Light and Shadows, E.S.S., Webster Division, McGraw-Hill. Short, pictures, quick transmission of interesting, concrete ideas.

Attribute Games and Problems, E.S.S., Webster Division, McGraw-Hill. Many concrete ideas and directions for math and other logical-thinking games. 87 pages.

Talks for Primary Teachers, Madeleine Goutard, Educational Solutions Inc., Broadway and 12th Street, New York. Short, pithy, theoretical guide to the use of Cuisenaire Rods according to the pure math of the authors of the method. A bible for people really into math teaching by rods.

What Is Music for Young Children?, Elizabeth Jones, National Association for the Education of Young Children, Washington, D.C. Anecdotal and suggestive description of music in nursery schools, encouraging experimentation, $1. Can be ordered from Publications Dept., NAEYC, 1834 Connecticut Ave., N.W., Washington, D.C. 20009.

Staff

The Teacher Paper, 280 North Pacific Avenue, Monmouth, Oregon 97361. A periodical that presents experiences of teachers in various situations: successes, failures, problems. The paper avoids the usual professional jargon. We haven't seen the paper ourselves, but we've heard good things about it from several different people.

Anger and the Rocking Chair, Janet Lederman, McGraw-Hill, $4.95. A book that focuses on the use of Gestalt Therapy techniques and perspective with elementary school children. A good source of inspiration for discouraged teachers.

Behavior and Misbehavior, J. Hymes, Prentice-Hall, $2.95. A short, simple book that can be read in a couple of hours before bed on the most frustrating day of the year and let you wake up the next morning ready to try again. Talks about why kids become "discipline problems" and how to deal with them.

General

New Schools Exchange, 701B Anacapa, Santa Barbara, California 93101; telephone: (805) 962-2020. If you want to know about schools, books, or clearinghouses, this is a decent place to start. The New Schools Exchange has been operating for three years. It serves as a national clearinghouse for alternative education though in the past it has not been particularly strong on the problems of schools in the Black and Third World communities. Twice a month, the exchange publishes a newsletter, including articles by well-known writers in education as well as profiles of schools. In 1970, the Exchange published a directory of alternative schools throughout the country. Newsletter #61 is a supplement to the directory. Also particularly useful are newsletters #55 (a bibliography) and #65 (a list of clearinghouses).

Shasta School, 499 Alabama Street, San Francisco, California. Shasta School was initiated by four students who were unhappy with their public school and decided they could do better. They did. The school is run entirely by its students. People there would be very helpful to other groups of students interested in initiating schools. If you have any doubts about whether students can really start and run a school you ought to get in touch with them and show yourself otherwise.

Inside Summerhill, Joshua Popenoe, Hart, $1.95. Written by a student at Summerhill, it gives an insider's view of the joys and sorrows of that particular institution. A very enjoyable example of how students view their schools. Popenoe also did the excellent photography.

New Schools: A National Directory, October, 1971. Available from Ralph Sama, 1878 Massachusetts Ave., Cambridge, Mass. This is the most up-to-date listing we have seen. It contains information about the composition, size, finances, and outstanding characteristics of each school listed, as well as a bibliography and a listing of 24 "coordinating and information centers" around the country.

Teacher Drop-Out Center, University of Massachusetts, Amherst, Massachusetts. Serves as a clearinghouse for information about education and particularly about available jobs in alternative schools. Sympathetic and attentive to teachers dissatisfied with the public school system.

Summerhill Society of California, P.O. Box 2477, Van Nuys, California 91401. This groups offers conferences, workshops, and films for people interested in Summerhillian educational ideas. In addition, the Society publishes a bulletin, a book list, and a list of Summerhillian schools in the western United States.

Alternatives for Education, 1778 S. Holt Ave., Los Angeles, California 90035; telephone: (213) 839-6994. Emphasizing Southern California, this group deals with a wide range of alternatives. They have a daily radio show, a monthly newsletter, a book list, and a list of day schools. The group is energetic, dedicated, and friendly.

Modern Play School, Play Mountain Place, 6063 Hargis, Los Angeles, California; telephone: (213) 870-4381. One of the oldest "Summerhillian" schools in the country (23 years), the school is interested in helping others start. Workshops in non-authoritarian teaching are available to any group of 15 interested people.

Summerhill Collective, 137 West 14 Street, New York, N.Y. 10011. The Collective is a split-off from the New York Summerhill Society. It emphasizes its collective nature and is particularly concerned with organizing for youth liberation. A newsletter is available.

Regional and National Clearinghouses. Following are a *few* of the places throughout the country interested in disseminating information on existing alternatives, starting schools, changes within public schools. Regardless of your location or the type of school you want to start, there is a clearinghouse nearby to help you. If no nearby group is listed here, it can be located by contacting New Schools Exchange (see page 134) or looking in *New Schools: A National Directory* (see page 135).

Wisconsin Coalition for Educational Reform, 3019 N. Farwell Avenue, Milwaukee, Wisconsin 53211. The Wisconsin Coalition, working throughout the state, is interested both in alternatives and in organizing for reform within the state educational system. The group offers information, for example, on legal means of dealing with inequities in the public high schools.

New Schools Movement, Earth Station 7, 402 15th Street, East, Seattle, Washington 98102. *Center for Urban Education,* same address. These two groups, originally one, have recently split. The New Schools Movement deals primarily with free schools and aims at establishing the best possible independent alternatives. The Center for Urban Education is concerned mainly with alternatives possible within the system and concentrates on organization and development of educational tactics to change the existing educational scheme.

KOA, Goddard College, Plainfield, Vermont. One of the most radically coalition-oriented groups on the east coat. Also write c/o Arrakis, RFD #1, Jeffersonville, New York.

New Schools News, c/o Bea Gillette, 407 South Dearborn, Chicago, Illinois. New Schools News is an information service for alternative schools in the Chicago area. Special attention is given to students seeking alternatives. The service operates with the cooperation of the American Friends Service Committee.

New Schools Network, 3039 Deakin, Berkeley, California 94705. The Network serves as a clearinghouse for both public and private alternative schools in the Berkeley area. It helps both parents and students looking for schools and teachers and volunteers looking for jobs through listings in its newsletter.

Federation of Boston Community Schools. Ann Pettit, 76 Highland Street, Roxbury, Massachusetts. A loose affiliation of community schools serving the Black community in the Boston area.

Federation of Independent Community Schools, 2637 North 11 Street, Milwaukee, Wisconsin 53206. These seven schools used to be Catholic schools in Milwaukee. Instead of closing the schools outright, the church turned them over to community groups. The director there is Jesse Wray.

National Association of Community Schools, c/o Don Stocks, 1707 N Street, N.W., Washington, D.C. Just beginning as a resource for community schools.

Education Switchboards. A number of education switchboards have been established as clearinghouses for information on new schools. Their general function is to put interested schools, teachers, students, and parents in touch with each other and to help get the word around that new schools exist. If there are many new schools in your area, there's probably a switchboard. Try to find it. They generally are in touch with a wide variety of situations and people.

Vocations for Social Change, Box 13, Canyon, California 94516. This is a collective that publishes a bi-monthly newsletter directed toward people who are redefining their sense of work, money, and style of life. They have centers in various parts of the country, and if there's one near you, it would be worth going to talk to people there about new schools. They're usually well grounded in what's going on in their part of the world. The current representatives are listed in each issue of the VSC newsletter, which is published in Canyon.

Clearinghouse, Department of Education, University of Massachusetts, Amherst, Massachusetts 01002. This innovative project was established to serve people who are exploring innovative learning environments. They've had their problems, but should have good information on what's going on.

Educational Confederation of Metropolitan St. Louis, 5555 Page, St. Louis, Missouri. The Confederation consists of a mixture of types of schools, some community-based, some free, some traditional private schools. Several of the schools in the Confederation are investigating the possibilities of becoming part of the public school system.

Other clearinghouses:

Teachers Organization Project and *Chicago Teaching Center,* 852 W. Belmont Avenue, Chicago, Illinois.

Washington Area Free Schools Clearing House, 1609 19th Street, N.W., Washington, D. C. 20009.

New Jersey Alternative Schools, c/o Terry Ripmaster, 16 Crestwood Drive, Glen Rock, N. J.

Innovative Education Coalition, 1130 N. Ramparts St., New Orleans, Louisiana 70116.

Southwest Education Reform Committee (SWERC) (!) 3505 Main Street, Houston, Texas 77002.

Center for Student Citizenship, Rights & Responsibilities, 1145 Germantown St., Dayton, Ohio 45408.

This Magazine is About Schools, 56 Esplanade St. East, Suite 301, Toronto 215, Ontario, Canada. A quarterly journal on educational issues, both theoretical and practical. It is published by a group of Canadians who work in and around Toronto. This Mag has recently moved away from a concentration on free schools and is now helping to promote and facilitate community control of public schools.

Center for New Schools, 431 S. Dearborn, Room 1527, Chicago, Illinois 60605; telephone: (312) 922-7436. The Center, a nonprofit corporation, aims at developing a technical assistance group to help schools in the Midwest, primarily those within the public system. Originally part of the Urban Research Corporation, the organization helped to start Metro High School, a school without walls within the Chicago public school system. The Center for New Schools consults with community groups, state educational agencies, and school staffs. Two publications are available, both relevant to starting schools: *The Metro School: A Report on the Progress of Chicago's Experimental School Without Walls,* $2.50; *Student Involvement in Decision-Making in an Alternative High School,* $6.00.

Affective Education Development Program, Norman Newberg, c/o Philadelphia Public Schools. Papers are available discussing various philosophies which might lead to the starting of new schools.

New Nation Seed Fund, Box 4026, Philadelphia, Pennsylvania 19118. A small fund to help new schools through emergencies.

Technical Problems

Legal Services Offices (OEO). Most areas are serviced by an LSO which provides free legal help to those who qualify under poverty guidelines. Good especially for incorporation, tax certification.

Volunteers in Technical Assistance (VITA). A bank of technical consultants (free to you) which has local offices in many cities. Poverty criteria apply. National office is VITA-USA, College Campus,

Schenectady, New York 12308. Harvey Pressman, VITA, 115 Gainsborough Street, Boston, Massachusetts 02115 is especially experienced in helping schools nationwide.

Alternative Schools: A Practical Manual. Available from Law & Education Center, 38 Kirkland Street, Cambridge, Massachusetts. An example of a full description of legal requirements and available government resources (for Massachusetts only).

No More Public School, by Hal Bennett, Random House. A detailed review of California's legal standards for nonpublic schools, private tutoring, and other legal alternatives to public school. Also contains suggestions about curriculum, materials, and teaching.

Afterword

A Case for Parent Control
by Dorothy Stoneman

Community control of schools has many advocates, most of them members of the community that wants to gain control. Their analysis of why community control is essential is basically a political one, seeing the school as a colonial institution that reflects and perpetuates our society's oppression of minority groups. Community control to some represents an opportunity for oppressed Black and Hispanic people to hook into political power, gaining control of a central institution; to others it is simply and wholly a way to reclaim the parental right of providing for your children's future.

The opponents of community control have been, for the most part, professional educators on the one hand and legislators on the other. They insist that poor people are not qualified to run the schools; they imply that poor people in power would be corrupt and torn by violent power-struggles; they insist that the impulse behind the struggle for control is a desire for jobs or for power, not an interest in the children. It is not difficult to understand why educators and legislators see community control as a threat to jobs and power.

As a professional educator convinced not only of the political need for community control but of its superiority as a structure for an educational institution, I'd like to present a theoretical and educational defense of community control.

For simplicity, I will talk about a parent-controlled school, rather than a community-controlled school. In the best of all political systems I believe there would be no essential difference. In America, where we are raised to take care only of our own, the general population of any community cannot be trusted to look out for some people's children as well as the people themselves can be trusted. Also, where routes to power are limited and competition intense, in a country that condones selfish uses of power, it is best to exclude from power those people who have no immediate and personal interest in the quality of the school as it affects their own children. Of course, in saying this I immediately alienate that minority of people who favor community control as a stepping-stone to political power. That's okay. My argument is not that community control is a necessary part of the political revolution. It is that parent control is a necessary part of the education revolution.

My argument is based on the following assumptions:

1. That schools for minority children run and staffed by people of the white majority have failed.

2. That members of the white majority cannot free themselves from racist and class attitudes they have been taught unless the power relationship between them and the minority group is dramatically changed.

3. That members of minority groups cannot free themselves from the racist and class ideas they have been taught unless the power relationship between themselves and the white majority with whom they come in contact is dramatically changed.

4. That children cannot get a good education in an environment where adults are divided by racist and class attitudes.

5. That racist and class attitudes are often as much a problem between nonwhite professionals and parents of poor children as they are between white professionals and the same parents. Therefore the problem of these attitudes and their effect on the children cannot be solved simply by hiring more minority-group professional educators. Professionalism is itself a class attitude, and often includes racist overtones, regardless of the professional's race.

6. That a good education for children includes the development of pride, hope, responsibility, the expectation of growing into a fulfilling adult life within a community, and the motivation to use opportunities for growing.

7. That in a ghetto area the only kind of school which has the possibility of developing these attitudes and feelings is one which is

itself a responsible and cooperative community within which a child's parents have an opportunity for a fulfilling adult life, for pride, hope, responsibility, and for personal growth.

8. That the only kind of school offering this opportunity to parents is one in which the parents have primary responsibility for the operation, development, and direction of the school.

9. That a child's identification with his parents and with his own community is a more important determinant of his expectations than any particular school experience.

10. That the best school will combine an opportunity for the student to respect and identify with his own community and an opportunity to master the skills of the dominant culture.

11. That a school presenting skills and mastery as a means to separate oneself from one's own community is destructive of a community's development.

12. That a community's development is more important to all the children residing within it than is the provision of an escape route for a small minority of a community's children.

13. That only a parent-controlled community school has the possibility of providing community identification and relationships along with academic skills and mastery.

14. That professional teachers tend to forgive themselves for not succeeding fully at their job because their job is so very difficult.

15. That, having forgiven themselves and needing still further justification for their failure, professional teachers tend to blame parents for the failures of children in their classes.

16. That this defensive process of externalizing the causes for failure tends to exacerbate racist and class attitudes, tends to create a self-fulfilling prophecy for the performance of some children, and tends toward an ever-decreasing effort on the part of the teacher.

17. That this defensive process of externalizing also acts as reassurance to the teacher that he deserves to keep his job regardless of the results of his work.

18. That the only way to cut through this defensive process is to make the teacher accountable precisely to the group of people he tends to blame for his own failure. His defensiveness can no longer be a source of reassurance concerning his job security; it will become a

source of insecurity and there will therefore be pressure on him to stop blaming the parents.

19. That only if a teacher is not blaming parents for a child's failure is a teacher in a position to work creatively with parents to insure a child's success.

20. That parents in a position to hire and fire teachers, as in a parent-controlled school, will not tolerate teacher failure and will not tolerate being blamed for teacher failure.

21. That this refusal to tolerate failure will generate in teachers a new commitment to success.

22. That this commitment to success will be accompanied not by blaming parents, since this is not to be tolerated, but by a willingness to cooperate with parents.

23. That cooperation between parents and teachers is inherently better for the educational process than mutual suspicion, contempt, accusation, or fear.

24. That teachers tend, also in a defensive process of justifying their own failure or their own limited success, to divide their classes mentally into those children they consider reachable and those children they consider unreachable. They forgive themselves more easily for not reaching the "unreachables."

25. That parents as a group will not tolerate a teacher's blame of any parents nor the dismissal of any child as incorrigible or uneducable. This group pressure on the teacher will prevent the teacher from mentally dividing his class into the educable and the non-educable.

26. That a school that refuses to consider any child unreachable is a better community for all the children.

27. That a school that is accountable to parents is less likely to consider any child unreachable.

Appendix

The Schools

The Learning Place is an alternative junior and senior high school in San Francisco, founded in 1969. Its purpose is to help its members develop the emotional strength and personal skills necessary to forge individual and collective alternatives to working class and middle class life styles. The student body of 60 is racially and ethnically mixed but predominantly white working and middle class in origin. Founded by four teachers, the school is presently governed by all-school meetings and committees having student majorities. The school is supported by a sliding scale tuition and by fundraising projects of parents, students, and staff. The parents have given active support to the school, though they play no formal role in its governance. The school operates in the Summerhillian tradition of allowing students virtually free choice of how they spend their time and use the school's resources.

The East Harlem Block Schools are a complex of parent-controlled day care centers, a tutoring program, and an elementary school in a poor, predominantly Puerto Rican section of New York City. The elementary school was founded in 1967 and now enrolls 110 students. Parents hold all positions on governing boards and committees and fill a majority of staff positions as well. The educational program is open and innovative, but places a high priority on giving children the academic and other skills which the parents consider necessary for survival. The school is open to any child in the neighborhood, free of tuition, and is supported by government grants and contributions of foundations and individual benefactors.

Presidio Hill School is a progressive school in San Francisco founded more than 50 years ago. Its primarily middle class, but racially integrated, student body of more than 200 is drawn from throughout the city. Most of the students are in the equivalent of grades one through six, but a junior high school was recently established. The school is legally a parent cooperative, supported entirely by tuition, with a governing board of parents and staff elected by an annual meeting. The educational program is in the tradition of John Dewey and has recently been influenced by the British infant schools.

The Berkeley Montessori School in Berkeley, California, is 8 years old and enrolls more than one hundred students from mostly white middle class families. It is run collectively by the teaching staff with the active support and cooperation of the parents. The structure and curriculum are based on Montessori methods and materials, but the staff has adapted them to the particular community and group of students. It features a unique outdoor classroom, staffed and available to children all day long. It is supported entirely by tuition.

The San Francisco School is a modified Montessori school for children ages three through twelve. The student body of 125 is middle class, integrated, and comes from all over the city. It was founded six years ago by a group of parents and is still controlled by the parents although they have turned the day-to-day operation of the school over to the staff. The school is located in a bright and spacious building inexpensively constructed with a lot of parent labor. It is supported by tuition and parent fundraising projects.

Berkeley High Community School is legally and physically part of the Berkeley public school system. It opened in January 1969 and presently has 225 students, selected by lottery from among Berkeley high school students who apply. Its racial and sex composition reflects the same proportions found in the population of Berkeley high school. The school is divided into four tribes, each of which has its own physical space and meets once or twice a week to decide operational questions and resolve interpersonal conflicts. General policy is set by an Inter-Tribal Council of students and staff. Each student is free to choose his or her courses or to develop new ones within the liberally interpreted requirements for high school graduation.

New Community School, in Oakland, California, sees itself as an active participant in the struggle for social justice. Its 50 high school age students, half of them white and half black, half low income and half middle income, come from the surrounding community of North

Oakland. The school takes stands on community issues and the curriculum is developed out of the perceived needs of the community as well as the skills individuals need in order to survive. The budget is raised partly from tuition and partly from foundation grants. It is governed by a board of directors comprised of students, staff, parents, and other community representatives.

Primary Life School is a parent controlled and operated school in San Francisco for four to eight year olds. There are about 30 students of mixed racial and economic backgrounds. A head teacher and assistant teacher provide continuity for the children and guidance for the parents. A rich environment coupled with a structure similar to British infant schools allows the child to pursue his interests freely without interfering with other students' activities. Tuition paid by parents provides the financial base for the school.

The Group School is an independent high school for working class white and Black youth from Cambridge. It was originated by students in 1970 and is presently governed by a community meeting and board, each of which is composed of more students than staff. The thirty-eight students range in age from 15 to 21 and participate in a non-graded program designed to teach basic skills, integrate employment into education, and provide for emotional and intellectual development in an atmosphere which is conscious of the history of the working class in America. A sliding scale tuition provides a small percentage of the school's budget, with the remainder coming from private and foundation support and government contracts.

The Highland Park Free School is a parent-controlled community school enrolling over 200 students between the ages of 5 and 14. The students, who are admitted on a first-come, first-served basis, are predominantly black and come from the Highland Park section of Roxbury. The curriculum is a mix of basic skills taught in small groups within each class and less formally structured, student-centered afternoon projects. Each class is run by a community teacher with the help of a professional teacher. The school charges no tuition and is supported through foundation grants and local fundraising activities. Highland Park is one of three Black community schools in the Federation of Boston Community Schools.

Michael Community School is a non-graded community school serving about 235 students ranging in age from 5 to 13. The school began when St. Michael's, a Catholic parochial school, was forced to close because of financial difficulties. The school is governed by a board elected from the neighborhood and stresses parent involvement in all phases of its governance. Though the school does lease its building from the church, it is no longer a Catholic school in its curriculum, staff, or form of decision-making. The student body is mixed Black, white, and Spanish-speaking. Michael Community School is one of seven members of the Milwaukee Federation of Community Schools, all of which were taken over by the community when the church could no longer support them.

The Ironbound Children's Center includes a preschool for 45 children ages three to four, the beginning of a primary school now enrolling 21 children ages 5 through 7 and an after school enrichment program for youngsters ages 6 through 12. All these are governed by a parent board. The center is the outgrowth of a series of parent meetings and seminars which discussed personal experiences with school and new methods of teaching. The classrooms are open structure, and have three teachers—a head teacher, an assistant teacher, and a parent. All have the same status within the class. Twenty-five percent of the students are Black and the remainder are mixed white ethnic including Spanish-speaking and Portuguese. All come from the Ironbound district of Newark, New Jersey. Funding comes from the State Department of Education, federal grants, private donations. There is no tuition.

Index

In Search of a Therapy

EDITED BY DENNIS T. JAFFE

HARPER COLOPHON BOOKS

Harper & Row, Publishers

New York, Evanston, San Francisco, London

A hardcover edition of this book is published by Harper & Row, Publishers, Inc.

IN SEARCH OF A THERAPY
Copyright © 1975 by Dennis T. Jaffe.

First HARPER COLOPHON edition published 1975.

LIBRARY OF CONGRESS CATALOG CARD NUMBER: 74–10444

STANDARD BOOK NUMBER (paperback): 06–090392–9
                    (hardcover): 06–136163–1

Contents

Introduction

DENNIS T. JAFFE

In the past decade what is called therapy has broadened from the traditional activities of physician-psychiatrists and clinical psychologists to include many new forms and styles, often practiced by people who do not have the usual credentials or training. Another trend has been increasing criticism of the use of psychiatric institutions and therapy to deprive people of their civil liberties without due process and to enforce conformity with social standards. Common therapeutic practices are increasingly questioned, and the myriad new forms that are also called therapy make it seem that once a person decides that he or she wants to become a therapist, there are still infinite choices to be made. With such questions about values and ethics in the air and such a proliferation of forms, a therapist can no longer learn a skill in professional school and then practice it, with a few modifications, for the rest of his or her life. This social context is leading each individual therapist and each therapist-in-training to ask difficult questions about what to do and how to do it.

The contributors to this book all "practice therapy" in certain ways based on certain values, experiences, and commitments each of them will relate. The purpose of bringing their accounts together is, however, to shed light on the nature of the basic choices and definitions of the work we call therapy. What is it? What kind of social institution has it become? Is the practice of this art, science, or skill consonant with the social rewards—prestige, fees, power—that many of its practitioners gain from it? What contradictions are there between therapists' professed values and the ways in which they are trained and organize their work? What effects do various ways of doing therapy have on society? Can therapy be harmful as well as helpful? Must therapy be

subservient to the dominant values of the society within which it is practiced, or can it be a force for social change?

This book presents personal answers to these questions, not in theoretical form, but as they evolved in the work and growth of each of the contributors. Collectively, they represent some of the breadth of the activities that have come to be called therapy. Their work is quite different from most of what is taught in medical schools and in the psychology, counseling, and social work departments of graduate schools. Some of the contributors went through such traditional training and tell how they grew to question or resist much of what they learned, while others learned therapy independently of such programs.

Rather than simply becoming a critic, each contributor has looked for ways to help people that go beyond the professional schools and associations. Many of them have started new projects or alternate therapy centers that try to redefine the basic goals of helping institutions. None of their projects is billed as "the answer" or "what therapy ought to be." None of the contributors claims to have discovered a new form of therapy that alone will cure humanity's social or psychic ailments. In fact, most of them admit that so far their attempts are little more than floundering, looking for a valid, satisfying, and ethical means to help others.

That is why the book consists of personal statements rather than glowing accounts of new projects or fully formed alternatives ready for widespread adoption. I got the idea for this book while talking with friends who were trying new things, and at the same time I saw the dilemmas of students who were generally critical of what they were taught in school but unable to envision concrete alternatives. People who were trying new things often did not present their "findings" at professional gatherings because they did not have "hard data" to "prove" their effectiveness and because the often stifling atmosphere and rigid formats of such meetings made it hard to share half-formed models and tentative ideas. So what they had learned was only available to a small, like-minded group of friends.

My idea was simply to invite statements from a group of therapists who I knew were trying to move from a personal critique of therapy as a social institution toward new ways of helping people. I asked them to write first person accounts of where they had come from, their background, their professional training, and why they felt they had to change their work in the directions they did. We thus have accounts of people who find themselves drawn to a profession that tries to serve others, who were initially put off by the realization that the ideals of

that profession were often a put-on, helpful not to the clients but to a social order that distorted relationships and human growth. Thus, if they did not originally intend to change, they felt driven to it. Hopefully, their life journeys and work styles will open up an array of possibilities for people who presently (or are preparing to) work in therapy settings in which they do not feel entirely comfortable by showing how a critique can open a path for action.

Naturally, my personal biases led me to select particular contributors. As I read over their essays, I discovered several common themes running through them. One was the integration of personal truth with political ideals, not only continuing the movement for basic social change of the 1960s through one's work in therapy, but also making sure that one's behavior—as a person and as a professional—is congruent with one's beliefs about society. My own search for a way of helping young people, Jim Gordon's redefinition of the basic system of the psychiatric ward when he became chief resident, Bob Lifton's collaboration on Vietnam veterans' rap groups, Tom Cottle's research style, and Michael Rossman's search for integration of himself with the social contradictions flowing around him—all represent examples of this kind of process.

Another common thread is the contributors' realization of the bankruptcy of many social institutions, even those which ostensibly are there to help others. Then there is the movement from feeling betrayed toward trying to reform at least the way they practice themselves, if not the whole institution. The people I selected have not changed by embracing an alternate system whole—becoming a gestalt therapist or a transactional analyst—although many of them feel in harmony with the new learning coming out of these traditions and are able to integrate them into their work.

The accounts here often focus on doubts and confusions in training, such as, Jim Gordon's and Tom Cottle's about medical school, and my own and Ted Clark's about paraprofessional clinical training, which led them to ask more basic questions about what therapy is. In general the therapists represented here would be called more political or radical in their awareness and in their consideration of the large-scale effects of therapy on people than most innovative therapists, and that is intentional. I feel that therapy has too long been allied with other social forces against individual change, and the main purpose of assembling the accounts here is to show how it can be used to promote change both in individuals who have already rejected or at least are ambivalent about the conventional options, whether they have chosen group marriage, madness, political activism, or simply running away from

home, and in society through the collective effects of helping many such people realize that the nature of their suffering lies not only in things they do to themselves but in the basic social arrangements that characterize our society.

1. Psychiatric Miseducation

JAMES S. GORDON

James Gordon is a psychiatrist with the Public Health Service. He was graduated from Harvard College and Harvard Medical School and completed his psychiatric residency at the Albert Einstein College of Medicine in New York City. This essay focuses on some of the destructive consequences of psychiatric education. In "The Uses of Madness" (Chapter 8) he presents examples of a therapeutic practice that grows out of this critique.

Currently Jim works with a number of alternative services for young people in the Washington, D.C., area, including a hot line and a runaway house. He is particularly concerned with the power of collectivity to transform human relations and conventional notions of "mental illness." He lives with the writer Sharon Curtin on a farm near Lovettsville, Virginia. His writings have appeared in *The Atlantic, The New Republic, The Washington Post,* and *The New York Times Book Review.* The two articles that are included here were first published in *Social Policy.*

Ever sensitive to the motes in their patients' psychic eyes, psychiatrists are too often beam-blind to the influences of their own training. What follows is an attempt to outline, from the vantage of my own experience, some of the dangerously obscure areas of residency training—unquestioned premises and unexamined contradictions that shape and distort psychiatric education.

Although my interest in psychiatry has many roots—socioeconomic, familial, and intellectual—I will touch only on those that in medical school fed my expectations of a psychiatric career. I wanted to help other people in a way that would be rewarding to me. In college, entranced by the stories of peoples' lives, the language peculiar to them, and the twists of character and fate that helped define their

passage, I had majored in English literature. Psychiatry would, I hoped, enable me to help people through my understanding of their lives. Wondrously I would make a living by the intimate and interpersonal exercise of imagination, investigation, and understanding. The sensitivity that novels and poetry nurtured would not grow dusty in classrooms and libraries but would bloom in service to others. In my more optimistic moments this seemed a reasonable approach. It sustained me through boring hours in medical school laboratories and helped enrich otherwise pressured and anxiety-provoking experiences on medical wards.

I had also read a good deal of Freud, Jung, and Erikson; Binswanger's *Case of Ellen West;* Frieda Fromm-Reichmann's essays on psychotherapy; R. D. Laing's *The Divided Self*—as well as Nietzsche and Kierkegaard, Tillich and Buber—before I set foot on a psychiatric ward. It was to these "psychologists" that I looked for help and understanding in working with patients.

I felt that the first obstacle in working with someone would be our mutual unfamiliarity, and I expected as I approached my first day of work on a psychiatric ward that I would be almost as anxious and tentative as my patient. I was shocked then—and still am—by the enormous power over the patient's life that was routinely delegated to me and to the resident who supervised me. For one thing it seemed absurd for a twenty-three-year-old medical student to tell a woman twice his age, whom he had just met, when she might or might not go to the corner grocery store. Although she was dressed in pajamas and "restricted to the ward," she did not appear sick in any ordinary way. Besides, even on a medical ward, I learned that one could not legally stop a patient who wanted to from leaving.

I knew the most intimate details of her life, duly recorded on her chart, and she knew only my name. Not even that I was a "student" and not a "doctor." I had immediate power over her life and had not yet spoken to her. Both she and I were dubious about what help I could be, and yet I was in a position to "harm" and humiliate her in innumerable ways. Where was the possibility for Freud's respectful analysis, Erikson's wise benevolence, Fromm-Reichmann's gentle understanding? It wasn't Kierkegaard or Nietzsche who could provide a frame of reference now but Kafka. Wherever I moved, I stumbled on painful ironies of power and mystification.

Some of the contradictions that beset me during my clinical clerkship and in residency seemed to have their origins in more general aspects of medical education. The habit of critical thought that the best teachers tried to inculcate in medical students is often undercut by the

rigidity of the structures in which the students must learn. One may question a diagnosis, argue the fine points of arrhythmias or electrolyte balance with a professor, but not challenge his attitude toward a class. In clinical work one may gripe about scut work or unnecessarily long or redundant medical workups, but not challenge the hierarchical setup of the ward itself.

Medical school teaches respect for human life. Too often that respect is limited to the physiological process of life, severed from the day-to-day relations of staff and patient. The tyranny of the operating surgeon over his subordinates, the long-winded pomposity of the attending physician, the sarcasm of senior residents to their juniors, are all well-known and long-suffered caricatures. If one protests them too strenuously, he is regarded as "difficult" or—on psychiatrically informed services—as "troubled." Medical students who spend time simply talking with their patients are suspected of being "unprofessional" or of "overidentifying with their patients."

It is clear to me that one doesn't have to go to medical school to be a competent therapist. To me medical school was valuable because I gained a familiarity with some of the mysteries of the human body, a sense of the complex interplay between the physical and the emotional, and an acquaintanceship with the processes of birth and death. It helped me assume a deep responsibility toward my patients and unintentionally provided me with a prolonged education in my own alienation. In retrospect it may well be that this last, unintentional result has been the most important to me in understanding the alienation of my patients.

The Hospital Ward

Like most psychiatric residents I began my training on an inpatient service. Amply staffed and comfortably furnished in spite of its location in a state hospital, the ward was to give me six months' experience in "the treatment of the hospitalized patient." It was one of three wards in what was ambiguously called "The Training Unit." Patients who heard about it had vague thoughts of vocational training. In reality it was the resident's training that was referred to.

Patients came at the beginning of a six-month period and left toward its end. If they were not ready to leave, that was too bad. They had to, because a new group of residents was coming. They were either helped to find a place in the outside world or transferred, usually without their therapist, to one of the other, less well-staffed wards. The

ward staff—nurses, aides, psychologists, social worker, occupational therapist, recreational therapist, a schoolteacher, and an attending psychiatrist—were permanent. Subject to biennial changes of chief resident and first-year residents, they sought to maintain a certain degree of consistency in an atmosphere of changing philosophical orientation and personnel.

The six-month time limit was said to provide "an inpatient experience" for the residents, a time for "long-term work with psychotics." Whether one thinks in terms of experiencing a new life situation or in terms of individual therapy, six months is not "long-term." By the time a patient or a resident was reasonably comfortable in the ward situation, the specter of departure loomed large. Though more "democratic" than that of private hospitals, which dismiss patients when their money runs out, the training unit policy was no less arbitrary.

Residents planned to see their "psychotic," "severely regressed" patient three times a week for several months and perhaps once a week thereafter. At the same time many of the residents were entering a personal psychoanalysis. Functioning rather well, they anticipated seeing their analysts four or five times a week for a number of years. The disparity between the treatment given the residents by their analysts and the ward patients by their residents was usually rationalized as follows: Psychotic patients are best treated with minimal contact and medication; psychotherapy is of dubious use. Neurotics and character disorder (almost by definition the residents are one or the other; at any rate they are not too regressed, or otherwise they wouldn't be residents), on the other hand, are more amenable to psychoanalysis. The most obvious contradiction is that the residents *do* attempt intensive individual therapy for six months. If one believes in the neurotic-psychotic distinction dictating different therapies, then this contact would seem to be counterproductive; but it is necessary for training. Therefore, the patients are given psychotherapy not for their good but because they are good "clinical material" for the residents. The goal is eventually to treat neurotics, who, like the psychiatric residents, will have enough "ego strengths" to accept the limitations of psychoanalysis. These patients will also presumably function well enough to pay for analysis.

The six-month time limit also reflected the current psychiatric emphasis on "brief hospitalization." But this phrase, like its corollary, "returning the patient to his community," seemed totally unexamined. Often patients did not want to return to their community, did not feel that it was either theirs or a community. Hospitalization was a way out; the ward was a potential new community. But the institution barred

its doors with arbitrary time limits.

Psychoanalysis provided the main intellectual basis for the residents' work. But against its wisest teachings of patient understanding was poised the necessity for "rapid reconstitution" and speedy exit from the hospital. As the six-month period drew to a close, residents and patients alike became anxious. By and large the residents—acutely aware of their inability to prolong the hospital stay and of their patients' need for more time—withdrew from their patients. The patients, angry and baffled, erected defenses against their anticipated loss and became, at least for a time, "resistant." Some of them never returned to see their therapists and over half were soon back in the hospital on another ward, usually without their therapist. Occasionally dedicated residents would continue to see those patients who wound up on other wards—usually incurring the displeasure of the new ward staff.

The difficulties and barriers that the time limit created were compounded by the therapeutic attitude that the residents were encouraged to assume. In seminars one discusses the ambiguities of the unconscious, the many-leveled ironies of transference and countertransference. Perhaps one reads the tender but tough writings of Fromm-Reichmann and hopes for the same warm depth of understanding. In practice residents soon come to adopt their supervisors' and the ward's language of "control" and "limits."

One ought to "discourage regression" and "strengthen the ego"; one should not "overidentify with the patient" or "encourage pathology." The language is one of dominance and submission, of disease and cure. Tortuosities of feeling, strange mixtures of love and hate, courage and despair, are compared to tubercular lesions. Medicine is prescribed to isolate and dissolve complicated thoughts and complex emotional states.

The language is also moralistic. A particular set of values—middle-class, white, work-oriented, male-dominated, puritanical—is the standard against which "mental health" is evaluated. Patients are to behave in accordance with certain norms prescribed by their therapist and the ward staff. "Resocialization" is defined by the values of the ward staff. On the other side therapists are either condemned or excused if their patients don't live up to these standards. Either they are encouraging regression or acting out or it is the severe nature of the patient's "pathology" that is frustrating their efforts. It is either in the resident's control or out of it. The possibility of entirely different standards of conduct is only rarely admitted.

In a therapeutic session the patient is encouraged to open up to and

trust the person who may numb him with tranquilizers or roust him out of bed in the morning or lock the ward door against his exit. Residents, at first hesitant and self-questioning, become stiffly righteous when their patients do not "get better," "produce material," or "act more normal." They have worked long and hard and have only the patient's interest in mind. Why is therapy so difficult? Perhaps an increased dose of Thorazine will make the patient "more accessible to treatment."

The physical structure of the ward frames and reinforces the estrangement of therapist and patient. The residents have tiny offices in which they spend most of their time. The patient comes to the door for his appointment and takes a seat to the side of the desk. Across the corner of the desk the resident conducts his therapy. There is no place to move, no place to go in moments of fear. If the patient does not come to the door, the resident is reluctant to leave his office. If he does it is usually to coerce or coax the patient into the session. Rarely do residents feel comfortable conducting therapy in a place of the patient's choosing. More rarely still are they encouraged to do so. Therapy must take place on the doctor's turf and according to his rules. A patient's protestations are evidence once again of resistance.

A patient will tell his resident that "everyone is watching me and talking about me," or "I feel like a guinea pig," or "I'm in prison," or "this place is driving me crazy." The resident answers reassuringly that he cares about the patient, or perhaps he reminds the latter that he was "sick" or "troubled" when he first came to the ward. But in order to dismiss the patient's protests as "paranoid," the resident must deform and constrict his own perceptions of the ward setting.

There is, after all, a glass-enclosed nurses' station in which the staff observes, discusses, and sometimes laughs at the behavior of the patients. The patients line up several times a day to receive pills that "tranquilize" them and fairly often cause unpleasant side effects. They *are* being treated by inexperienced therapists who are in training. The ward often *does* have as many locked doors as a prison and as little freedom (the resemblance between a mental hospital and a prison, a ward and a cell block, a seclusion room and solitary confinement, is quite striking; and in both institutions inmates are frequently told that they are there for "their own good"). As for being "driven crazy," put yourself in the patient's place and consider your responses and the responses they would elicit from a ward staff and the sum of the effect on your mental state.

I believe that the way mental hospitals, even "enlightened" or "liberal" ones, are set up is destructive of their patients' efforts to find a

sense of personal wholeness and worth. And I believe also that the enforced complicity of the psychiatric resident in this system undermines his efforts to define his own wholeness. The resident must adopt all or part of the hospital's view of the patient in order to survive in the hospital. Insofar as he does this, he must invalidate his patient's perceptions of the situation. And he usually does this by first invalidating his own perceptions. "This is a hospital," he may say (I have said so), "not a jail." It is true there are locks on the doors and only the staff has keys. If a patient is disruptive he will be forcibly injected with a tranquilizer (every patient *must* have a standing order for "agitation") and confined to a "seclusion room." True, it is often cruel or impersonal. But think of what might happen if we didn't do this. It really is in the patient's interest, for his own good. If he doesn't see this, it is because he has "poor reality testing" or is "delusional" or is "acting out."

My impression is that this process erodes the *resident's* "reality testing." More specifically he takes on the hospital-defined reality and thereby estranges himself from understanding his patient's reality. If he were to share more completely his patient's experience, he might have to take a very strong stand against the hospital that defines him professionally and supports him financially. He might in fact have to leave the hospital.

Understanding, exploration, and challenge, rather than "limit setting," "order writing," or the rationalization of any particular social order, are the stated purposes of therapy. And it is this understanding and this exploration that the constraints of the hospital structure, the physical setup of the ward, and the medical definition of the therapist's role vitiate.

The Outpatient Clinic

When at the beginning of my second year of residency I began to work in the outpatient clinic, I felt, like many of my colleagues, both uprooted and relieved. The feeling of community, however slight and compromised, that existed on the ward was gone; but so were the constraints and struggles of working with a tension-filled group of people in a rigid, hierarchical setting. Also gone were some of our patients from the first year.

We were discouraged from seeing most of those with whom we had worked long and hard. Held together by tranquilizers that previous supervisors had advocated, stranded in welfare hotels, reenmeshed in

the toils of their families, or isolated in other wards, they were not considered to be "good cases." "You have to take so and so many new cases," we were told; and besides, they are "interesting"—that is, young, attractive, bright, promising, and "not psychotic."

Time coerced and "interest" seduced many of us from our former patients. A callousness that should have been sharply questioned was fostered by our transition to the outpatient clinic and by the supervisors that we met there. Those who resisted were challenged about their motives for continuing to see their patients so intensively. Didn't we want to learn how to deal with "neurotics"? Did we really think our attentions were so vital? Wasn't there something a little "strange" about our concern for our patients? Perhaps some "unanalyzed countertransference problem"? The curriculum demanded that we move on and our objections were "resistances" to be analyzed.

Whereas the overarching issue of the first year was control, that of the second was analysis. This reflected a change in structure—from a large hospital with wards to an agglomeration of private practices—as well as a change in the diagnoses of the patients and the concerns of the supervisors. Freed from the necessity to control his patients, the resident could now simply listen. But the clinic had a fairly good idea about who should be listened to and how much.

There were "insight" and "supportive" patients. The focus of the resident's work was on insight patients, whom he would generally see twice a week for fifty minutes. Supportive patients—more numerous, generally older, darker skinned, less well-educated, and bearing more pessimistic diagnoses—would be seen once a month for a half hour or so. The latter would usually be given medication (tranquilizers and antidepressants), the former only occasionally. Psychoanalytic psychotherapy for the privileged few, the medical model and small comfort for most.

What is so remarkable is not that this happened, but that it was so little questioned. Somehow the residents allowed themselves to be convinced that this arrangement was reasonable, if not adequate. And in the process they became party to an unexamined elitism. Some people were worth listening to and others were not. Roughly speaking, those closest to the residents in age, class, socioeconomic standing, education, and aspirations could be heard. The others would be medicated. This process could not help but make it harder for the residents, become psychiatrists, to hear the plaints of these people, plaints that are already deadened by a far greater barrier: poor people, even with Medicaid, cannot pay the fees of residents once they finish their training, leave the clinics, and become psychiatrists in private practice.

The emphasis, then, was on psychoanalytic psychotherapy with a small, carefully selected group of people, on the analysis of an individual's problems as he presented them in fifty-minute sessions. Supervision was aimed at understanding these problems and the interaction between therapist and patient. I object not to the validity of this approach but to its exclusiveness. Some residents took a group therapy seminar, others took family therapy, still others learned about behavior therapy, and occasionally someone took an elective in community psychiatry. But these were courses, compartmentalized (and, incidentally, less stressed) aspects of a curriculum.

Nowhere was an attempt made to understand modern psychiatry, particularly psychoanalytic psychotherapy, in a historical context as a product of certain socioeconomic, cultural, and scientific developments. Just as supervisors would ferret for evidence of castration anxiety or orality in an individual session, so the whole curriculum was geared toward the detailed understanding and application of psychoanalytic principles.

An atmosphere of timeless, unquestionable verity develops; residents, like scholastics or Talmudists, enthusiastically dispute the fine points of dogma. Why had one let a patient stay more than fifty minutes? "Why not?" was a response met at best with a bemused tolerance. From fixed boundaries the process circled ever inward, experience fragmenting before analysis. Yes, residents do learn about psychoanalysis this way, about the laws of unconscious displacement and projection, about the power of infantile sexuality, and about the "psychopathology of everyday life." What they do not learn is that they see only one aspect of the reality of everyday life. We see what we are taught to look for. So dedicated and anxious are we that we forget how narrow our vision is.

Just as on the ward, so in the outpatient clinic the physical structure reinforces and confirms the basic ideology. The entire world funnels into the resident. Patients move progressively from their home through their neighborhood to the waiting room, to the therapist's office. The patient's world is never glimpsed at firsthand. His understanding of it is subject to an analysis of distortions that one has no way of documenting. All experience becomes the end product of a series of intrapsychic mechanisms. Even the experience of therapist and patient is put at one remove by a too exclusive focus on the processes of the transference and countertransference.

The resident never sees a patient in his or her natural setting, at home, on the job, or in school. In fact he almost never thinks of doing so; and if he does he is warned that such action would seriously tamper

with the transference. The fact that it might also be plain common sense to, say, be with an anxious dental assistant while she works or sit on a subway with a claustrophobic patient is never considered. Even when residents see families together, they rarely visit in the home. Ethologists have learned that animal behavior—including basic patterns of relating—is very different in artificial and natural settings. Psychiatric training still insists unquestioningly that one understands more about human beings in an artificial, isolated, doctor-determined situation.

The problems with training in the outpatient setting are finally not all that different from those in the hospital. In both cases a too rigid distinction is made between the inner and outer lives of patients. Psychopathology is said to exist in a person's mind. The world in which he or she lives is composed of both projections and facts. It is subject to distortion by fantasy and confirmation by reality testing. But the psychiatric resident is in a position to point out only certain distortions, to confirm only particular realities. In a classic instance of a double bind the resident is trained to distance himself from certain kinds of understanding and then to deny that he has so distanced himself.

He takes for objective fact a particular subjective evaluation such as a diagnosis. He accepts as given and acceptable a particular world— inpatient ward or individual therapist office—and does not question, much less try to alter, the nature of the world. Instead he elevates to the heights of truth certain constraints that may be purely institutional: Psychotic patients *need* controls or tranquilizers or limits. Rather than derive his attitudes toward those he is trying to help from their relationship, he allows it to be determined by the medical model and its authoritarian institutionalization in the hospital setting. Rather than try to observe the "problems in living" in the life of the person who comes to see him, he chooses to observe only the created problems of the therapeutic setting and then, relying on the efficacy of the analogy, to analyze these.

Individual psychoanalytic therapy in an office is a technique designed to promote understanding of a human mind. Hospitalization is one way of dealing with certain people who are disturbing and worrisome to others. The former is analogous to shamanistic techniques, the latter to thought reform and correction. Both depend in our society on a belief that the person so indicated is sick and must be dealt with in isolation for his or her own good as well as ours. Whatever good anyone may experience from either process, they both function as instruments of a particular society. It is a society that cherishes both individualism and conformity, a measure of individualism for those

who can afford it financially, conformity for those who cannot.

Psychiatric residents foster at times one, at times the other, function. In a hospital setting individual understanding is undercut and vitiated by institutional constraint. In outpatient therapy it is truncated by a narrowness of perspective. The feelings of estrangement that bring the patient to therapy are too often perpetuated in the therapeutic setting. The resident, at first a hesitant, questioning partner, becomes, through his training, the bearer and arbiter of this tradition.

Possibilities for Change

There are no easy solutions to the problems and processes that I have described. They are rooted in the very structure of medical and, particularly, psychiatric education—in the language, the politics, and the architecture, in the economics as much as in the "clinical evidence." If I do not see another person as the victim of a disease, I will not try to use medical or surgical means to cure him of it, nor will I confine him to a hospital. If I do not consider my reality as normative, I will be less likely to stigmatize his difference as deviance. If I do not depend for my livelihood on the ability of my patients to pay my fees, I may find that my techniques are applicable to more people than I previously suspected; I may also find that other techniques are more capable of alleviating the suffering of those who come to me.

The possibilities for change are enormous. We must begin by examining those biases that we have come to call basic principles or necessities. Psychoanalysis began when Freud listened to what people said and took seriously words that others had ignored—accounts of dreams, memories of childhood, slips of the tongue. If we situate ourselves so that we can hear afresh, we have taken the first step. At present we too often assume that we know how to treat our patients' problems. Training is a time for passing on and perfecting this knowledge. We forget that we choose to look from one perspective at the problems of a small, select group of people. We too easily accept the felt problems of the vast majority of people as "reality"—even as we help, in our institutions and through our training, perpetuate that reality.

To begin with, we must think anew about why psychiatrists are only medically trained and what consequences this has. We might remove psychiatric trainees from a hospital setting and sponsor the creation of small living communes in which they and their "patients" might interact more freely. Perhaps residents should spend time listening to, being with, people in a bar, luncheonette, shopping center, or school-

yard. Perhaps their powers of analysis should be brought to bear, not merely on individual patients' "problems," but on the social and political situations that affect these patients. Rather than play with a child in an office and send his mother to a social worker, one might visit the house, walk in the neighborhood, stand on the welfare line with mother and child, other family members, and neighbors. Psychiatrists should read Frantz Fanon as well as Freud, Dostoevski as well as Karl Abraham, Emma Goldman as well as Helene Deutsch, Buber as well as Skinner, and Richard Wright and Malcolm X as well as Hollingshead and Redlich. We know so much less than we need to, and psychiatric residency—hurrying young doctors through their "training" and into their "subspecialties"—confirms rather than questions our and their ignorance.

2. The Words of Those Other People

THOMAS J. COTTLE

I first heard of Thomas Cottle through reviews of his book *Time's Children*. Like him, I was a social scientist interviewing and writing about young people, and I was surprised to hear a book labeled "poetic," "lyrical," "warmly human," when I expected it to contain generalizations about the life experiences of contemporary youth. As I read it, I found out how it could be so: it was a series of encounters between Tom, fresh out of graduate school, and young people from the ghetto, from high schools, and from colleges in the Boston area. He played with them, rode school buses with them, and tried to share as much as possible *their* experience. As I came to the end, I was still waiting for the obligatory theoretical essay, the tying together that I had come to expect. It wasn't there. Since then, I have read his work in *Harper's, The New York Times Magazine, Daedalus,* and his recent book, *The Abandoners,* and have come to admire his method, or perspective, enough to want to try to be more like him.

In this essay he talks about how he came to that style, which he contrasts with the scientific, professional, objective style and attitude that was preferred in the medical and graduate schools he attended, in his research, and in his clinical work. Like Jim Gordon, he is saying that the popular assumption that the scientific attitude of the professional is *more* complete or superior than everyday perception is definitely wrong. It often masks a hidden insensitivity and loss of humanity. His suggestion is to alter that equation, change that bias, and allow people to remain people, even as they are also professionals and therapists. Tom is affiliated with the Children's Defense Fund of the Washington Research Project.

I have discovered that when I say my values or attitudes have changed over the years, it often means that I am merely realizing that my current "adult" perceptions have little in common with my childhood perceptions of adulthood that I still carry. It isn't exactly that my values have changed. Rather, how I imagined I would be as an adult, how I thought things worked, is not coinciding with how my life is actually evolving.

The practice of psychotherapy and, even more appropriately, the conducting of research provide good examples of this "false change" in values. As a boy wanting to become a doctor, I imagined that one did something with patients in private, a little something that had science and magic mixed together, and patients went away happy and well. Somewhere along the line I would be living pretty well myself. One day a week, the fantasy continued, I would, as they used to say, give some time to charity, which meant working with poor people, who, while they couldn't pay, presumably developed illnesses like the rest of us. Even as a child, I imagined charity work as a far less private affair. It was open ward and emergency room work, on the street work, not small, sanitized office work. There was another difference: you didn't talk much with charity cases. You performed your service, they thanked you and left, perhaps holding you in awe as well. And something else was different: you went to their part of the city, while your regular patients came to you.

The policy in many medical schools—as, for example, the school I attended for one year—actually substantiated some of these fantasies, just as the practice of medicine generally must have encouraged the fantasies in the first place. Medical students in their third or fourth year took off two weeks to deliver babies in poor communities. An uneasy balance was established between using these babies and their mothers for educational purposes and providing doctors for families who could not afford them. What I heard from the medical students returning from these obstetric visitations was first, that they were nervous and didn't know what to do, and second, that the women who supposedly "needed" them instructed them more articulately than any professor. There was always the story, too, told with astonishment, of the woman with seven or ten kids who helped the doctor help her give birth and four hours later was back cooking or scrubbing the kitchen floor. It was all incredible—the women, the families, the children, the neighborhoods. But in the end only a few people, seemingly, took away from these experiences the lasting idea of the strength, physical courage, and difficult conditions facing these families.

Childbirth was the exceptional moment, the unique case study. It

was not viewed as yet another process that had to be endured within the tangible contexts of poverty. "Those people" were still out there, having their babies without proper medical attention, being under-nourished, and probably having nothing to do in their lives but *have* babies. No one pursued the idea of their stamina, their eloquence, but only how awful it was where they lived and how much the women had helped them when they timorously entered those shabby homes. How in God's name was anything alive going to come out of that woman who, with her water burst and the baby practically crowning, had gotten up off a putrid-smelling mattress to open the door for the doctor?

Even during graduate training in sociology and psychology I maintained similar images about "those people out there," although "out there" was getting closer as the university was sprawling into those "out there" regions. The lives of those people were constantly being separated from us by one thing or another, and it wasn't always that ubiquitous creature called culture that kept us apart. The question of how to study those people, reach them, and work with what they told us was becoming quite a source of separation from them.

Now here was a perplexing problem: the methodological techniques we were learning as young social scientists involved keeping data pure, free from anything that would spoil them. Indeed, one apparently treated the data with greater antiseptic precautions than the doctors were treating those mothers in labor. So we were learning the appropriate techniques of interviewing patients, clients, research subjects; and we were being moved by these people, I suppose, but not according them full human stature. When we got what we wanted, we had right away to analyze it, interpret it, and wonder about how much we could generalize about human behavior from what these people had said. Gradually, the child who had volunteered to be in our study or the woman who consented to be interviewed or the man who brought to us, strangers, his anguish and overpowering sadness became a case history, a representative of society.

Soon the interview was over and a discussion about it followed with a dozen other students who had observed through one-way mirrors or in the darkness hidden by partitions. Then the term papers and examinations were written and someone recalled the guy with the Italian name and the depression who came in that dreary afternoon three months before, the man who had been labeled a "borderline." "What the hell was his name? Whatever happened to him? They hospitalize him?" "Someone gave him three bucks and sent him home in a cab!" "You ever read Frieda Fromm-Reichmann on depression?" someone

would ask. "She's got this great thing about . . ." And then all of us were gone.

I oversimplify numerous aspects of my education when I say that professionalization quieted my involvement with "those other people." What seemed natural and straightforward, the regular sort of chat with a new friend, even if that friend ran a pool hall or was found waiting in an emergency room of a city hospital, was being discredited. Professionals, we had learned, transcend these simple anybody-can-have-them types of relationships. They learn how to initiate encounters without becoming implicated, and they do so in such a way that the data they collect remain systematic, clean, analyzable. They learn, moreover, the importance of collecting the kind of material that someone after them can collect. Indeed, the notion of replication seemed to imply that material had to present itself to the next person exactly as it had to us, otherwise the investigation's validity, stability, and reliability would forever be questioned. But always at stake was the issue of not becoming involved with those one studied. (Strangely, I discovered later, the people with whom I now speak in the course of doing research face these same issues with me. Some take seriously the friendship we have established. They are concerned about the material they provide me with and wonder how *they* are performing their part of the bargain and whether their contribution to the research is adequate. Others, of course, see the relationship strictly in research terms. They receive nothing from our conversations and might terminate our association at any time.)

It was the professionalization, the unseen spirits, dogma, and tradition that actually affected not only our cognitive apparatuses, but our private impressions and aspirations as well. Psychology should be practiced in an office with a tie and jacket and, of course, a fee, for one must never forget what Freud wrote about the symbolism of payment. Sociological work, moreover, must be pursued, for want of a more elegant phrase, from afar—afar and above, more likely. One had to be on top of situations, protected by one's understanding and analyses. Hunches and wonderings were appropriate for accomplished elders who appeared to rely on intuition when actually they leaned on all varieties of empirical findings.

This is not to say that there weren't moments of humanism. Spring showers is what they were, soft downpours lasting for so short a time the flowers were barely moistened. But they helped. Once, for example, in a class of sixty of us towering intellectuals watching a movie of a social worker speaking with a schizophrenic child, the professor, an eminent psychoanalyst, was unable to budge our vision and make us

see what was happening. We found transference, repressed rage, condescension on the part of the social worker. He saw a woman kneeling down in order to make eye contact with a small boy. "And what do you think when a person comes into your office," he asked gruffly from a high podium, "who appears to be having a psychotic episode?" We answered drugs, crisis intervention, examination of the entire family not just the "labeled patient." "You think," he corrected us angrily, "there but for the grace of God . . ."

Actually, most of us had been thinking something like that. I remember after that class how we joked that if we treated a psychotic person we would be thinking, "I'm glad it's you, pal, and not me." So we were close enough to the "correct" answer, except that our prepuberty professionalism did not allow this thought to be expressed and become part of any living ethic.

In contrast to those who showered us with a gentle humanness were those professors of medicine—and this was in the 1960s—who actually reported to the dean the names of students carrying books of poetry in their lab coats. My own illicit package was the works of Wallace Stevens. Because they had never studied the dynamics of urban public schools, those medical policemen never learned that the reporting to the dean becomes the critical incitement to rebel. Wallace Stevens was poignant, moving, but not yet influential in shifting values or determining that old values were not being sustained. I would draw on the poets later on, however, when I needed support for a type of inquiry many social scientists found meager, frail, and unmanly—the subjective.

Then there was the actual research work and psychotherapy. Case reports, a form of literature that always stimulated us, also served, I fear, as a form of divertimento rather than as a full-fledged symphonic form. Glimpses at patients were "better" than reading turgid prose. But always, like those women in the poor neighborhoods, the case studies were teaching us to consider humanness with a controlled posture. I remember asking once what was the personal and literary significance of calling someone by his or her psychoneurosis or letting a letter stand for her identity? It was more than confidentiality being preserved, I said, when Dr. T. treated the thirty-eight-year-old female Caucasian Madam L. The representation of a whole human being was being withheld.

The case study, in other words, although a blessed relief from purely theoretical and empirical writings, was offering up a victim in the very mode practiced in introductory anatomy examinations. Here a tray was presented to the student. A reddish wax had been poured in the

bottom of the tray, and pinned with straight pins was a tiny chink of flesh, blood vessel, or, more tricky, a wholly unidentifiable object. Then, while the liberal arts graduates grumbled about the insidiousness of encountering body parts desecrated in this way and uttered words like "gestalt" and "neoimpressionism," the anatomical dandies searched their memories and found the secret words. In the bar after the examination there was always talk about walking down the street and finding—how fortuitously—a lonely chip off some poor fellow's epidydimis like the one on the red wax tray.

Case studies had a bit of that same effect on us. Instead of a slice of an epidydimis, we had a bit of anal aggression or a soupçon of schizophrenia. But the patient's—dare I say person's—whole life was never revealed. Nor for that matter was the therapist's life or his or her remarks during the treatment. Out of clear blue skies the thirty-eight-year-old female Caucasian just began speaking, and the invisible recorder-therapist began writing or transcribing. So people, social situations, and human engagements were coming at us in the most fragmented fashion.

I am not certain that those of us being socialized in this way could articulate such feelings at the time. But surely one of the major forces urging us to read novels we had read already or had always heard we should read was the need to witness human relationships unfold in the aesthetic, imaginative, and holistic ways in which they genuinely unfold. Although appealing, the case study seemed inadequate because the fascination with a single human being or the concern with life and death, history and evolution that novelists had portrayed for us was too often missing. Frequently, even the demeaning "slice of life" peek at men and women that newspapers and magazines published under the label of "human interest story," was more telling of the way life truly was led. In a sense, the case study and not the novel was fictive.

During this period of training and early professionalism, a similar set of constraints was imposed on research. Here again people were not people, were not meant to be people, but were instead transformed into quantifiable units. Everybody knows about this. We were aware of the process in those days, too, in the same way that we knew about brutality in schools and prisons. Yet, most of us bit into the pie as it was served up to us. We learned how to transfer people's responses to our questions onto IBM cards and then stuff the cards into the machine itself. We learned computer programming and how to clean the data and, alas, analyze it. The complexity, ambiguity, and richness of even the limited interviews I conducted contrasted markedly with the linear beauty and quintessential order of the data as it appeared all

categorized up and analyzed in gorgeous printouts. In the first moments of inspecting the material from the computer, human behavior
was, in effect, interpreted, understood. While someone beginning a
practice in psychotherapy could not readily admit to this sort of reaction, the truth was that the computer did bring that proverbial order
to that proverbial chaos, and the feeling actually was satisfying. For the
moment, anyway, my reactions to those I was "studying" could be
denied, especially in the light of such glorious scientific(-looking) results.

The effect on me of the computer was the constant separation of
myself from the people I had studied—the very people whose utterances I had transformed into numerical coefficients. If anything, I was
implicated in the IBM system, but not in the lives of those *lower status*
people kind enough to complete my questionnaires, the people whom
I mentioned in the footnotes of professional articles.

Perhaps the most frustrating of all the principles I learned in graduate school was the principle of interactive indifference. In the name
of science and psychotherapy one stood apart from one's "subjects"
and "patients." One emphasized analysis or understanding and wor-
shiped results and the usefulness and beauty of ideas and books rather
than the spirit and everyday action that constitute human existence
and survival. Quotations from authors could be inserted in manuscripts
when they illustrated something or provided the reader a bit of therapeutic ambience. But long quotations, descriptions, or meanderings
about one's *friendship* with someone were deemed inappropriate,
unprofessional.

Furthermore, when one included in a manuscript pages of conversations rather than mere snatches and anecdotes, the person written
about was inevitably labeled a patient. When a psychotherapist talks
to someone, particularly someone living in a poor community, like
those mothers the medical students befriended for two weeks, then
that someone becomes a patient. Even today, I find that no matter how
many times I write that those with whom I speak have not come
seeking psychological treatment, that in fact I went to them, many
critics, well-meaning to be certain, label these people patients. Why
else would a professional therapist be speaking with them if not for
purposes of treatment or change? To report what they say, it is also
argued, is not enough. One must do something with the people or with
their words. Reveries, opinions, reflections, feelings, whatever anyone
tells us in our travels to their homes, must be transformed into one of
the world's professional currencies. We have been instructed to abstract the findings, analyze the words, which means impose classical

objective analytic criteria on them. Sadly, the myriad forms of subjective analysis that underwrite the type of research many of us perform continue to remain invisible to those schooled only in objective forms of analysis.

Let me pause on this idea of people speaking for themselves and letting their words be the final "product" of research. Throughout our training there was always a message that words had to be transcended, lifted into some greater plane of human significance. Well and good, for the analysis of the written and spoken word has a long tradition, and among the cognitive operations of listening are coding, decoding, organizing, synthesizing, and other forms of interpretation. That these processes are a fundamental part of human exchange testifies to the necessity of transposing individual word units into categories of more comprehensive meaning.

But there is an important political point to be made as well. The words of patients, of poor people, of those mothers again, could not attain the highest level of significance to us because of the relationships we had established with these people and the status we had thereby accorded them and ourselves. This was the fundamental distinction that struck me, not during my years of training, but afterward. Good doctors must shoot for a greater ideal—the ideal of making science. Anything resembling literature—and certain forms of psychotherapy resemble forms of literature—was not deemed consistent with the scientific enterprise.

I believed this. I would love to be able to say that in my mid-twenties sophistication I argued with professors on the nature of truth and untruth and the experiencing of multiple realities. But I did not. Indeed, I remember idolizing a man who practiced several forms of psychotherapy while at the same time being an expert on matrix algebra. The latter work, I concluded, *compensated* for the airy and rarified activities of the former work. The latter work, moreover, stood squarely on the road to making science, whereas the former represented merely listening and responding sensitively to people.

For years the words of people, the forms of their survival, the substance of their everyday and everynight needs, activities, and wonderings loomed as grist, data to dissect, material to be poured into the architectural forms of theory building and empirical analysis. Words by themselves counted for little, except that certain colleagues rather admired anyone who did a great deal of interviewing "in the field." To acquire reams of notes from conversations with "ordinary" people— we weren't, after all, anthropologists engaged in a year of field work in New Guinea or the bush—was a demiaccomplishment. Further-

more, to follow the procedure of psychotherapists and social scientists of speaking with people week in and week out for years seemed even a greater achievement, although as I understand reactions to this type of work, it still wasn't considered science.

In time, I found there was a natural way to perform the work in the homes I had rightly or wrongly invaded. I described the lives of people I had come to know and let them speak for themselves. No conscious decision was made regarding the major forms of the work. When long passages of speech were recounted, there simply was not that much else to do.

The reader may question this approach. If someone has spoken about something that matters to him or her, why does this necessarily preclude analysis in the manner, for example, that Freud performed it in his elegant and clearly literary case studies? The person's identity can be hidden, so what constrains the researcher in making further analysis?

The answer to this question rests partly in the contract one establishes with the people about whom one writes. It is a contract essentially of friendship, of mutuality, and not merely one of questioning and answering. It is a contract predicated on a request that persons share moments of their lives. Research of this type does not constitute psychotherapy. I go to people, and they give me real as well as symbolic moments of their time. I go, moreover, to speak to *them*, not strictly to research a problem or gather material that might elucidate some greater issue of which the other person is merely a convenient example. The person is not an informant in the sense anthropologists use this term. The person's life or, really, the tiny fragments he or she gives *me*—for to other investigators other fragments are given—represents the entirety of the inquiry.

In the selection of conversations, naturally, all sorts of political, economic, moral, educational, or religious issues play dominant roles. No one can hide his or her biases, prejudgments, or the visions produced by professional training. No one can hide the fact that when research takes someone into neighborhoods of poverty that poverty itself may emerge as the nonabstract hero (or antihero) of the final work. Still, these issues may not be paramount in the moment-by-moment conversations that constitute the research. The work is nothing more than talking and listening, having one's mind wander, sometimes in step with the story, sometimes in counterpoint to it. This is the quintessential aspect of this form of subjective inquiry: the interaction, the friendship, the mutuality, the encounter. This is why the actual words spoken become so important and why no further "objective" analysis is left to

be undertaken. It is research based on aesthetic judgments and human intuition, both fundamental ingredients of the dramatic or dramaturgic. One seeks to know how life is led.

Each of us senses the private inner sphere of human reality and what influences it, and the exterior sphere and what seems to affect it. And everyone senses the ways in which these two spheres shift so that their boundaries are at times indistinguishable and how this shifting may result from changes in either sphere or in the interplay between spheres. Essentially, this interplay lies at the core of the subjective inquiry. I mention this notion of spheres so that no one will think I am arguing that nothing existing in the mind of one person can ever be known by (to) another. The subjective encounter underlying this research includes the interviewer, intruder, who possesses an inner sphere which is at all times having impressions made on it by another human being and the environment of this other human being. The writings of philosophers, scientists, psychotherapists, and novelists ripple my mind as I write that all I know is what I experience in the mutual presentment of selves that constitutes any encounter of which I am a part.

My work, then, is based on paying attention more than interpretation and on reaction more than abstract analysis. It is a sharing of lives in which the asymmetry established by dint of the original interview relationship is never fully righted. But always there are the words, the other persons' and my own, and the exchange which must get into the research and into the friendship as well. The dramatic quality of the interaction persists in all interactions, if one accepts the metaphor, but it is especially salient here because of the nature of the friendship and its special purpose as established at the outset. For this reason I refer to myself not only as a friend of those who share their lives with me, but as an intruder as well. This fact psychotherapists and counselors know, too, for the feelings of intrusion exist in the therapeutic alliance even though the person called patient or client seeks out the therapist precisely because the therapist's role allows for a degree of symbolic invasion.

I mention the dramatic aspect, too, because it reminds us of the public and sociological parts of research and psychotherapy. When we speak of authentic engagements, we must consider the public, situational, cultural, aspects of this authenticity. Events and processes outside our private selves contribute to the determination of the authentic. Physical as well as psychological settings shape encounters and the eventual presentation of authenticity to another and to oneself. A description of these settings, therefore, must also be included in the

documents one writes about another person.

One final issue relates both to the type of research I have been discussing and the practice of psychotherapy. An easy way to validate our writing is to show it to those we have written about. This gives them the opportunity to delete passages that they feel are incorrect, unfair, or hurtful as well as the chance to recall or elaborate certain points. It also lets them see how we have perceived and recalled our friendship. This is easy enough, but the principle of confidence and confidentiality implied in it is more complicated.

It is presumptuous, to say the least, to undertake a friendship in which one may write about that friendship. Still, certain precautions and forms of decency may be practiced. For example, we may not say anything about those we "research" until a manuscript is approved. I am appalled in this regard by the extent of divulgence exhibited by researchers and psychotherapists. Not only are real identities made known, but people's words are bandied about even though they have been promised secrecy. Consulting with one's husband or wife when a patient is unaware that this occurs is part of the violation of trust, and yet many who practice psychotherapy do not agree that this constitutes a violation. A psychiatrist laughingly responded to my position on confidentiality by asking, "You mean I should tell patients, when things get hot in here I may talk to my wife about it?" "That's exactly what I mean," I answered. Our discussion had been initiated by his mentioning that videotapes of families in treatment were to be shown at a conference, although none of the families knew that their sessions would be revealed in this way.

I can be accused of oversensitivity about my position on confidentiality. One woman once admonished me that the days of secrecy about psychoanalysis have ended. Now, one could send out announcements that one is in analysis, she said, just as one sends out birth announcements. I was incredulous, and she was incredulous that I would find her analogy outrageous. Still, the charge of hypersensitivity remains.

Many people, apparently, care little that their therapy experiences or even their names are the subjects of party conversations. As long as their therapists continue to care for them and do not wish to hurt them, then the therapists may speak as freely as they wish. The problem, however, is that once confidentiality is broken, one cannot assure another person that something hurtful will not happen. Control over outcomes is now forfeited; the material becomes public property. Patients, clients, and interviewees will speak to friends about therapy or the research in which they are participating, which means that numerous stories will circulate about therapists and researchers. The tempta-

tion is to reciprocate but it must, I feel, be denied.

Another problem is that too many of us are in touch with the world only through television, our patients, or those in our research projects. Retelling their stories makes it seem as if we were authentic travelers in the world. With good intentions we may support an argument by revealing what people have disclosed to us, but again I wonder whether this is a legitimate act. These people have not come to us or allowed us to enter their homes with the understanding that they are informants. It is the enhancement of their lives that we have promised, and while value may accrue from bringing their words to those who might otherwise never hear them, an equally enhancing gesture is to keep their secrets and respect their privacy. It is, after all, the same thing we do for our friends.

An important political distinction underlies the preservation or violation of confidentiality. I notice that when we speak about poor patients, much is divulged and often a name is dropped. Confidentiality is more likely to be preserved when patients are affluent. While the matter of therapists deferring to the wealthy or patients deferring to their therapists is a serious one, it ought not mask the notion that even people seeking treatment must decide whether or not to reveal private matters. The decision to reveal oneself in therapy is based on trust, but trusting is not a purely psychological act. Sociological features of the relationship like ethnicity, age, credentials, economic background, and status contribute to one's willingness to trust. Social standing cannot be the basis on which practioners and researchers establish the limits of confidentiality.

I have perhaps touched on these last points merely to remind myself of the precariousness of therapy and interviewing. I am preoccupied with the question of overromanticizing another person's life, just as some of us are preoccupied with the power of our work. We believe strongly that our writing, research, or forms of treatment bring our "clients," our friends, into the light or, indeed, make them come alive. Granted, it is often through someone's writing that we learn of some person or condition. It is also true that those we work with and befriend are very much alive when we are not in their homes nor they in our offices. They may appear "larger than life" during the magical fifty minutes of therapy, but soon they are shut out again from us.

I return to the issue of professional training and the positivist brand of research and practice that was advanced. It supported a separation of people, an assumed heirarchy of human significances, and a belief that people may properly be used for certain purposes and that these purposes were essentially good. To be sure, we deal only with bits of

roles when we deal with others. But this fragmented and abstracted treatment of human beings gradually assumed a rational justification for us, if not a genuine scientific importance. It was good analyzing other people's lives, sifting through people on the basis of criteria convenient to us; it was good listening only for certain utterances or attitudes and letting the rest go by; and it was good presenting one's findings in the traditional forms that excluded personal expression and made the rendering of science preeminent.

There is, however, an aesthetic form of doing research, practicing therapy, and describing one's experiences. It has not yet been fully explored by social scientists, for some of us still dress in scientific trappings and fear that our work may be moving nearer humanistic traditions. "Is it fiction or nonfiction?" we are asked. The events are true, we answer, the conditions and the people real as the very days of their lives. Did we get permission from them? We did. Did we use tape recorders? Sometimes. And are these people our patients? No. All are valuable inquiries, but none of them touches the crucial questions: Is what we are doing truthful? Is it respectful of the truths of the single human life as it evolves within a culture, within psychological and sociological spheres, and according to the constraints of history? Is it mindful of the truths of ourselves, and the space, time, and movement that are uniquely our own and subject to change because of the research or therapy we practice? Is it respectful of the truths of the civilization in which these brief life moments are exchanged, then to ramify in the private and public spheres of ourselves and others? And finally, is it mindful of the fact that we cannot know directly the life of anyone but ourselves?

This last question haunts me, particularly when I see the aging computer printouts on my shelves and the notes I have taken on a conversation with a child only hours ago. I find myself wanting to deny this undeniable principle of human reality. But then to comfort myself I will say the child does not wholly know me either, and at least in this one sacred realm we stand equal. So now we might both continue our work and our friendship from this ideal premise.

No doubt, the word "premise" has a precarious quality about it, the very quality that makes me uncomfortable about practicing therapy and doing the type of research I do. One source of this precariousness lies in the nature of the role one assumes in establishing any premise for human engagement. Surely, we are beyond thinking that "playing a role" is, by definition, unauthentic. Like pretending, playing is not automatically an unauthentic gesture: it is the role and the demands it makes that cause us in our self-consciousness to feel dishonest or

incomplete. Understandably, different personalities are attracted by different role demands: some of these demands are found to be satisfying, some oppressive. No matter what we believe about therapy and research, an ideology of some sort dominates this work and distinct levels of power underlie it. Forms of truthfulness and equality exist in both enterprises but so, too, do forms of deceit and inequity.

Once I thought I had resolved the conflict between truth and untruth in my work. Traditional methods of research, I decided, were unauthentic, contemporary styles of therapy that spoke of wholeness and authenticity were genuine and true. Later, still hunting for simple resolutions, I shifted attitudes and decided that the subjective inquiry yielded the truth in contrast to even the most humane styles of psychotherapy. With each change in attitude my feelings were transformed. First I felt healthy doing therapy, then I felt healthy doing research. Then I concluded that an old personality trait lay behind my shifting dissatisfactions. The instant I felt half-way competent at something I lost interest in it and sought something new, using the earlier activity as a symbol of what I no longer valued.

Presently I have a new assessment of my work; it overflows with ambivalence. There is truth and untruth, equality and inequality in whatever I do, and each moment brings new gratification and new concern. I am not now speaking of the phenomenon we all recognize, that one is a "good" therapist one session and inadequate the next. Rather, the culture, its politics and economics, its values and styles of human transaction necessarily influence every assessment of my work, every instant of my therapy and research. I hear the sounds of ideology, power, manipulation in every encounter, in the same way, probably, that some people hear the words of angels or devils. At times, when I am able to hush these sounds, I feel the work to be glorious and even presume to think I have helped someone. But gradually the sounds are loud again, and I resume questioning my efforts and wonder whether I have not been deceived, or worse, deceived someone else.

"Denial" was one of the important psychological words we examined in graduate school; "delusion," in all its senses, is the word I have used again and again with myself since embarking on a career. Have I created situations under the banner of humanism and enhancement of life that, in fact, convenience *me* philosophically, intellectually, financially, politically, all ways? And do I therefore find in these exquisitely prepared situations only those gratifications, truths, and equalities, as well as frustrations, deceptions, and inequities, that I am able to deal with or safely agonize over? It must be this way because I do not experience the inconveniences and oppressions that the hurting

peoples of the world experience. Knowing their anguish only by report, perhaps even first-hand report, causes me to feel unauthentic no matter what I conjure up in response to it. Still when one is directly confronted by anguish, suffering in the form of another human being, something in one's soul changes and never changes back. From that time on laughter and crying take on different meaning. But the fear persists that I encounter human beings according to premises convenient for me and with devices that protect my vulnerabilities more than theirs.

I have not remained unchanged by the albeit limited encounters that constitute my therapy and research work. At least two signs convince me of this. First, I now take greater personal risk, in subtle and in not so subtle ways, than ever before. Something about risk suggests that my conceptions of life and death have been altered in the course of doing my work. The second sign comes in the form of a sadness mixed with anger, a disconsolation tinged with outrage. I call it a depression, thinking that if I label the mood, it might magically disappear. Surely many events and long-standing experiences play into this depression, but whatever its cause I feel it connected in some important ways to the therapy and research I perform. And no matter how mightily I try to let go of it, it hangs on and makes me think I will never be free of it.

3. The Mythology of Professionalism and an Emerging Alternate Role

TED CLARK

Ted Clark and I have been co-workers for several years. Before that we were both nonprofessionals at the same mental health center, and our experiences there led us to join Yvonne, now my wife, to form an alternative to that center oriented toward young people in crisis, in New Haven, Connecticut. Ted and I coauthored a book about our work in alternate institutions, *Toward a Radical Therapy: Alternate Services for Personal and Social Change.* Then we were researchers for a study of youthful drug use and young people's responses to government drug programs, *Worlds Apart: Young People and Drug Programs.*

Last year Ted created a video resource center through which he teaches professional psychotherapists how to operate and apply video in therapy, as well as the use of video as a tool for institutional and social change. Ted is the author of *The Oppression of Youth* and *Going into Therapy.* Presently he is the director of the Coventry Counseling Center, in Coventry, Connecticut. The center is primarily focused on youth and family issues.

The importance or, more precisely, the power of mental health professionals[1] should not be easily dismissed nor taken for granted. Often the

---

1. In this article the term "professional" is used to refer to the group consisting of clinical psychologists (Ph.D.) and psychiatrists (M.D. plus a psychiatric residency). It is understood that generalizations about the trends established by

influence of this elite is derived from false beliefs people have about the capabilities and qualities of anyone who has a doctorate. Over the last ten years I have worked as a nonprofessional psychotherapist, and from my experiences I conclude that the myth of the doctorate has a detrimental effect on communities. The power derived from myth, unlike the influence earned by an individual based on demonstrated abilities to address the needs of the community, is generally used to exploit vulnerable individuals. In addition, to preserve the benefits granted by society to the professional elite, nonprofessionals are oppressed and discriminated against. There are, however, creative and meaningful alternatives open for anyone who wants to help people with emotional conflicts and problems in living but who refuses to participate in either the academic rituals necessary to earn a doctorate or the mystification of the professional.

I do not reject the value of some graduate schools and psychiatric residencies as *one* means of learning the fundamentals of knowledge and skill useful in psychotherapy and related areas. It must be recognized, though, that these programs have limitations. For instance, one psychology professor remarked to me that he thought his department made learning so stressful that many graduate students refused to continue educating themselves once they achieved the doctorate. The benefits of membership in the elite are conferred simply on the basis of the credential, and there is no extrinsic pressure on many professionals to continue to educate themselves. Programs dominated by conservative faculty long out of touch with the needs of the community are another example: hence, the content of graduate studies is often irrelevant to the real work of the professional in the field. In such a program one is trained to be incompetent. Students generally lack the comprehensive experiences and familiarity with contemporary developments in the field needed to make accurate judgments about the relative value of course material or training. The point is not so much that graduate programs have limitations, but that the training provided by these programs falls far short of the beliefs the public has about the knowledge, authority, skills, and ethical consciousness of anyone who has earned a doctorate.

People tend to assume everyone who possesses a doctorate is therefore competent, knowledgeable, and trustworthy. The degree is offered by professionals as a credential which legitimates these claims. The public tends to believe every "doctor" is competent in any role

---

these individuals and their professional associations do not reflect the thoughts and behavior of many individuals who are also professionals but who are not exploitive, oppressive, or discriminatory against nonprofessionals.

(administrator, teacher, supervisor, consultant, social critic); they believe any professional may speak authoritatively on any area of human experience (sexuality, politics, child raising, alternative life styles, the mental health of public or historical figures); they believe any professional has skills adequate to cope with any problem (families, marriages, parent-child relationships, emotional disturbances of any severity, school systems). Rather than explicitly denying these grandiose expectations, professionals tacitly accept them as valid by either responding to any and all requests from the community for advice and help or using the opportunities available to professionals because they are in control of clinics and institutions to act as if the expectations were not only realistic but, in fact, were being met through these programs. Often, of course, this is not what is happening.

Whatever reasons may account for the deification of the "doctor,"[2] it is clear little effort is made by professional psychotherapists or their associations to establish clear limits on the powers of professionals, much less to educate the public as to how they may accurately evaluate the potential of any individual professional to help them with their specific needs. When I was a co-director of a crisis intervention center for youth, the primary concern expressed to us by professionals in the community was that we recognize our limitations and make them clear to our clients. In the next breath they added that they would offer to see *anyone* we referred to them, to work with us in *any* capacity *we* thought would be helpful, and to provide the necessary guidance to ensure what we did do (a then director of a local mental health center suggested we only make referrals of youths to professionals) was of high quality. By implication, of course, *they* were able to work with any kind of person, with every kind of problem, to accept any role we considered helpful with equal skill and authority, and to set meaningful standards of quality of service. Experiences with professionals who approached us in this manner[3] demonstrated the fallacious and mis-

2. Some suggest the psychotherapist has replaced the priest or shaman in society. Others believe that psychotherapy is a *science*, that only scientists (psychologists and doctors) are therefore competent to be psychotherapists. The authority and respect earned by scientists and doctors in the field of medicine is therefore extended to include "doctors" specializing in psychotherapy.

3. An exception to this was a psychiatrist named Terry. He came to the crisis center and offered to see if there was any way he could be helpful without making any implications that because he was a psychiatrist there necessarily were contributions he could make. He watched and listened for several weeks, responding to situations only when he was asked to. Instead of acting as if he had all the answers, he tended to draw out the complexities of situations and offer alternative directions. The staff accepted him without reservation as an

leading character of these implications, causing resentment and disillusionment in our staff.

It should be obvious I am not arguing that every professional is incompetent or that it is impossible for any one professional to have expertise in a variety of roles. These propositions are demonstrably false. I am suggesting that professionals tend to ignore or at best minimize differences in competence, knowledge, maturity, and so on lending support to the myth of the doctorate and to present to the public (and to a lesser extent themselves) an image that encourages unrealistic expectations that can only lead people anxious for help to be disillusioned, resentful, and finally rejecting of psychotherapy.[4]

The failure of professionals to meet many of the needs, not to mention the expectations, of the community has occasioned the development of alternative sources for psychotherapy. Many of these alternatives are offered by paraprofessionals (social workers, psychiatric nurses, etc.) and nonprofessionals, some by professionals themselves disenchanted with the mystification of professionalism. Nonprofessionals have demonstrated they can be sensitive and skillful psychotherapists, and one presumes that if they had the opportunities they would make fine teachers, effective supervisors, and creative administrators. Yet professionals are using their power to exclude nonprofessionals from positions of influence, affluence, and status and to oppress those in subservient roles in clinics or institutions. This discrimination against and oppression of nonprofessionals is in the self-interest of the elite. While deplorable, particularly in a field which claims to offer services to the oppressed, it is common enough in our society that people with power, wealth, and status act in ways to ensure they keep control over these gains.

In college I worked as a counselor, and during a two-year separation from academia I was employed in a residential treatment center for disturbed children. But it wasn't until I began work in a state mental health center that I began looking forward to a career in the field.

---

authority because he demonstrated expertise and knowledge rather than made claims or implied powers. He was explicit about what he could and could not do, as well as about areas where he was unsure, anxious, and defensive.

4. Evidence of this alienation can be seen in various political groups, including radical therapists, gay liberation, women's liberation, insane liberation, and in the popular attraction toward critics of professionalism like Szasz, Laing, and Perls. Among my own clients fully 90 percent have tried traditional professionals and, finding themselves no better off, seek a "radical" therapist almost as a last resort. If such disenchantment is commonplace among even middle-class people of conventional tastes, this is a serious problem.

Technically I was a psychiatric aide, although my first role was as a community organizer. I worked in the field, offering home treatment and crisis intervention as means of gaining access to the community. The program was innovative and eventually was suppressed. However, while in the field I had extensive training in psychotherapy and considerable autonomy. Consequently, when the program began to be altered I requested to be moved into the institution to work on a ward. My responsibilities changed rapidly. I was now expected to do custodial and supervisory work with patients and to report on their activities to first-year residents (psychiatrists in their first year of training).

I still believed in the myth of the doctorate and was obedient to professionals. In turn they allowed me continued and exceptional access to training opportunities but still prevented me from being a psychotherapist on the floor. There was an implicit expectation that when the nonprofessionals were ready, we would be *allowed* to do psychotherapy. In fact, we were inferior in role, status, power, and income to all professionals, even those in training.

Nonprofessionals in clinics and institutions are dependent on the professionals, and this dependency is used to oppress them. On our ward the professionals were the "primary" therapists, and we were extensions, acting out their directives, providing them with information, caring for "their patients," and behaving deferentially toward the professionals. Our sense of value, of our worth, came from how well we succeeded in meeting the expectations and desires of the professionals. We were dependent on their approval.

Institutions are under pressure to create more responsible roles for nonprofessionals. One source of this pressure is the increasing numbers of people seeking psychotherapy, which made it necessary, it is thought, to increase the size of clinics and institutions. It is prohibitively expensive to hire professionals to fill the numerous positions opening up on the lowest levels of the institutions, even if there were enough available for the jobs. To increase the number of professionals would decrease the value of the credentials. Consequently, nonprofessionals and paraprofessionals were hired to handle the day-to-day, face-to-face work with clients.

Professionals have moved up in the hierarchy and have created positions of control over paraprofessionals and nonprofessionals. They are in positions where they determine the priorities, organizational structure, and evaluative criteria for the institution. Ironically, one sign of status for many professionals has become their distance from direct services to clients. Although some choose to see a few clients, psychotherapy for professionals is increasingly an elective. Their pri-

mary responsibilities are as administrators, as faculty, as supervisors, and so forth. Even among professionals in private practice a sign of success is their ability to choose which patients they will see and which will be referred to others. The more successful professionals in private practice make one of their selection criteria the ability of the client to pay considerable fees. For nonprofessionals therapy is *work*, not a vocation, a demand made upon them. Usually they do intakes, seeing everyone who comes in.

Some nonprofessionals attracted to the mental health field have considerable education, although they lack doctorates. They may be paraprofessionals, for example psychiatric nurses (nursing developed masters programs in psychiatric nursing for positions as clinical specialists whose main responsibility is to supervise nursing staff, train them, and administrate, under the control of both nursing hierarchies and professionals), college students, divinity school students studying to be pastoral counselors, social workers, and so forth. Combined with the need of the institution to see clients on demand, to have appropriate clients referred to professionals, and to carry increasingly heavy caseloads, pressure from nonprofessionals has led to their being given limited but responsible positions as psychotherapists. However, their continued inferior and dependent status is evident in the label "paraprofessional."[5]

One can see that the response to pressure in this case has been to create increasingly larger hierarchies rather than to address the critical question: can an organization encourage staff, without regard to their credentials, to move into increasingly responsible positions based on demonstrated competence and knowledge? Instead of keeping the focus on therapy as a service, it has become a demand to be avoided. The intrinsic satisfaction which can come from helping people has been obscured by the emphasis on position, income, influence, and status. Professionals have created a system which protects their elite while focusing everyone's attention on evaluating their personal success in terms of extraneous and alienated goals, all of which have no

5. A clear indication of the oppression of nonprofessionals is the fact their vocational identity is established by reference to the elite group. One is constantly reminded, before one knows anything about what the people do or what abilities they have (a positive identity) that they do *not* have a doctorate, hence are to be accorded less authority, prestige, and status. It is not just a matter of identity; nonprofessionals are in lower salary categories than professionals, do not define the priorities and structure in which they work, have less autonomy, and are under the control of professionals, some of whom have less experience and knowledge than they do.

direct connection to effective, humane psychotherapy.

Much has been lost by this self-serving response to the developing needs of the community. Helping the client has become a means for the professional psychotherapist to increase his or her prestige, status, wealth, and power object rather than the primary concern of psychotherapists. The client has become a source of income, a record-keeping problem, a potential source of disruption who must be kept tranquilized, an object of fear and contempt. This focus is evident when a therapist terminates treatment because a client can no longer afford the cost or when a close and supportive relationship to a client is cut off by institutional policy.

The concept of service is being lost. The intrinsic joy and meaning in being helpful is often submerged under concerns about job security, advancement, and the acceptance of one's efforts by superiors. Even in a crisis-intervention center that I co-founded after leaving the mental health center, this process of increasing alienation from client-centered work occurred. I found the responsibilities of being a co-founder and co-director took me into areas more concerned with staff conflicts, fund raising, and program development. My dissatisfaction resulting from reduced contact with young people led me to be more desirous of security, affluence, and greater recognition "in the field" as a compensation.

When I left the mental health center I was another casualty of the system. Disillusioned with the field, filled with feelings of inadequacy exacerbated by my experiences as an aide, I was determined to enter a different field entirely, and only circumstances beyond my control compelled me instead to accept employment as a consultant on youth to a church, during which time I co-founded the crisis center and discovered an alternative path (although not without difficulties) to my long-time goal of becoming a psychotherapist. People still ask me when they hear about my achievements, "If you are really as good as your record indicates or you object to how you are treated as a non-professional, why don't you get a doctorate?"

First, feelings of inadequacy (a consequence of the way professionals had treated me) persuaded me that I would not be accepted in a doctoral program, nor, because of my "attitude," would I be successful even if I were accepted. Second, none of the professionals I knew were positive models that I wanted to emulate, although I envied a few their knowledge and skill. Third, I had become alienated from academia for reasons similar to my objections to professionalism: the devaluation of the student or aide; constant promises of future gains in return for obedience, conformity, and drudgery in the present; the dependence

on faculty and professionals for recognition, advancement, and opportunities, often given in return for ego support rather than demonstrated abilities; and the fact that many of the required courses are irrelevant to what I consider the tasks for psychotherapists.

My primary objection to credentials is a moral one. Participation in the academic process of graduate school and in the professional club is a tacit acceptance of an exploitive and discriminatory system. To become a psychiatrist or psychologist for the convenience involved, I would have to ignore the fact that professionals use their elite status to charge high fees to support living standards far above the majority of people seeking help. I would have to ignore professional discrimination against nonprofessionals which disregards the abilities of many of these individuals. I would have to ignore the criteria for acceptance to graduate schools which exclude many nonprofessionals who lack academic skills or are unable to go to college. I would have to ignore the damaging effects the myth of the doctorate and the elite status of professionals have on the community both directly for clients who have unrealistic expectations and indirectly through the denial of opportunities to others who can make substantial contributions to the community's problems.

The myth of the doctorate persists because professionals claim that their system ensures a high standard of quality in psychotherapy. The admission criteria to graduate programs, the grading system, internships, licensing (in Connecticut professional associations must approve the graduate program and the place of internship before the state will grant a license), and professional control over clinics, institutions, and nonprofessionals are all supposed to support the system.

The complex issue of quality control is critical to anyone like myself who lacks a doctorate but wants to work independently. I have already discussed the oppressive environment of a professionally dominated institution and the self-contempt I felt about my aspirations and abilities in the field of mental health. But in the community, without a doctorate my claim to be a psychotherapist is suspect. People are wary of the quality of therapy offered by a nonprofessional, particularly if there is no professional who has assumed responsibility for such work. Consequently, in order to earn a living I have had to develop alternative means of convincing people I am competent rather than rely on the myth of the doctorate.

The professionals' claim of maintaining quality control through credentials and licensing rests on four specious assumptions. The first is that professionals have criteria for evaluating the quality of psychotherapy. The second is that they can identify unacceptable and poten-

tially harmful characteristics in doctoral candidates or psychiatric residents. The third is that the available evidence supports the belief that the general quality of psychotherapy is high. Finally, that professionals are objective enough to be the arbitrators of who may claim to be a psychotherapist.

The fact is there are no generally accepted criteria for determining whether therapy is effective. Indeed, psychotherapy occupies a unique position in the academic world. It is an area of knowledge and skill claimed by medicine (psychiatry), psychology (clinical psychology, which also stresses psychological testing and research), divinity schools (pastoral counseling), social work schools (M.S.W.s are trained in both psychotherapy and group work), nursing (psychiatric nursing), masters programs in counseling, and so forth. Each area has its own extensive literature on the subject. No one is sure about the proper or most effective methods; hence, numerous approaches exist without clear guidelines for deciding what is *the* appropriate study for anyone else, since personality and style make a critical difference. To suggest in such confusion that any certainty exists as to the quality of therapy, enough to ensure that clients seeking help will receive it, is arrogant.

In this context the confusion perpetrated by professionals between science or medicine and psychotherapy is almost dishonest. Psychotherapy is a kind of relationship between two or more people, where at least one person assumes the role of a client (a person seeking help in a specific and deliberate way) and at least one person assumes the role of psychotherapist (someone offering help to another person). But the formal characteristics of the role relationships are open to dispute, and in practice a wide variety of contradictory but apparently acceptable interpretations are available. Sciences, on the other hand, are exceptionally formal, and are generally based on empirically or mathematically verifiable premises. Theories organize facts to support hypotheses, however the scientific method minimizes self-deception, while theories are useful only to the extent that they *predict* as well as explain phenomena. Psychotherapists rarely use *any* method for eliminating self-deception, have no theories which predict behavior (nor will many therapists state whether or not they can help a client; they don't know until it happens), and the field is replete with theories attempting to explain all or part of human experience, yet few, despite their age, have been disregarded.

Analogies which are presented as integrities are not only confusing, but almost deliberate attempts at mystifying both the public and professionals. For example, psychiatrists, because they are doctors, see psychotherapy as analogous to medicine. Psychotherapy is far from a

highly-defined relationship, and to assume psychotherapy is treatment and labeling and evaluating personalities is diagnosis is confusing and probably erroneous. Neither is psychotherapy the application of a science. Theories abound about emotional and interpersonal conflicts because psychotherapy is not refined enough to offer collaborating or rebutting evidence, even to theories about the best methods of *doing* psychotherapy. Psychotherapy is a *relationship* which seeks to help people, and it has not been (if it ever can be) formalized sufficiently to be considered anything more than, *at best*, well-intentioned efforts on the part of people assuming the role of therapist to *try* to understand and help others who ask for help, using whatever methods and knowledge they have (from literature, life experiences, social science, the client, friends or relatives of the client, ad infinitum).

Furthermore, it is difficult, given the ease with which students can conceal unacceptable and potentially hurtful behavior patterns or desires, to assume that graduate programs or internships can recognize individuals who will not be helpful. The evidence from homosexuals, women, countercultural individuals, youth, and schizophrenics in increasing numbers is that many therapists with professional status are prejudiced, sexist, exploitive (in cases where treatment is prolonged unnecessarily because of the high fees involved), seductive, brutal, insensitive, domineering, etc. Clearly someone is fooling someone in maintaining that quality control efforts are effective in making sure psychotherapy with licensed professionals is safe, standardized, or scientific.

If it appears that the general level of competence is high, it is because the majority of therapists (in my experience) are well-meaning, nonmalicious people, regardless of their professional or nonprofessional status. Furthermore, since individuals abused by a therapist rarely go to court or join a political group of people with similar experiences there is little chance that his or her experiences will have much effect on the image. The limits actually placed on professionals are meager. Professionals tend to ignore or deny rumors about their colleagues (many times rumors exist with no basis in fact) or to speculate about the motivations of the client in encouraging or permitting the situation to develop. Furthermore, it is often standard procedure and therefore not thought of as especially significant for professionals to commit people to institutions against their will and in violation of their rights or to coerce young people by threats of commitment, use of tranquilizers to create suggestible states of mind, subtle undermining of the youth's values through interpretations, and so forth.

Finally, it is clear that the claim that professionals can be the arbitra-

tors of quality control given their expertise and authority is self-serving. The assertion disguises the effects of the power of professionals to control admission to doctoral programs, access to positions of authority and influence, income levels, nonprofessionals, and so on all in the name of quality control. It is a claim which cannot be disproved! No objective criteria exist which are not controversial. In the absence of self-confidence people have turned to professionals as the obvious group to determine what is acceptable and unacceptable help. However, people are seduced into trusting "professional judgments" as absolute authority because of the myth of the doctorate. The claim to this authority and expertise, symbolically granted to professionals with the doctorate, rests on claims to expertise by professionals who in turn claim to be the only people capable of determining what is expertise. Hence a tautology prevents critical questioning of the professionals' claims upon which their status and power rest.

In this morass of controversies it is clear only that the legitimacy accorded professionals does not incontrovertibly rest on demonstrated abilities, but on the community's trust. The nonprofessional wishing to work independently from the professional system must develop trust in the community which can be the equivalent of the trust in the value of the doctorate. Several factors help the nonprofessional: widespread feelings of resentment and disillusionment with professionals, demonstrated inadequacies of professionals in coping with community problems (youth, drugs, life style changes), and a developing tolerance in the community for alternative life styles. But people are still wary of a nonprofessional's claim to being a psychotherapist. Even more critically, many nonprofessionals are still convinced there is essential truth in the doctorate myth and devalue their own abilities. Without alternative learning experiences the nonprofessional will remain where I was when I left the mental health center: feeling inadequate, pretentious, alone, and without support, valid skills, and knowledge.

After circumstances involved me in a youth crisis center, I was still dependent on professionals. I saw the center as a means of making contact with young people but felt unable to handle the problems they presented. I thought the center could refer young people to professionals when we had reached our limits. Two things happened which forced me to alter these convictions. First, young people we did refer failed to find help. In all the cases they would go once, twice, rarely three times and then drop out, often to return to the crisis center. Second, young people didn't want to see professionals. They distrusted them, often because the professionals' values were identical with their parents', and they received little or no support for the way they

wanted to live and for things they wanted to do. If they were to be counseled, it appeared that by default they would have to be seen by the staff at the crisis center. And they *wanted* counseling!

Despite my feelings of trepidation and self-doubt I began to counsel the young people we saw, and I often counseled their parents as well. Many times I found that what I had learned at the mental health center, was not always helpful. Without supervision, but with support from my friends and co-workers, I began exploring new approaches to psychotherapy and new theories. Such self-directed learning, through independent work on a project, has been the core of numerous learning experiences of people seeking alternatives. In fact, Antioch and the Union of Experimental Colleges, Goddard, and the Humanistic Psychology Institute offer graduate programs based on students working independently on projects and determining for themselves what they want to learn.

Gradually my therapy relationships became clearer. My subjective distortions of what was happening were being ironed out (primarily through feedback from clients), just as my skills became more definite and refined through experience and experimentation. My confidence in myself developed. I began doing such related work as leading workshops, research, and publishing. After leaving the crisis center, I continued to seek new areas of learning, while continuing to develop as a psychotherapist (my central commitment), including videotape applications to therapy, developing a model of radical therapy unifying the skills of psychotherapy with the political and psychological literature, as well as community action—activism based on support in the community developed from counseling relationships. In other words, there was *confirmation* of my increasing skills and expertise through publication, grants, speaking engagements, and leading workshops for professionals and nonprofessionals.

This confirmation was much needed. At first I wanted to be recognized as an equal by professionals. My identity as a therapist still rested, to some degree, on the approval or lack of it from professionals. I sought to create huge, undeniably brilliant achievements so there would be no doubt that I was just as good as any professional. It didn't make any difference if it was clear I was more skilled or knowledgeable than some individual professionals. Relative skill, relative expertise, and authority were meaningless. I wanted mythic powers. I wanted to be the personification of the myth—without the doctorate—on my terms. This irrational need was gradually diminished as my genuine helpfulness in counseling relationships became clear. By learning from doing I was able to mature. The basic fact was that at no point was

anyone ever going to take my abilities for granted if I intended to remain independent. I would have to be able continually to demonstrate my abilities, generate access to new opportunities.

In my experiences with a crisis center, a videotape resource center, writing four books, working on an HEW contract to study drug use among youth, I created, in each case with autonomy, a meaningful and significant series of learning experiences. Simultaneously I developed operational values which served to build trust between myself and members of the community. In other words, I was able to create structures and contents in my work which allow the people I come in contact with to develop trust in me.

Through my experiences working in the mental health center I had come to dislike and distrust secrecy. I was repelled by staff discussions about patients when they could not be present and by the closed door policy of therapists so clients are always alone and unsupported with a therapist, that is, a person of considerable authority and often very real power. I wanted to be open, and I wanted people to be able to experience openness directly as a means of being more secure and confident in themselves. I began by inviting clients to bring anyone they wanted to along with them for any session or to talk about what happens in a session with others if they are anxious or curious about something. This ended the implicit control I as a therapist had over the privacy of the situation. Privacy not only leaves a person feeling slightly overwhelmed by a therapist, but allows therapists who have a mind to, to use the privacy to their own advantage.

I extend this openness to include personal information about myself when I believe it is relevant to an experience or to any question from a client. This helps break down the irrationally elevated position that anyone considered a psychotherapist begins with and builds trust and sharing. It is difficult for clients to trust someone who is himself remote and silent, whatever rationalizations come to mind for this behavior.

Ambiguity about the therapy relationship is another source of anxiety and fear. I want to be clear and definite. First, I begin by developing explicit contracts with my clients. These contracts specify our goals for therapy and at the same time my estimation of how long it will take for observable changes to occur. If I am ineffective, the client has a right to know; and without an idea of how long the therapy process should take, they cannot. It is true that change in therapy takes the cooperation of the client with the process. But it is easier for me to identify resistence in a client than it is for the client to identify ineffectuality in my behavior. I have the advantage. If I want to, I can call clients on their attempts to undermine therapy and avoid change,

calling attention to contradictions and the like. What can clients say to an incompetent therapist?

Finally, I discovered I was put off by contradictions between what I said and did. If I wanted to persuade people in the community to trust me, I would have to model my values. For example, I could not subject clients to therapy approaches I would be reluctant to experience myself. As I am developing politically, I expect people to be willing to make certain changes in their life styles, for example, working out sexist issues in their relationships. Consequently, I am working on sexist patterns in my own relationships as much as possible. I object to therapists exploiting the needs of clients to the extent that they support affluent, upper-class standards of living for themselves through large fees. After thinking through the issue of fees, I decided to charge individuals a maximum of ten dollars a session. Each session lasts an average of an hour and a half to two hours as I attempt to resolve as many emotional issues as arise in a session during that session, rather than cutting the individual off arbitrarily at the end of fifty minutes or an hour. If anyone cannot afford to pay for sessions, I am willing to barter or to accept alternative means of sharing energy, time, and skills.

The expressions of these values in my work are neither unique nor original. Many professionals are living and working in this direction. The difference for me is that I use these values and their manifestations as the basis of an alternative credentialing process.

I started counseling in college, informally, with my friends and acquaintances. These relationships developed out of my concern and their willingness to share themselves with me because I was concerned. They experienced these relationships as helpful and told people they knew, who wanted to talk to someone about their problems. Gradually these relationships became more deliberate: the people I talked with and I both intended that they would be helped by the relationship, and other possibilities (like developing a sexual relationship) were considered confusing and were avoided because they seemed to diminish the helpfulness of the relationship. Only after I had reached this point did I learn of psychotherapy. I did not realize this kind of relationship was formalized to the point of being a "professional" career until I had been doing "psychotherapy" for two years!

My career is still based on this informal but effective credentialing process. People I know find out I am helpful. They tell people they know. Everyone I see is a referral from friends, acquaintances, and clients. This network is sufficiently large so that even people strange to the area may meet someone who knows of my work through some-

one who has been a client or knows me. Professionals go to graduate school instead of attempting this longer, more risky (if a nonprofessional isn't helpful, people tell you) process. They use the doctorate as a shortcut. People "know" the doctor is helpful because of his or her credentials. Many professionals must work in institutions or with referrals from other professionals because they could not generate sufficient community support based on their demonstrated competence. The elite avoids the free market of experiental learning and community validation through direct relationships with the therapist as friend, acquaintance, therapist, or activist. Such a process conceals incompetence as long as the professional makes a good impression and is successful academically. As the number of people involved with psychotherapy increases, potential clients will more and more depend on recommendations from friends.

In summary, I have had to overcome issues concerning my "inadequacy" as a psychotherapist exacerbated by my contacts with professionals in order to return to a vocation which had begun naturally and spontaneously. I have developed an alternative learning process for myself through reflection, study, projects, feedback, and mutual relationships with other people in the field. This kind of independent, self-directed alternative is being recognized as equally as valid as more orthodox doctoral curricula in programs like the Humanistic Psychology Institute or the Union of Experimental Colleges. Through my personal qualities and a deliberate effort to create forms and structure which reflect my values (openness, clarity, specificity, mutuality), I have been able to gain the continued trust of my community sufficiently to earn a living as a psychotherapist. This trust functions as an alternative credential because it is communicated by members of the community to other people. They feel they are helpful when they can recommend someone more helpful. This trust is finally and, I think, only grounded in direct experiences, whether or not the therapist is a professional or a nonprofessional, rather than in the myth of the doctorate.

4. The Healer, the Community, or the Bureaucrat

DENNIS T. JAFFE

The fable "The Emperor's New Clothes" illustrates a basic choice that every therapist must make. The emperor has bought the illusion that he has a magic suit of clothes that will help him spot disloyal subjects and eliminate any threats to his rule. Perhaps his illusion is not as destructive as the ones used today to buttress our foreign or domestic policy, but just the same he feels he has to use all the power behind his authority to punish those who do not appear to share it. A child, symbolic of clear perception which has not yet bowed to conventions exposes the charade, demystifying the situation by stating openly what others are afraid even to think—the emperor has no clothes.

Let us imagine what might happen then. The populace might be catalyzed by the child's remark into laughter or rebellion, or, more probably, they will simply remain silent out of fear. The emperor might still save his power and his dignity by reacting as those in power do today against people—such as the hyperkinetic child, the illegal drug user, the welfare poor, the insane, or women and black people —who force us to question some of our basic assumptions about social order and who make us nervous or angry by questioning their places. The emperor could define such people as misguided, out of control, or sick and then order them to receive treatment from some kind of therapist until they are back on the road to adjustment and social decorum.

The child's ability to see through things and share his perceptions suggests another kind of therapy, one that might also lead people to

change but is not allied to the view of reality and the needs of those in power. Today we can witness therapists of either persuasion defending their vision of their work as the "true" or "scientific" form of therapy, denouncing those who disagree as misguided, naïve, immature, sick, or destructive. I set out to become a therapist at a time when many kinds of people—psychoanalysts, community psychiatrists, encounter group leaders, sensitivity trainers, soul healers, gurus, body therapists, master game players, rappers—were laying claim to the title "therapist," and my own development consists of trying to put these various pursuits into context: How do they all relate? Whom do they serve?

I think that I can distinguish three somewhat overlapping and not mutually exclusive kinds of activity which call themselves therapy. I call them the bureaucratic, the healer (or guru), and the community. The bureaucratic style predominates in mental hospitals, as well as in prisons, schools, and community mental health centers, where the aim is to isolate deviants and compel them to behave properly. The healer helps people change by the force of his authority, whether it be his medical credentials, his personality, or his technical expertise. He does not necessarily see himself as an agent of society and can thus serve any of a number of value systems. Many people change due to the influence of the community or the environment around them, whether in a consciousness-raising group, by talking to friends, or simply by living in a certain kind of environment. I have come to reject the bureaucratic style of therapy, have become highly ambivalent about but somewhat accepting of the healer style, and see the most promise in the community as a force for therapeutic change. What follows is a sketch of some of my encounters with these forms of therapy.

I discovered Freud when I was fourteen, at around the same time that I discovered masturbation. Both became personal modes of self-discovery, which dissociated me from and made me critical of current adolescent society. If Freud could do it, so could I, and with his guidelines I began to free associate on reams of paper, dreaming of the day when I would help others to go on this exciting voyage. While the psychoanalyst was an austere, intellectual, almost solitary figure, he had taken up the noble calling of helping humanity toward greater reason and truth and away from self-delusion. In college I took philosophy and literature courses, as well as the required pre-med sciences, to prepare for this role.

This fantasy received a rude injection of reality in my junior year of college. For an hour a week I became a companion to a back-ward

patient at a state mental hospital, after which there was a seminar at which we discussed our experiences. This was my first contact with a real patient, a schizophrenic. I discovered that there was a whole other world of psychiatry, consisting of a lower class of both doctors and patients, in which the primary task was to house, feed, semiclothe, and drug thousands of lost souls, the mentally ill who occupy 50 percent of the nation's hospital beds. I soon learned that to call this hospital care, with associations of comfort, nurses, and constant attention, was a distortion of reality as gross as the emperor's.

In the seminar I was told that the people in the hospital were psychotic and, hence, incurable. The first part of our training seemed to be to give up the fantasy of seeing them change at all. For a year my companion hustled me for cups of coffee, walked with me, and told me how he didn't think he could ever conquer his anxiety enough to go home, if indeed a home awaited him after twenty years. At the seminar we were titillated with psychological test results, medical workups, and nursing notes, which we would compare with what the patient said to see how out of touch with reality he was. The message was that there is nothing we can do with people like this and that these medical records fulfill our responsibility as therapists to such patients. I began to feel that my career might not be as romantic and fulfilling as I had thought, but I was assured that I would only have to spend one year of my residency in a place like this.

A group of us, graduates of the companion program, felt that many of the people we had met in the hospital were there simply because they had no other place to go. We decided to try to raise funds to purchase a house which would be run democratically as an expatient-student cooperative and which could support itself through rent payments. It seemed like an absurdly simple, humane, reasonable solution to one of the dilemmas of the hospital. The next year, in the month of my graduation, the house was ready to open, and I decided to live there during my first year of graduate school (which I chose because I could not see the relevance of medical training to therapy, a belief which none of my subsequent experience has shaken).

For a year prior to moving into the halfway house I had another experience with institutional psychiatry, this time as a half-time psychiatric aide at the new community mental health center, which had just opened as a clinic for the community and a training and research center for Yale psychiatrists. The community mental health movement seemed committed to values I was forming about psychiatry: It proposed to offer care according to the needs of the community, as much as possible in that community, with a sliding scale of fees. I began

work as part of a task force consisting of undergraduates, high school students, community leaders, and professionals, whose job was to help the new center determine the real social needs of the people in the center's inner city catchment area. This group, which would operate "without professional blinders or preconceptions," would enter the community and ask the people what a mental health service might do to help them.

The effort was destined to be frustrating, because the center was starting in a new $5 million building and was committed to training a medical staff in psychiatry, despite the needs of the community, so that the freedom of self-definition the center had was limited. The group disbanded, writing a report indicating that the priorities of the community were meeting its physical needs, educational and government reform, self-determination of the type of mental health services desired, and storefront clinics staffed by indigenous people with a preventive, public health orientation. What we found, of course, was that such concerns represented a dilution of what to Yale was "real" psychiatry—psychoanalytically oriented individual therapy. Community oriented therapy was considered less difficult, less intellectual, and more appropriate for a lower status social worker than a psychiatrist.

From that job I went to another part of the center, the inpatient unit which was to be run as a therapeutic community. My three years of part-time work on this unit, which overlapped with my residence at the halfway house, provided a study in contrasting environments which I now look back on as the key element in my unorthodox "training." Being part of two communities which held similar values, but which nonetheless were polar opposites in so many ways, greatly developed my ability to demystify, to see through the psychiatric jargon and ad hoc justifications to what was really happening to people in each of those environments. Indeed, many halfway house residents came from the ward or had relapses and were sent back to it, so I had the rare opportunity to see the same people behaving in different environments, which was the most vivid way I can conceive of to see how much of the behavior which is labeled "symptomatic" on the hospital ward is actually a function of the tensions caused by the ward itself and of defenses the patients erect against it.

The central contradiction of the ward was that while it espoused democratic decision making and collaboration, when a patient was not progressing or behaving as the staff desired, authoritarian and coercive tactics were substituted for self-exploration. While patients were told that they were there to learn to take responsibility for their behavior and make decisions about their future, in practice more often than not

decisions were made by the medical staff meeting in secret. The psychiatric residents and their medical supervisors spent no informal time on the ward. They saw patients a few hours a week for individual therapy, and nervously, with no formal instruction, they attended group meetings, putting up emotionless, inscrutable façades and saying little. In case conferences they debated therapeutic tactics and classification, while the nursing staff asked occasional questions about how they ought to "manage" the patient for the time he or she was living on the ward.

What the staff seemed to be denying and the patients often seemed to be pointing out was that the ward was a very anxious, nervous, depressing place to be. A new staff member has that initial impression, as does a new patient, but the staff member learns to accept it as natural, while the patient learns that the feeling is part of his or her problem. To my knowledge nobody ever felt or expected that a psychiatric ward ought to be a place where people would feel comfortable sitting down and discussing what was bothering them and working together to decide what ought to be done. That would never happen because the tension seemed to stem from the fact that while the ward staff gave lip service to collaboration, they were actually obsessed with secrecy—keeping their records, notes, and deliberations from the patient's knowledge—and control over behavior. I began to feel that the formal, rigid, stylized medical tradition might not be the best one to help people in distress. But, I was told, what else was there?

The halfway house was an old rooming house with about ten bedrooms and a living room, dining room, and kitchen furnished with Goodwill throwaways. It was to be a mutual support community, with everyone participating in the work and contributing rent. It was open to people who had been hospitalized, mainly people just out but also those who felt in danger of having to go back. Each semester a few students could also become house members. There was a house director and a board of directors, but actually the house was left to settle its own affairs and to run itself. Like the hospital, it was based on the idea that patients need to take responsibility for themselves; but unlike hospital patients, residents of the house had no superior authority figures who would make decisions for them if they did not make "proper" ones.

The house was messy, loud, impulsive, and had the highest tolerance for odd behavior of any environment I had seen. I shared a room first with a teenager coming from five years in a state hospital and then with one just out of two years in a plush private hospital. There was always a crisis threatening to disrupt the house, taking up the energy

of the weekly house meeting and of late night conversations, yet the house never fell apart. It occurred to me about halfway through the year that grappling with constant crisis was what made the house therapeutic. For most of us who lived there (whether former patient or student) the opportunity to offer help to someone who really needed it, to help someone find a job or stay away from speed or not commit suicide, helped us, probably more than we were helping the ostensible focus of our efforts. The desire to help and a community to support a person seemed to be a much more potent healing force than the bureaucratic efforts of the ward staff.

There was always one person in the halfway house who was playing the role of patient. That is, he or she was more demanding, more angry, more weird, more irritating, and less responsible than the others. When that person became the center of house attention, very often nothing we tried seemed to work. However, as I looked at those who were offering support, listening, thinking the problem through—remembering that all of these people had a few months before been patients themselves, totally dependent on the authority of a hospital ward staff—I began to see that helping was probably more therapeutic than being helped. In becoming helpful people learned self-confidence and were established as human beings who mattered, which is one of the essential goals of therapy. I sometimes think that if a hospital ward were designed so that a person was hired to be more disruptive than anyone else on the ward and the patients were all asked to try to help that person, hospital wards would be changed for the better.

My personal experience living there told me a lot about why professionals have not yet created many communities like the halfway house. The major problem I faced was not how to help those poor expatients, but how to keep myself together. We would joke about how both students and the others were escaping from total institutions. It was a little frightening to live with a former "schizophrenic" and see the common ground between us. After two years of analytic therapy in a hospital, my younger (by three years) roommate had learned enough of the analytic game patiently to point out to me all of the ways I withdrew and did not share myself with the community. Such behavior on his part made me angry and not a little uptight. He assured me that was how he had felt on the ward when it was done to him. Therapists made one's natural defenses into accusations of symptoms, pointing them out in a way which nibbled at one's self-confidence, as if one were the only person with such an obvious and glaring defect. All interpretations in the hospital were one-way, with no opportunity for rebuttal or exchange. It was clear that the traditional therapeutic

distance and detachment and the one-sided nature of interpretations were very clever ways of protecting the therapists from having to look at their own behavior. They could never be confronted, never see how close their own feelings and doubts were to those of their patients; thus their own superiority and fitness for analyzing others would remain unassailable. The mutual exploration, the acceptance that what the current or expatient says may be just as valid as what the therapist says, that characterized the halfway house simply did not fit the professional conception of the omnipotent therapist. Such therapists remained forever protected, like the emperor, from any information that might deny their closed and self-fulfilling theory of treatment.

By working at the mental health center as well, I was continually at the interface of the two systems. It was hardest to explain the halfway house to the people at the center who agreed that it was a good idea. Despite invitations, few of these professionals ever came to dinner at the house. Only one of the therapists who was treating residents of the house ever visited it, and yet I continually heard, third-hand, about their criticism: that the house refused to enforce limits or that there were no controls on the behavior of their patients who lived there. I would point out that we cannot prevent anyone from doing anything, but they continued to believe that if we were to be helpful, then we would have to learn how to exercise control over residents. Also, I would be asked to come to clinical conferences about people living in the halfway house, and when I said that I would do so only if the person concerned were present as well, they were puzzled and put off. Evidently the presence of a patient interferes with the professional decision-making process. If knowledge is power, that is the last thing that hospital therapists want patients to have. For such behavior we were made fun of, criticized, and dismissed, which was evidence to me of how different the values governing each institution were, despite their rhetoric of basic agreement. Thus, I became increasingly critical of therapy as it was practiced in clinics yet increasingly dedicated to the practice of therapy as I had begun to experience it in the halfway house.

The late 1960s was a time of basic questions about how social institutions ought to function and of demands for a total break from the past into any conceivable personal or social experiment—mass demonstrations, psychedelic drugs, building takeovers—which might create a better *now*. My personal odyssey, going on alongside the events just described, included a year of personal psychoanalysis and much experimentation with drugs. In terms of therapy the technique of per-

sonal change which seems to have had the greatest social impact during that time was the small group encounter.

In my first year of graduate school I enrolled in a sensitivity training course, which was an application of democracy to learning with many parallels to the application of democracy to therapy in the halfway house. The course began with everyone on a first-name basis, sitting first around a table and then on the floor, relating to the course instructor-trainer as a peer, as just another resource person among many. The purpose of the group was to learn by watching ourselves and the process of the group, to share feelings and ideas, and to create a collaborative learning community in contrast to traditional authoritarian learning structures. For many of us this change in the role of the teacher forced us to examine our own assumptions about learning and our ambivalence about authorities. Learning came as part of the group ethos from any one of a number of people who were key figures in the group. This simple structure was a model of some of the key demands being made by students on the rest of the university and society.

The role of trainer, who was "just one of the guys who happened to have been in a few more groups than the others," in the personal growth movement quickly changed. That change—from the democratic community model to the master therapist, healer, or guru model —presented to me what is currently the primary unresolved issue of how I ought to be as a therapist. Out of the democratic protestations of group leaders, growing authority and specialization crept into the group leader's role. Today's group leader, whether gestalt therapist, psychodramatist, transactional analyst, or primal or bioenergetic therapist, has once again, like the early Freudian analyst, become the sole and unquestioned bearer of a skill at analysis or catalysis who is thereby indispensable to the growth of the other group members. Personality cults have grown up around the charismatic medicine men and gurus of various new forms of therapy. While new forms of therapy have left behind the disease model which plagues psychiatry and some of the societal strictures on expression of emotions and exploration of deep aspects of the self and the body, I feel that the structure of the leader-participant relationship has not changed very much. The leader has expertise in releasing feelings, unraveling hidden parts of oneself, and exploring relationships, but increasingly he or she seems to do this like a wise teacher demonstrating knowledge to mystified pupils. The leader is once more sealed off from potentially negative feedback from the group, while the group participant, like the patient, cannot question the basic assumptions of the environment.

I am aware of the counterargument, sometimes even convinced by

it, that the leader can be truly facilitative, like a Zen master, in unlocking hidden truths for the learner. I cannot deny that highly skilled gurus, true healers, exist, but I know that they are much rarer than the many growth-oriented therapists who claim that status. The issue of licensing group leaders, which I would support if only we could devise an operationally sound method for certifying expertise, points up the concern that people are starting to have over which new kind of therapy to trust. On the other hand, I continually see that almost any group of moderately aware, sophisticated, and self-critical people, armed with books by Fritz Perls, William Schutz, or Alexander Lowen, can have a productive encounter group. The master leader is not necessary, and some research suggests that the more democratic self-directed encounter group or one with a noncharismatic, democratic trainer will start slowly and have less psychodynamic fireworks but will tend to produce a higher degree of change in group members which is maintained over a longer time. It seems to me that the vitality of the personal growth group phenomenon is that people have decided to take charge of their own course of personal development, utilizing a variety of means and methods, for an end which they will define for themselves. I feel that for myself and for the people around me the small group has led to a democratizing and self-directing of the process of therapy away from the bureaucratic and controlling influence of organized psychiatry but sometimes also into a new style of the authoritative healer role.

In the fall of 1969 following Woodstock and after dropping out of graduate school, I joined several other critics of the mental health center to try to form a community which would redefine the basic structure of a service organization. I mentioned earlier my participation in the task force to determine the mental health needs of a poor community. We found that their needs were for the direct provision of basic services—food, shelter, work—and for participation in defining and operating these services, as well as the rest of the decisions that affected their lives. We felt that the bureaucratic structure, whether of a welfare office or a hospital ward, mainly got in the way of providing both service and human dignity and did not offer the recipients of help any role in the provision of the service. We wanted to create a simple, direct human service agency which would cater to the needs of the growing migrant community of young people who were moving across the country and living at barely a subsistence level, greatly in need of medical help, counseling, and unique services to deal with their interest in drug experimentation. We observed that such services had to be

provided in the style and with the values their potential clients had chosen, and we assumed that the people most likely to be helpful to them were each other.

We borrowed a storefront and organized a hotline and counseling center where people could find help, talk to others, stay overnight, and participate in a community. All meetings were open; anyone could be on the staff and learn to do telephone counseling or help out in other ways. We were a big attraction. Students from high schools and colleges responded to a great need in themselves to be helpful; and the fringe people who live on the edge of every city and the street kids who were restless and on the move responded to our message as well and began to hang around our storefront. The center was a maelstrom of released energy, forming a learning laboratory for our intuitions about helping others. The boundary between staff and client was nearly nonexistent, and the boundaries between tasks and roles were blurred to the point where anyone was welcome to do what he or she felt he or she could. Each regular member of the staff was regularly in a personal crisis, and the people who came to the center in a personal crisis, on a bad trip, or as runaways often became staff and helped out themselves. We bought a condemned house, which was fixed up to become a staff residence and a place for people who had no place to live to stay temporarily; we received surplus food; we became expert on temporary employment and welfare regulations. At any one time about half our staff were young people on leave from college and the other half were street people, most of whom had spent time in a psychiatric hospital. Ted Clark and I have already told the story of this center in *Toward a Radical Therapy,* so here I will dwell only on the way in which our work raised or answered some basic questions about the nature of therapy.

The center validated the proposition that participation in the governing of a community is in itself a therapeutic act. I am using "therapeutic" to mean gaining greater self-esteem and confidence, a sense of involvement in meaningful work, and growing competence in whatever one chooses as one's task. Our first full-time staff member, who had known one of the founders of the center when he was a patient at the mental health center, came to us on a bad acid trip and stayed for two years, learning to be a counselor and helping others through crises he had experienced himself. He now works in the hospital emergency room as an admission counselor and has completed several years of college. The connection of becoming a whole person with meaningful citizenship, of therapy and politics, was never clearer. The fact that society ordinarily offers former mental patients little more than a per-

manent stigma and marginal social status probably has a great deal to do with the recidivism and demoralization of those who are unfortunate enough to become patients. The existence in our helping community of a positive identity—"I've been there and know what it's all about"—for people who had been hospitalized and our offering anybody a useful job was probably more important to people's changing than our theory of therapy or the kind of counseling that went on in our center.

However, I grew to feel that there were certain defects in this concept of therapy. In all of our confusion, lack of structure, blurred roles and boundaries we never established an idea of what therapy, helping people grow, actually was. While political participation might be therapeutic, it is not *all* that therapy is. Most of the staff, working out of an intuitively Rogerian model, felt that counseling or therapy was synonomous with honest, deep, personal encounter or rapping. But it also was obvious that simply listening, providing shelter, and asking people to help out were not sufficient to help some of the people who came to us. There was also some additional skill and theory and technique to the process, and if it was not skill in the sense of traditional psychiatry, what was that skill? After working at a hospital, a mental health center, a halfway house, and an alternate service, I was still uncertain of how I wanted to answer in my practice the basic question: what sort of work does a therapist do?

Most of the preceding account has been of the conflict of style and values I experienced between the bureaucratic model of therapy, practiced at the mental health center and the state hospital, and the community model, which we tried to implement at the halfway house and the crisis center. Society has placed nearly all of its resources at the service of the bureaucratic model. The halfway house survives today because it is self-sufficient; the crisis center is barely alive because it has been unable to find any ongoing source of funds. New services of this type are rarely seen because resources—funds, social legitimacy, and community support—are all centralized and monopolized in the bureaucratic repressive institutions. There is very little experiment with new models of service, because the community is basically satisfied with the performance of existing institutions as a funnel to label and remove people who present a problem or create anxiety in society or to pressure such people to alter their thoughts and behavior to fall into line with community standards. They also "promote the general welfare" by setting standards of morality through diagnosis of what a "healthy" person is and exerting control on the boundary when people

stray from such a standard. Thus, they emphasize limits and proper behavior, rather than self-determination and creative expression.

I do not feel that a society does not have the right to exercise control over its citizens. By comparing bureaucratic psychiatry in China, Russia, and the United States, I think I can define more clearly why I particularly resist current American bureaucratic therapy. In China someone acting crazily is temporarily hospitalized and subjected to coercive demands that he understand the politically reactionary nature of his behavior and struggle against his illness to regain the proper revolutionary spirit. From the evidence we have, after a few months of such reeducation, which includes drug therapy, acupuncture, lectures, and group therapy, most patients are returned to their homes and welcomed back to their community and jobs. There is no stigma attached to mental illness, which really is treated according to the medical model (there are no social aftereffects of the cure). Another reason for the success of this form of treatment, I believe, is that Chinese society is not wracked with dissension and contradiction; most people accept its basic values and goals.

The use of Russian mental hospitals to stifle dissent and house political prisoners has recently been publicized but, interestingly, has failed to attract the criticism of the American Psychiatric Association. The reason for the lack of outrage by established representatives of psychiatry probably stems from the fact that the function of psychiatry is similar in Russia and the United States. Both Russian and American society seem beset with conflict and contradiction, and psychiatry has been harnessed as one major means to stifle dissent covertly. As psychiatrist Thomas Szasz has amply documented, society projects onto psychiatric victims—drug users, schizophrenics, homosexuals, young people, and women—its weaknesses, doubts, and fears. The people who are victimized by therapists are, coincidently, those who have been most victimized by society in other ways. Thus, in all my experience I found that the concentration of therapists in child guidance clinics and private hospitals on young people's anger and aggression and on their experiments with sexuality and drugs masks a political concern that such values not spread in society. That is why therapists do not like a treatment setting which does not emphasize limits and control.

I feel that the model of the democratic, supportive, expressive community I have experienced represents an alternate style of therapy, which is also a direct assault on these repressive values in current bureaucratic therapy. Ironically, such communities resurrect democratic values on which our nation is already premised, in rhetoric if not

deed. Thus, the current search for alternative communities represents a conservative movement against bureaucratic encroachment on individual self-expression and self-determination. Similarly, in its original concept psychoanalysis rested on a noninterfering reflection on the patient's goals and aspirations, which eschewed all direct intervention and decision making for the patient as antitherapeutic and unlikely to increase his or her freedom.

What of the third role of the therapist, that of authoritative healer? The healer role spans such disparate activities as the work of the medical director of a private hospital, the psychoanalyst, the encounter leader, and the guru. Its basic definition is that the therapist is a person who has superior authority and the skill to create changes in the patient. As a therapist, this is a role I both aspire to and am ambivalent about. I have spoken of how this role can be abused, when the healer becomes a tool of a covert value structure, like an agent of the emperor or a bureaucratic ward administrator or an encounter leader who dispenses wisdom and creates encounters but who is not affected by the group members. To me, the key issue in becoming a healer is mystification, the theme of the fable at the beginning of the essay. In all cases where the healer had cut himself off from change, did not see his role as susceptible to change or alteration based on what the client-patient was saying, the healer entered the rarified air of self-fulfilling predictions. Psychiatrists who do not subject their case histories to the scrutiny of their patients or encounter leaders who have an unchanging, stylistic response to being confronted are all defending themselves against the very process of self-examination and change that they are asking of their patients. For therapy to remain an open system, the therapist must always be potentially able to change as a result of the encounter.

The second issue for the healer-therapist is the value system under which he works. Therapy is not value-free; all of my work has assumed a set of values which are represented by the institution I worked in and the nature of the work I did. Since the issues that the people I helped were engaged with were intimately involved with the style and the skill of their participation in society—for example, often their behavior, running away from home or using drugs, was illegal—I had to be aware of the values I was espousing and my relation to those of my client. For example, I know that my values about marriage can decisively influence a couple to stay together or get divorced, simply by the nature of the questions I ask or the interpretations I make. I could easily convince a young person to go back home, stop using drugs, or do the opposite, according to whether I focused the counseling sessions

on his fears or on his goals. All therapy is covertly directive.

I happen to believe that many of the issues which people bring to therapy stem from the internalization of contradictions which are rooted in our society. I think that one ought to act on one's perceptions of injustice, and in many cases this means adopting behavior which is considered deviant by much of society. I find that, whether by self-selection or my own influence over the therapy process, people who come to me for counseling tend to share my beliefs. My personal definition of therapy is one which is often at odds with prevailing norms, but one which I hope will be compatible with a new type of community in which healing is a part of the entire social environment. At that time therapy will cease to be a skilled trade and will be simply one more property of the growth-enhancing, person-valuing culture.

5. "I Can't Read Minds, but if You Want to Try Something New . . ."

LARRY L. CONSTANTINE

For a therapist the task of creating a boundary between one's life and one's work is difficult. While therapists have traditionally paid a great deal of attention to one direction of this transference, taking one's personal concerns into one's work (counter-transference), they often deny the other direction, the effect of coming home from work after dealing with people's deep personal concerns and its effects on one's relationships. When the therapist is part of a husband-wife co-therapy team and when the issues they deal with are those that they themselves face in their lives—the nature and style of family life—the boundary between work and life can become nonexistent. When to that situation is added the further fact that they came to the profession of therapy through trying to solve an issue in their own lives—the feelings surrounding the collapse of a group marriage—you have the situation of Joan and Larry Constantine. Since, like Joan and Larry, I do counseling mainly out of my home, often with friends, and work with my wife, I know that such an arrangement can be exhilarating, demanding, and helpful (to both oneself and one's clients). The traditional boundaries of the professional therapist who works only in the office, within fixed time spans, without personal self-disclosure, and allows no relationship with clients to exist outside of the office may be norms devised not for the good of the client, but rather for the protection of the therapist.

The Constantines spent several years traveling around the country with their children in a car and trailer with almost no money, interviewing and learning about the lives of people who, like them, had been involved in group marriages. Their results have been published in several magazines and journals and in their book, *Group Marriage*. In their research and their friendships they found themselves asked to help with personal problems arising in the lives of people in group marriages, and, to their

surprise, they also found that they were helpful to them. Like Ted Clark they were therapists before they consciously took on the title and trappings of therapy as a profession. They entered training at the Boston Family Institute and are now in private practice with all kinds of families in all kinds of settings. They continue their research under the auspices of the Center for Family Change, and Larry is on the faculty of the Tufts University School of Medicine. They live in Acton, Massachusetts, in a house they have nearly finished building themselves.

When I was a little boy, my parents once threatened to take me to a psychiatrist. I was really scared. I believed that psychotherapists could read minds. The moment I walked in the door he would know my deepest, darkest secrets, even that I masturbated! And now I am a psychotherapist. I can read minds. Mine, at least, or parts of it. Sometimes. But I do sometimes have trouble convincing people at parties that I can't read *their* minds.

There have been other changes as I became a therapist, a family therapist, a radical family therapist. There is a change in how I see myself.

Somewhere within, near the places where daydreams begin to percolate into awareness, is enshrined our very personal art collection, a gallery of deeply felt images, self-portraits, maps, as it were, guides to our priorities and directions. We know these images, though we know them only indirectly. Mostly we know them when they are touched or seen by someone else. The feelings evoked are unexpected in their swiftness and intensity.

I receive a telephone message that a client, Mrs. Nalons, called. I reach her at home and ask what's up. "I don't know," she mumbles. "Do you want me to see you?" "I don't know," she drones. "Is anything wrong?" "I don't know," she sighs. My intuition and my newly installed critical-observer-computer simultaneously conclude—God knows how —that she is suicidal. I arrange to come to her house. As I pull out of the drive a bit too fast, Mitty-like, I become . . . the Blue Knight!

Well, that *is* an improvement. Once I thought I was the Avatar (as I've learned seven out of ten people think they are). Knighthood is so much more achievable. Knights are not divine; they are skilled, competent, well-equipped, effective, ever-ready, and on rare occasions even courageous but nevertheless only human and ultimately as soft and susceptible as anyone. The change in this heroic imagery is one cell in a matrix of changes. As other people give me feedback, steadying their mirrors so I may see myself in them, I learn that I *have* changed. Change is possible. If I change, then there is hope that I,

person-therapist, Blue Knight-Country Doctor alias me, might be instrumental in others' changing. I will try to share some more images of changes, a little history, and a lot of random meanings. But then, I am random and to present myself that way is easier, more honest, and harder.

I didn't start out to be a family therapist. Who does? I started out to be a computer scientist. Before that I wanted to be a biologist, but chemistry killed me; and besides, before that I wanted to be a theoretical physicist and wrestle with cosmic and ultimate things, but math kills me, too. It all does make sense in a disordered way, at least viewed from here. Would you believe, my degree is in management!

In 1968 I only knew that I had a nagging and intensifying dissatisfaction with my career as boy-corporation-president and iconoclastic consultant in computer science. It was a challenging, well-paid way to stretch my intellect and leave a few fecund footnotes on the theory of information systems, but it left me feeling unwhole, segmented, with a deep longing to be involved integrally with some of the transcendent goals I held for myself and humankind.

Purpose and pattern emerged as I became first an intellectual advocate of alternative family life styles and, later, a very emotionally involved participant in a group marriage with another couple. I now see that the group marriage research with which Joan and I have become identified was begun for many reasons. Sundered by that short-lived but very stuck family experience, we were reaching for some task to pull us together. We wanted reassurance that we were neither alone nor crazy. And it tapped into our shared images of ourselves as Crusader Couple. Somewhere along the line I realized that this was where I wanted to be and made a commitment to work with families as a way of life.

The entire way is paved with chance events that seem, nonetheless, to have a logic of their own. Meeting David Kantor at a workshop on alternative life styles was such a touchstone.

David was my final guru. The radar in me which was tuned to respond to big-loving-knowing-answer-daddies went off like a fire alarm. He does that to people. His guruship is still a hassle for him and problematic to others equipped with the radar. But he helped me to turn my own to more interesting channels. While I was still idolizing him, I signed up in benevolent ignorance for the Boston Family Institute training program in family therapy. That interest started on our cross-country research trips where we were often asked for therapy or counseling by friends and research respondents.

Alas, degrees in management are not tickets of admission to gradu-

ate work in marriage counseling. We made one feeble attempt to apprentice ourselves to a sex and marriage counselor we knew. In the end I think I really entered the BFI because they would take me. They may or may not have known what they were in for; I certainly was unprepared for the changes that would be expected of me.

I think therapy is about change, and the changes I have in mind are ones which free people by undoing some of the internal knots which tie them up. To me, "mental health" is really a matter of one's psychological degrees of freedom, the interpersonal repertoire within which one is internally free to move. Of course, that freedom depends on external realities, including political and economic ones; but there are many fronts, and I have chosen to work on this one.

I consider myself to be a radical therapist (lower ease letters) but not because I work with people in alternative life styles. Joan and I are both still deeply committed to alternatives, though fully half our work is with very conventional families. I find I can work comfortably to help people find their own options in either sphere and never be tempted to "convert" anybody to book answers, whether the text is traditional or revolutionary. Untied and with their eyes open, I think people can make choices for themselves. I trust us with an ordinary family much more than I would trust most other therapists, even some very good ones, with an unconventional one. To some I'm sure it looks like we've left the movement, been co-opted, but they wouldn't be looking very carefully. Our "cause" has just broadened.

My style of being a therapist feels radical to me in two ways. I place a very high premium on being effective. This demands a systemic or ecological overview which takes into account the total web in which we are all enmeshed and which shapes and is shaped by our every interaction. Being efficient in such complexity requires accurate models of real processes, that is, the active use of solid theory, continually tested and revised. I'm talking about leverage, because I'm interested in facilitating *change*, not merely consoling or counseling.

Second, there are no clear-cut lines separating my life as therapist from my private and personal life. The image I have is of the country doctor who comes all the way out to the farm to deliver a baby, then stays for dinner and gets a hand from the family starting his jalopy.

I do therapy with friends and become personally involved with clients. Not always, of course. This is a messy issue—therapeutically, ethically, personally—and I try to meet messy issues head-on. I have no easy, precut answers, even for myself, and to be therapeutic with friends and lovers means evolving new, custom-made answers on a continual basis.

More and more, I try to be person-therapist. Being me, at least part of the time, comes naturally. Therapy is an acquired skill. What's sometimes tough is to be therapeutic and just be me at the same time. Just-me, I have to admit, isn't always all that therapeutic; neither is just skill. Putting it together means changing me, increasing my own internal repertoire.

I do a lot of therapy in daily, nontherapy life. That's a no-no to many therapists, but to me, if I know the difference between what might be useful to someone else and what probably won't be, it would be wrong not to act "therapeutically." If I don't know the probable impact of my own behavior, I'm off the hook temporarily. Either I don't know that person as a person well enough, don't know enough about therapy, or don't know myself, all continuing processes. I just accept the complications and refuse arbitrarily to compartmentalize my life experiences.

We got a card this Christmas from a woman who had been in a group marriage, one of the groups in our research. The card contained news of her remarriage and a note of thanks. I remember that therapy vividly. We were living in a trailer parked outside our half-built house. The house had no electricity, plumbing, or walls inside, but it had a phone. The phone started ringing one summer evening around midnight. Eventually, it awoke us in the trailer. I fumbled for the house key and ran naked for the front door, certain that the call was important but equally sure the phone would stop ringing just before I reached it.

It was long distance collect. "Remember how you always told us when we were in your research that if we ever needed help, just call? Well, I'm sorry for all the trouble we gave you about the questionnaires and, well . . . ." Well, I spent an hour and a half bare-assed on bare concrete, talking her through the first shock of her group marriage collapsing. She called us because her therapist was away. I spent the wee hours of several mornings trying to be therapeutic by long distance. I was only half-way through training and really got scared when she started talking suicide. By day we tried to locate alternatives-oriented help in a distant city we didn't know. At last we got through to a hotline there and convinced them we were for real. I arranged for them to contact her. About that time her mother arrived on the scene, her therapist returned, and the effect of our "sessions" began to take. He wasn't there, but the Blue Knight would have approved.

We do some therapy with clients in our home, and in many other ways our whole family is involved in the family therapy world. Our two girls call felt-tipped markers "therapy pens" because we use them in our work. Joy, who is five, has already decided she wants to be a family

therapist. She is a perceptive observer of process, as are many kids, but has also picked up the vocabulary to express her insights and enough of the tools of the trade to be able to observe even our own family process and comment on it. She even tells *me* when my yelling is coming from somewhere else rather than what is happening here and now.

We direct a lot of our energies and skills back into our own marriage and family. Fortunately, the family systems perspective does not as readily become new ammo for old family games as some therapeutic *Weltanschauung* do. Our experience as family scientists doesn't hurt any, either. Building understanding of our own family to give us all more flexibility and room to grow is a pretty steady avocation.

Family therapy is engaging and evocative of one's own original family themes and hangups. This has been especially significant in my marriage with Joan as we went through training together. One of the ostensible advantages of co-therapy teams is that the team is the therapist. When the co-therapists split for home, they need not carry therapy issues with them. That is, unless they are a wife-and-husband team.

The family therapist has to learn how to get in and get out of each family's process, getting in without getting stuck in, being out without being locked out. When you get caught in another family's stuck goings on, you play their games, but you play them as you learned them in your family.

During the first two-thirds of training Tuesday nights were like a weekly injection of new insights and vitality into our marriage. Then we started doing co-therapy together. Intentionally each of us had done some supervised work with other co-therapists until we felt we were ready to bring what we had gained back into working together. It was an experiment; we really didn't know whether we would be able to work together effectively.

Things started to get tough with the first session. The father was drunk and still drinking. Their adult son, known to us to be diagnosed as paranoid schizophrenic, turned out to have psychomotor epilepsy. He, the index patient, walked out after twenty minutes and refused to reenter therapy for many weeks. The spatial and systems strategies we had learned went down the tube since no one would get up and try anything. I felt deserted by Joan, who let me carry the ball, deflated as it was, most of the time. It was an incredibly stuck family, and shortly we were an incredibly stuck part of it. We responded to their situation mostly with still-knotted parts of ourselves and our marriage.

For instance, we had always known that Joan had problems taking

the lead, being a mover, as David Kantor puts it. We had overlooked (funny!) that I didn't know how to be a follower in our relationship. Now how the hell can I follow if I have no mover to follow? And how the hell can Joan be a mover if she only gets countermoves or nothing from me? So, slowly, with much energy and no small amount of pain, we each began to learn some new strategies, to free ourselves, and, concurrently, to free that family.

One of the biggest changes for me has been in the way the world, people, families look to me. It has been like going from black and white to full color, stereoscopic vision. People's lives and actions to me seem incredibly rich, varied, and exciting. I marvel at the way the simplest daily rituals in "ordinary" families, when unfolded, reveal sheer genius in the way they balance and counterpoint the manifold concerns and interests of a number of people.

Incidentally, remember Mrs. Nalons? It turned out she had attempted suicide. I arrived to help clean up the blood and reassure her kids. In doing so I broke nearly every rule in the book of the agency I was with. I had made a *home* visit, then conducted *unscheduled* therapy back at the office. I had been *alone* with a *female* client in her home, then driven her in *my* car. But the message of my response to her pain and need got through. Over the weeks to come, we were able to turn the crisis into a creative one. I didn't last at the agency.

So the Blue Knight rides off, surrounded by caring friends and family, but looking for work.

I must add a postscript. Recently a group of my family therapy students gave me some caring feedback on the way all of the Blue Knight's equipment clanks and clatters when he enters a room. I am learning of the advantages of an unobtrusive black bag.

6. I Did It—Scribbles on a Note-book Wall

JOAN M. CONSTANTINE

There we were, Larry and I, sitting at our breakfast table discussing our three-year plan of researching multilateral (group) marriage in the United States. We had no idea where it would all lead, we only knew at that time no one else was studying this phenomenon and, since we had just separated from *our* group marriage co-spouses, we wanted and needed the perspective that contact with other groups might give us. Our ethic during the research was one of mutual sharing with respondents so that we all gained something from it. In the course of our travels and contact with groups, we began to be called on to intervene in their crises, large and small. Sometimes the groups needed an outsider to inject a bit of objectivity or simply needed to talk openly about their life style with someone who could listen without judging. We listened, and we could give an objective point of view, but there were times when the crises were beyond our abilities to deal with them productively and effectively. At first we simply maintained we were researchers, not counselors; later we did apply "first aid" or crisis intervention and made referrals to qualified professionals. But it was difficult to find people who understood the phenomenon of group marriage and who would be willing to work with such a group. As time went on Larry and I began to realize that we wanted the experience and training necessary to be really therapeutic ourselves.

After deciding on further training, we settled on the Boston Family Institute, which trains individuals in the science and art of family therapy. To be frank, I really didn't know at that time what I was

getting into. I wasn't sure what family therapy was, except that it meant working with "the family." And I was not sure if BFI knew what they were getting into by accepting me, someone without a college degree. Many of my classmates had all kinds of training and educational background; those who, like me, didn't have the degrees kept it to themselves. Over time I came to see that some of the less formally educated people did well and some of the experienced professionals had a hard time. The amount of college education we each had was not as important as what we did with it.

The issue of formal education has run through my life. My parents always expected their children to have college educations. The unspoken message we received was that we were somehow not ok until we had our degrees. So when the issue of attending BFI came up between Larry and me, it was difficult for me not to hear the message, "If you don't go, you're a loser, you're not ok." I began my training with a lot of anxiety, since it tapped into one of my big knots.

The training was didactic but, more important to me, experiential. In the process of learning about family systems and therapy, techniques, skills, videotaping, I was in process, too. When I was hung up over something, it would take me two months of intense anxiety before I could confront myself about it or ask someone else for help. I got stuck a lot, but I grew a lot, too. I applied what I had learned in class to myself. I gained perspective, distance. I experienced that I could use myself, who I am, effectively to help others. I learned to take my weaknesses and turn them into strengths. I had expected that once I had completed an educational program such as this one, I would have made it. After finishing training I felt launched on the *beginning* of a trip.

Another process began at the first BFI class. Larry and I had decided to function and present ourselves not as a couple, but as individuals. Yet at the first meeting, when an exercise called for each of us to define a space of our own and explore it, I felt shut out and hurt by Larry's keeping me out of his space. His notebook became a wall between us. I felt unsure about making a space of my own. At the next class it was Larry's turn when I did not come to his rescue when someone misunderstood him. By rescuing him in the past, I had prevented him from learning new ways of working out misunderstandings himself. I had always worked with Larry, played with him, grocery shopped with him along, socialized with him right there beside me. But I had not learned how to be with him and yet be separate. We spent the time driving home every Tuesday evening sorting out and processing what had happened at class. We spent quite a lot of time and frustration on the

people in the class responding to us only as a couple, until one Tuesday on our anniversary we walked in holding hands. From then on it was their problem.

I had thought of the training as a route to dealing with unconventional, alternative families. I had the impression that group marriages and the like were much more difficult to work with than the average family. After all, I had grown up in an average family and we all seemed to be functioning, average people. It was the group marriage experience which seemed too complex and intense to sort out. As I began to learn about families as systems, I came to see that we all carry the families we grew up in around with us. We all end up repeating our old family system regardless of how distressing it was and regardless of whether we choose to marry one person or many persons. It is fascinating that on so few cues from another person, our minds can attempt to choose or reject that person as someone who will repeat our old family's patterns. Looking back, our group marriage system just allowed me to repeat a stuck role I played during my childhood.

During my training I came to see that more conventional families were not as simple as I had assumed and that in some ways problems and ways of dealing with problems were the same in every life style. I began to look at any group of people living together as a family (with its own system) whether those involved are blood kin or self-chosen peers. What may make working with, say, a group marriage family easier for me is the experience the clients and I have in common.

Through our research and therapy experience I have found that alternative life styles in themselves are neither "sicker" nor "healthier" than conventional ones. What is more important is finding the life style which best fits and fulfills each individual. For some people the thought of anyone living in any but the modal marriage is threatening. How can that fear or sense of threat be changed to something more positive? Since I have learned so much through experiencing, I try to help people to explore their fantasies, to discover and share where they are coming from, and to *experience* for themselves in role play what it would be like to be in an alternative life style. Through getting inside and looking out in this new way, each now has a gift of knowing without becoming changed and yet has changed without knowing.

Family therapy is no longer a fuzzy concept. Life itself is less fuzzy, and I am more capable of choices. I still have problems to solve, old programs, stuck places. But the part of me which is the observer is more well-developed now: I can stand back and see what is really happening. If something seems fuzzy I stand back, or it stays fuzzy until I am ready to focus on it. More important to me is experiencing

the phenomenon of being therapist-person in and out of a structured therapy situation. It is not the same as when Larry is therapist-person, since being therapist-person is an expression of one's uniqueness. Therapist-person is not giving away a piece of myself, but rather opening up, radiating and being me without the programs and the dysfunctional old patterns and familiar feelings. It is feeling solidness, inner strength, power (not over another person but rather to live and be and choose), capabilities, willingness, flexibility, risk-taking, competence, good feelings, a sense of context, sincerity. It is talking straight and effectively and purposefully. It means choosing to help when I can and not to help when I cannot. It means to say what is happening instead of just feeling or seeing it. It means not always giving someone what he or she wants but what is therapeutic. It means getting in close, standing back to see, and then moving in close enough to help someone without losing perspective.

I feel that it is most difficult of all for me to be therapist-person in my own family with my husband of ten years who is also a therapist. Just think of the patterns which are ingrained in us all. Each day reinforces those behaviors. So we work on changing; it is more difficult from within since it is so difficult to be involved *and* have perspective.

Each new family I see puts me in touch with parts of me which are still ungrown or knotted up or which have changed. Hopefully, we all grow from the experience. For example, I notice an improvement in Larry's and my communications when we are concentrating on communications skills with clients. On the other hand, when Larry and I are working as a co-therapy team we tend to bring home with us any stuckness or knots which are brought out in us during therapy. During our training there were many times when we needed our supervisors or peer group to help pull us out of our stuckness, which was sometimes reflecting the clients' dysfunctional relationships. An effective co-therapy team is like a healthy marriage: The partners are capable of facing differences. They are able to be supportive and can fight creatively. If the co-therapy relationship is not functioning well, then the team is not going to be very therapeutic for the clients. With a non-spouse co-therapist I can leave him or her after the therapy session and go home; I can think about the problems or issues, get perspective, and still function well within my family. When Larry and I work together, a co-therapy issue may effect everything else in our system until we get unstuck or work it through.

7. The Uses of Madness

JAMES S. GORDON

I would like to share some thoughts on the uses of madness—not its etiology or phenomenology and not, in any systematic way, its treatment. By "uses" I mean simply the ways in which the madness of an individual may influence and bring about change in the people who are involved with that individual and the situation in which the individual is enmeshed.

For this purpose I will define madness as that condition which when it appears in one person prompts others—with or without the "mad" one's agreement—to seek a psychiatrist's assistance or counsel. I choose this definition partly because it is the lowest common denominator of many situations with which a psychiatrist is confronted, and partly because it avoids the distorting and denigrating prism of diagnosis.

It is my belief that an individual's madness sometimes reveals unexplored contradictions in a social situation. Its expression may prove enlightening to others in the situation and indeed can provide a lever for group change. One role that a psychiatrist may play is that of facilitator and catalyst in this process.

Perspective

Before I discuss two concrete situations, one of which occurred in a mental hospital ward, the other in a group foster home for adolescents, I would like to make a brief historical detour. All cultures have recognized members whose behavior was odd or disruptive and whose thoughts were unusual. Sometimes these people have been stigma-

tized by their fellow citizens; in some circumstances they have been venerated. The belief that they are "sick" and therefore in need of medical treatment has only in the past two centuries come to be generally accepted. And it is this belief that has dictated that madmen be cared for in hospitals by psychiatrists—the medical practitioners whose specialty is psychopathology, "diseases of the spirit."

And so we no longer seek, as men have for thousands of years, to exorcise demons, nor do we hear in mad speech the voice of God (to "act like a prophet" meant in ancient Hebrew to behave in an uncontrolled manner). We do not, at least overtly, condemn madmen as evil as many eighteenth- or nineteenth-century citizens did, nor do we regard their transports as evidence of shamanistic potential. The mad are pathetic, childlike, amusing, sensible, annoying, and interesting by turns—but above all they are "sick." They must be well "treated," properly medicated, and adequately controlled. Psychiatrists speak of signs and symptoms, of diagnosis and prognosis. If the mad are young and intelligent and especially if they are wealthy someone may want to do psychotherapy with them.

Against this prevailing current a few voices have been raised. Harry Stack Sullivan, resisting rigid distinctions between the mad and the sane, observed that "we are all more simply human than otherwise." More recently the British psychiatrist R. D. Laing and his associates have made an impressive case for the psychotic experience being not merely "human" but a "natural healing process . . . a voyage of discovery into self of a potentially revolutionary nature."

In an essay written in 1949 Frieda Fromm-Reichmann observed that "mentally disturbed persons who have withdrawn from their environment are refreshingly intolerant of all kinds of cultural compromises; hence they inevitably hold the mirror of the hypocritical aspects of the culture in front of society." And in a similar vein Laing suggested that "future men . . . will see that what we call 'schizophrenia' was one of the forms in which often through quite ordinary people, the light began to break through the cracks in our all too closed minds."

My own work has been greatly influenced by both Fromm-Reichmann, who retained the medical model and worked within a hospital setting, and by Laing, who renounced the former and created a new kind of setting. My own experience suggests that if one eschews medical categories and notions of psychopathology and deals instead with individuals and the situations they exist in, the very nature of madness as well as one's approach to it changes.

Customarily, pathology has been located in the individual psyche. More recently, therapists who work with families have concluded that

the family is "pathological." The individual who is presented as the patient is simply the receptacle for its most bizarre or socially unacceptable behavior and thoughts. Some contend, as Laing does at times, that the whole society is mad. Individual madness "that we encounter in 'patients' is a gross travesty, a mockery, a grotesque caricature of what the natural healing of that estranged integration we call sanity might be."

The ground in this territory is constantly shifting. The point I will make here—and I regard it as a point of departure—is simply that the mad behavior of one person in a group may provide a critique in light of which the whole group may see itself anew and bring about change in itself. My contention is that this in itself is therapeutic not only to the mad individual but also to the group as a whole. A dialectical process is at work in which the madness of one member provides a critical perspective on the prevailing norms of group behavior. Out of the conflict between one individual and the group, a new, potentially richer style of group life may emerge.

Peter

Shortly after I took over the administration of a state hospital ward, Peter's parents called me. Their son, who was twenty-one, "a college dropout, but very intelligent," had for the past eight months been committed to and had escaped from several mental hospitals. While unemployed and unsure of his future, he had had some "bad acid trips" and tried to "find himself" on a religious commune. He had ultimately returned home "acting very peculiar and speaking incoherently." His parents had brought him to a city hospital psychiatric emergency room. He had been committed and tried to escape, been tranquilized, sent to a state hospital, and discharged.

This process had taken place three times. On one cycle he had spent three months in a "therapeutic community" and had taken and then lost a clerical job that his therapist had suggested. Several times he had escaped from the state hospital. He took tranquilizers, which had been administered in doses of up to 2500 mg. of Thorazine a day, reluctantly, complaining that they slowed him down and made him feel like a "zombie." He resented having to work and maintained that he wanted only to "seek truth" and to "find love."

When we first spoke, Peter admitted that there was "something wrong," but he wasn't sure what it was. He felt that a "trick had been played," that he could trust no one and that a lot of work would be

required "to find out what was going on." He needed "freedom" and "respect" and did not need tranquilizers, strait jackets, being beaten up, or told what to do. He had experienced all of these in his previous hospitalizations.

Peter and I struck a bargain. He said that he would try to let us know when he wanted help or if he had to leave the ward. I replied on behalf of the staff that we would try to limit our efforts to helping him to experience and understand what *he* needed to. I also assured him that we would not interfere with his comings and goings except insofar as there was an immediate risk to his life: "For instance, if you said you were about to run out onto the parkway."

In "speaking for the staff" I was being premature if not presumptuous. My sense of what Peter needed—to be allowed to experience the "natural healing process of madness"—was shared by only one or two other staff members. The rest had evinced attitudes that ranged from qualified interest to open skepticism.

Since I am here discussing the uses of madness rather than its therapy, I will focus on how Peter's behavior over the next several weeks helped the ward staff to share, at least provisionally, a common point of view, how it helped individual members to enlarge on their therapeutic skill and, finally, how it helped us to shed some of the stultifying armor of our roles as doctor, nurse, aide, occupational therapist, and patient.

To begin with, Peter affected his individual therapist, a first-year psychiatric resident who was open to a noncoercive kind of therapy. Tranquilizers, restraints, and conventional psychotherapy had not been of much use to Peter. He resisted them consistently and persisted in behaving in such a way—sitting naked in his room for hours, refusing to work, speaking incoherently, shouting and laughing to himself— that he was repeatedly returned to psychiatric hospitals. No one had listened to what Peter wanted to do or to how he wished therapy to be conducted. Perhaps this path would meet with more success. The first step taken by Peter's therapist—simply listening to what his "mad" patient wanted and trying to implement the patient's sense of his own needs—in itself represents a profound shift in attitudes for a hospital-based psychiatrist. Peter's doctor like other residents was accustomed to diagnosing and treating, to writing "orders," "restrictions," and "passes."

In his first week on the ward Peter came to his therapist's office at the appointed time, said a few words, sat silent, became increasingly anxious, and left to return to his room. When the therapist asked what he could do, Peter replied that he could come sit beside his bed. The

therapist overcame *his* anxiety and daily, after ten or fifteen minutes in the office, returned with Peter to his room and sat with him silently. After a few days he felt comfortable holding Peter's hand until the latter had drifted off to sleep.

The therapist was puzzled and occasionally put out at the lack of "material" that Peter produced. But at the same time he recognized the intimacy of these moments and their function in building up Peter's trust. In addition he came to recognize a whole new dimension of therapy, a silent "being with" that was deeply fulfilling to both the patient and therapist and which, anxiously preoccupied with such matters as his "resistance," "transference," and "interpretations," the therapist had never experienced.

Peter's slightly unconventional use of therapy sessions was augmented after about ten days by "peculiar" behavior on the ward. As the Thorazine he had previously been given began to wear off, his anxious stiffness gave way to more fluid but furious activity. Peter was all over the place, embracing people, trying to get them to play tag, breaking up pool games, singing, shouting, and dancing.

Debate on "what to do about Peter" was well underway by the time the daily ward meeting began. The head of the Inpatient Service was making his first visit to the ward. An urbane, modly dressed, fiftyish analyst, he nodded his head when introduced and sat back and proceeded to take notes. I felt tense though I had taken the job with the stipulation that I would have autonomy in running the ward. My position with the staff was shaky and I feared that the postmeeting "analysis" might damage my credibility.

Into the circle of the ward meeting danced Peter, half-naked. He sat down, took one look at the head of the Inpatient Service and burst into song: "He's got the whole world in his hands." Shocked silence gave way suddenly to relieved laughter. Peter like Lear's Fool had exposed the absurdity of my anxiety and my boss's pretentions. He had diagnosed (literally, "seen through") the situation. The cheerful edge of his irony drained anxiety from the meeting, and we proceeded.

Later that day Peter took off all his clothes, "baptized" visitors to the ward with paper cups filled with water, and preached freedom from the top of the pool table. We called another meeting and decided together that we would try to let Peter go through whatever it was that was happening to him. One or preferably two of us would be with him at all times and our function would be to aid and understand rather than constrain or "treat" him.

The meeting broke up with a feeling of satisfaction. For the first time the staff (and some of the patients) had a common goal. We were going

to try something together—a new way of being with a mad person. Perhaps the staff would be more anxious, but I felt we might be able to handle it. I knew that the punitive and corrective role of a hospital staff diminished anxiety but also felt that it closed off relatedness and understanding.

Meanwhile a call came from downstairs. Peter was next to the highway, naked, dancing in full view of the traffic. I went down to get him and helped him back to the ward. Only a week later did I realize that he had signaled according to a code I had taught him; the "only time," I had said half-jokingly when he first came to the ward, that "we would stop him from leaving was if he was about to go out on the highway."

Over the next two weeks Peter went through an often bewildering series of changes. Contemplatively tasting his own excrement at one moment, he would suddenly leap up and embrace someone. A few minutes later he would be on his knees praying. During this period staff and patients spent time with Peter, sitting silently sometimes, at others participating with him in the dramas that he precipitated. Here are three examples out of a great many:

> If a woman and man are with him, Peter sometimes wants them to play "mommy and daddy." He asks a female nurse and a male psychiatric resident to hold hands. When they seem ill at ease, he points this out and assures them that "it's ok because it's just pretending for Peter." They hold hands and talk with some embarrassment about their feelings and the difficulties that they have previously had with one another. Peter watches them. After they have grown comfortable with each other, he puts his head in the man's lap and rests.

> Peter is downstairs. He has gotten some candy and is walking through a corridor with a male staff member. Suddenly he stops. The staff member is in a hurry and is anxious about a physical struggle with Peter away from the ward. Peter sits down and after a moment so does the staff member. Peter says there is darkness and danger ahead: "I'm frightened." The staff member sees only a shadowed patch of corridor. They sit together for a few minutes as others pass by. The staff member feels a little silly. Then quietly he feels Peter's anxiety and understands. The shadows are dangerous to Peter. A little while later both feel calmer, and they agree to go on.

> Peter is restless. He angrily tears the pages from a book of pictures. With difficulty, an aide restrains himself from stopping

him. Peter starts to paste them on the drab walls of the ward. Several people help and one or two others get pictures that they want to put up. An hour is spent doing this. Staff and patients exchange, in a relaxed way, their opinions of the various pictures.

Peter later described these days as very "important to me," a time of "going into hell and coming out again," of "dying and being born over." They were also important to me and to many others on the ward. At the very least we agreed that we understood more of the feeling of a "mad" person's world than we had before, and that this understanding came from changing our attitude toward Peter's behavior from regulation to inquiry, from treatment to cooperation and guidance.

Beyond this, however, we made some progress in knowing and trusting one another. Psychiatric wards are rigid hierarchies sustained by levels of job titles, partitioned by the walls and doors of offices, and strengthened by the struts of paperwork. By publicly granting Peter the greatest expertise in his own treatment, we allowed the possibility of an understanding that transcended role or status. By a shared openness to his experience, we simultaneously became more open to one another. By honestly confessing our ignorance of his needs, we were able to avoid premature and ignorant treatment. By refusing to do violence to Peter, we made legitimate and trustworthy the counterviolence we had to use if Peter drastically impinged on us. We could protect ourselves when endangered, but Peter would not be "controlled" or "punished" for acting bizarre or "inappropriate." By listening to Peter we began to hear, from under the cover of rules and roles and ideology, ourselves.

Tom

Psychiatrists are generally called into a situation when one member of a group—a family, a circle of friends, a company, a team—is regarded as too difficult or "troubled" to be effectively dealt with by the others. Among people whose field of competence is human behavior—social workers, guidance counselors, probation officers—psychiatrists are sometimes called in when someone is regarded as "really sick," that is, presumably in need of the diagnostic and prescriptive powers of a medical specialist.

If this medical definition is accepted, it becomes the role of the psychiatrist to prescribe medicine, therapy, or perhaps hospitalization.

The doctor and the patient—if he is lucky—will decide. But the situation may be viewed from more than one perspective. And the different perspectives, if taken into account, may point to a different reaction on the psychiatrist's part. It is a corollary that the desires and training of the psychiatrist have some bearing not only on how the patient is dealt with but, in fact, on who becomes "the patient."

For several weeks I had heard about "crazy Tom." Members of the helping arm of the local counterculture—workers at Runaway House, the Free School, and the Free Clinic—had read an article I had written on R. D. Laing and madness and thought I might be able to help Tom. After a few days I went to the group foster home where Tom, who is seventeen, lives with two counselors and four other teenagers—one boy and three girls. First I met the counselors, Ann and Fred, who are in their late twenties. They outlined the decline in Tom's condition.

A runaway and truant who left behind angry and bewildered parents, Tom had lived at the house for two years. He had been withdrawn and frightened at first, but gradually had "made progress" to where both Fred and Ann felt quite close to him, closer to him than to anyone else in the house. Then about six months ago, he had begun to act "peculiar." Where once he had been shy and passive, he became nagging and aggressive. His reticence turned to a suspicious seclusiveness. At times he abused the people in the house unmercifully, particularly Ann and the female teenager who was closest to him. He had pushed and punched each of them and seemed at times dangerous and "paranoid." Tom refused to go to school or to tell the counselors where he went when he left the house. He had, incidentally, been in individual therapy for over a year and his therapist was at a loss to help Tom.

Fred and Ann had been looking for someone to replace the psychologist who had come as a consultant to their house's weekly group meeting. But if I didn't have the time to do that, they hoped I could at least help them find some place for Tom to go. His behavior was becoming more and more intolerable and they simply didn't know what to do. I said that I would like to try to help by acting as a consultant to the entire house. I would regard the counselors' point of view about Tom as merely one among several. I added that though I respected their efforts to help the teenagers in the house, I felt in no way committed to any one person's point of view about what the house or its residents should or shouldn't be. I wouldn't come, I said, unless it was all right with all the residents.

By the time my first meeting was half over, Tom and Ann were at it: Ann gently, patiently explaining and inquiring; Tom shouting, swearing, demanding. Ann had simply wanted to know what subjects

Tom was taking at the free high school, and Tom replied that "it was none of your goddamn business." When Ann said she was "interested" in him and "cared" about him, he began to shout and swear at her, accusing her of "lying" and "fucking me over." When she asked for specific examples of "fucking him over," Tom maintained that this request for specifics was just one more example of "what you are doing to me." He insisted that Ann hated him. The more vehemently she, Fred, and the other teenagers denied this—"how about the time Anne sat up all night with you" or "took you on a camping trip," and so forth —the more incoherently furious Tom became. "You're crazy," his best friend said to him in conclusion. "You belong in a hospital."

The following week the group opened with a discussion about cleaning the house. Almost everyone had been negligent, but Tom rapidly became the focus of anger. "I'll clean up if I feel like it," he said. "And if I don't, no amount of prodding will get me to do it. The only reason I clean up," he added, "is because if I don't you'll throw me out." When the others denied this, Tom said that they were crazy, that they were robots. Several house members looked at me as if to say, "see what we mean, we're afraid its hopeless." I suggested that they hadn't really tried to understand what Tom meant, and that rather than deal with the substantive issues that he had been raising, they had decided that he was crazy. "What were the issues?" they asked. I suggested that Tom felt he had the right to decide what he wanted to take at school, if indeed he wanted to take anything at all. Ann, on the other hand, was sure that it was good for Tom to take certain courses or at least some courses, and this was not apparent to Tom. But it wasn't simply a matter of disagreement, because at one point—in fact, when Tom had first come to the house—he had been told that he had to either go to school or work in order to stay there. The velvet glove of Ann's concern for Tom's education and welfare concealed the mailed fist of banishment for disobedience to her wishes.

Tom was told not to dispute the rules and told not to recognize that the counselors didn't want him to dispute them. Finally, no alternative to the living situation existed for him. He was a "person in need of supervision," a delinquent who had spent months in a detention center and who would be subject to reform school the next time he behaved badly. The situation was very much a double bind and Tom's anger— to be mad is among other things to be very angry—represented the first cries of protest against it.

Over the next four or five weeks, more and more of the powerful but unacknowledged contradictions of the house's operation became avail-

able to the group's scrutiny. Each time the group threatened to ignore one, Tom escalated his "madness"—once he spat in Ann's face, another time he threw a table in Fred's direction. Often he sat rigid and trembling, his fists clenched, eyes rolled upwards. He accused the other people in the house of being "on an ego trip," "hypocritical," and murderous.

An important point about this bind, as about many others, is that it was embedded in cultural values that are only questioned with difficulty and altered with considerable pain. In this case the cultural frame of reference included that of the house, the charitable organization of which the house was one part, the city welfare system which financed and supervised Tom's living situation, and American society with its belief in productivity and compulsory education for all. Tom said, "You say you care about me, but you are willing to force me to do things I don't want to do, because *you*, with *your* values, believe they are good for me—it's clear to me that you care more for your values than you do for me."

By helping Tom to articulate this kind of anger, several processes were set in motion. The counselors acknowledged the disparity between their point of view and Tom's and admitted to the contradiction between "caring" about Tom and insisting he go to school. They turned their demand into a question: "What do you want to do?" Tom answered, "I want to stop people from fucking me over!"

Together, Tom and the counselors set about to gain representation for the teenagers on the governing board of the organization that controlled the house. Together also, they began to call into question the attitudes that permitted the counselors to "do things for the teenagers" whether or not the latter were capable of doing these things for themselves or, indeed, wanted them to be done. Since the counselors had felt uncomfortable in their patronizing role, the results of this process, though anxiety-provoking, were "liberating" for them as well. They began to feel free to challenge some of the assumptions of their jobs. And as they divested themselves of much of their power over the teenagers, they became more credible to them and more helpful to them.

The house seemed to function more smoothly. Tom's "craziness" receded from view and in group sessions he began to discuss his very real problems with other people. He never apologized for his previous disruptive behavior and was never asked to do so. He saw it as legitimate anger directed against oppression. "Besides," he added, "when I tried for months to talk coherently nobody listened."

A New Kind of Equilibrium

In both Peter and Tom, one who was so inclined could have elicited the "signs and symptoms of schizophrenia." During the period I have described, both of them were at times difficult to understand, angry, threatening, despairing, and disruptive. I don't wish to minimize the interpersonal strain that existed in their orbits or, on the other hand, the concern and anxiety that they provoked in those who cared for them. Nor do I wish to exempt them from "responsibility" for their actions. I merely wish to suggest that it was possible to view their behavior and words not as the signs and symptoms of an illness, but as comments on and criticisms of the social situation, and as a communication to people in that situation of needs, experiences, dissatisfactions, and insights.

Why do this? First, because Peter and Tom—not to mention many others who present themselves or are designated as patients—ask us to do so. And second, because we may be—or perhaps ought to be—concerned with the whole situation of which they are a part. The disturbance of one member of a group—family, team, or community—may help to reveal clues about a disturbance that exists among all members of a group. Beyond that, it may, if presented to all of them divested of "pathological description," suggest a basis for establishing a new kind of equilibrium.

The willingness of groups to open themselves to a high degree of disturbance is usually not great. And it is as limited in most "therapeutic communities" as it is in nuclear families, work groups, or social circles. The challenge that the "mad" person presents, beyond his or her need for attention, concern, and care, is often to the very social order on which the existence of the group is predicated. And very few groups are willing to question their fidelity to the assumptions that underlie their functioning, much less the assumptions themselves.

The situations that I have described occurred in groups that were ostensibly committed to the welfare of the individuals involved rather than to efficiency, competitive excellence, or profit making. In most settings—even those in which the stated commitment is to patients' or clients' welfare—attempts to value each member and his or her experience are seriously compromised by institutional values that are regarded as beyond question, for instance, the beliefs that "schizophrenics need to take medicine" or that "adolescents need controls" or that "ward staff must be professional."

My functions were to help the "mad" person articulate his implicit challenges to the established order of thought, behavior, or action; to facilitate experiments in feeling, thought, and action in which all members could see some value; and then to help the community define in open agreement new limits beyond which its members were unwilling to go. In doing this I refused to define thought or behavior as healthy or pathological. I tried instead to help put the responses of the various participants into a broader context, to explicate the situation rather than analyze the individuals in it.

Classical psychiatric therapy has depended on separating the "mad" individual from his or her context of family, job, and community and treating him or her as a patient. This act of designation and separation serves to reinforce the definition of one person as "the problem" and the social situation as normative. It is an act that often gives tacit consent to systematic inequities, social hyprocrisies, and interpersonal binds. A therapist's refusal to collaborate in this process may be the vital first step toward changing both the situation and the inner state of the "mad" person. By taking seriously the "mad" person's critique of the situation, one calls into question acts of social denial, isolation, and suppression and raises the possibility of mutual enlightenment and transformation.

8. Growing at Soteria

ALMA MENN

Jim Gordon has told us how he tried to have the staff of a state hospital ward simply listen to their psychotic patients and try to provide them with what *they* said they needed as directly as possible, otherwise interfering with them as little as possible. Another psychiatrist, Loren Mosher, tried a similar experiment on a hospital ward where I worked and met with a comparable lack of success. He then went to the NIMH as head of their Center for Studies of Schizophrenia. One of the things he has done there has been to fund a community which operates out of such a model, but which is independent of the hospital and functions in the community as a small, autonomous, sheltered household. This new community is called Soteria House. It is neither run nor directed by psychiatrists, but rather by a staff that are recruited not according to degrees or professional experience, but because of their intuitive, seemingly natural ability to share the world and understand the needs of a person who is going through an episode of madness. Alma Menn is the director of the project, and she writes here of what it has done for the people who live there—staff and other residents (not patients!)—and of how she came to work in such a project. The everyday experience of those who live in such a house challenges some of the conventional wisdom that psychiatry has propagated about schizophrenia: that it is permanent, that it is incomprehensible, that mad people are irresponsible and have to be locked up, and that only medically trained professionals and hospitals are equipped to deal with them.

Currently there are several similar communities starting, and after research is done on the outcome of the life crises of the people who live in them, the traditional assumption that not much can be done with psychotic patients may change.

I thought of starting this saga of myself with a smash. After all, I'm supposed to expand your mind, startle your psyche, and spur you on and out to change the field of mental health. But I can't do that. It's not my style; I'm a humble and honest woman. So I've decided to tell you the mundane truth. I am not a radical therapist. I am the principal investigator of a National Institute of Mental Health experiment which is attempting to develop and evaluate a new delivery system for the treatment of schizophrenia—an alternative to hospitalization. The Soteria project is a combined research and service program in which the psychotic episode is viewed as a crisis in development with the potential for positive growth. By guiding a person through, rather than encouraging him to repress, his "altered state of consciousness," our treatment is designed to help him emerge from his life crisis a stronger, better integrated person with the capacity to pursue a life which he himself will view as a success.

The idea of the psychotic episode as a potential growth experience is something each mental health worker discovers for himself; we knew about it before R.D. Laing spelled it out for us. If we were lucky, we learned it from the people we were supposed to be helping; maybe we began to get the idea from Thomas Szasz long ago, when he had the courage to question the whole notion of mental illness or even before we took on our professional definitions from Sartre or Kafka or, best of all, Rilke. Such discoveries were reinforced by our own personal transcendental experiences. For me, as I sat with psychotic persons in the hospital, it was the feeling in my insides that the thoughts of mad people, although sometimes terrible and painful and fascinating, are also efforts to reconcile, from the inner depths, the polarities of existence. It was this understanding of the people that made me able to continue working in mental hospitals. This attitude of mine probably interfered with accomplishing what the people who were paying me expected me to do. I spent much too much time allowing people to "talk crazy" and not enough time "strengthening the well part of the ego."

Soteria opened in May 1971 as a home in the community for people who are usually kicked out of their families and banished to seclusion rooms and large mental institutions. The house provides a family in which the disturbed person is not depersonalized but rather is related to in human ways. His bizarre behavior is regarded as valid and real and capable of being understood.

The house itself is a large, two-story, white barnlike structure in a declining neighborhood in the San Francisco Bay area. Most of the other big old houses in the neighborhood have been converted to rooming houses for students and ex-state hospital patients, and some

of the old buildings have already been replaced by new apartment houses and offices. The setting is much like the fringe of a growing, once-agricultural city anywhere in America.

Two staff members and a volunteer are always in residence at the house. The rest of us come in during the day or spend nights there on the living room sofa if it is necessary. Work schedules are negotiated, usually monthly, but they can be and are sometimes changed on a day-to-day basis, depending on the needs of the residents and staff. Each of us on the staff considers himself or herself on call at all times.

The day-to-day activities of the house are similar to those found in most large families: we buy food, bake bread, sew, tie-dye, plant our garden, play ping pong. Anyone who wants to takes a turn preparing a meal and cleaning up afterwards. We write diaries, play guitars, sit on the front stoop, collect data, go to the beach, do yoga and massage, in short, do things that are necessary and interesting to the people living there. We have house meetings from time to time to discuss house problems, such as people using up all the towels, annoyance at another person's freakiness, people running away and getting picked up by the cops or getting taken to the hospital. We have no nursing station, no ground privileges, no group grounds, no weekend passes, no medication room.

Normally, during the day doors and windows are wide open and residents come and go as they please. The degree of control a staff member might exert on a particular resident depends on how the resident is *at that time*. If he wishes to leave for a walk and we are concerned that he or she might be picked up and taken to the hospital or might disturb someone in the neighborhood, a staff member or two will accompany him. We sometimes use trips away from the house with a volunteer or staff when another resident's "freaky" behavior is upsetting a resident.

The one underlying belief to our work at Soteria is that the usually unacceptable behavior of someone in this altered state of consciousness called "schizophrenia" can be part of a growth process. Our next assumption is that one cannot choose another's resolution of this life crisis; the resolution can only come from within.

In other words, we as staff are not the judgers, the limiters, or the *curers*. We are there for the other to be used by him as he chooses. Our first task is to protect his physical body and that of those around him. Often we don't understand what the person is doing or saying, but we assume that we *can* understand if we continue to tune in to the other.

I think one of the major strengths of the staff at Soteria is our acceptance and awareness of each individual's right to choose his own real-

ity. I think we on the staff are aware enough of our own delusions, fantasies, and fears so that what is expressed during the psychotic experience is not perceived by us as remote and nonhuman. One staff member recollects an experience which he had with a resident:

When Susan was working on that big oil painting for her mother and her mother finally told her that she could not come home for Easter, she was really angry. She was looking at the painting that she had been working on for weeks, six to ten hours a day, and took the paints and started with the brush to make wider sweeps, finally using her hand, mixing all the paints together and smearing it on the painting until the actual painting itself was practically obliterated. But she was still doing it with a style. It was kind of another painting. At one point she stopped and looked at it and said, "What do you think?" I said, "It's the best painting you've ever done." I really liked it. It looked nice the way she was doing it. There was anger in the way she was using the colors. It had meaning to it, whereas the painting by numbers didn't have much meaning. She kept on doing it and finished it up. At the same time, she was getting back at her mother. When she finally finished it, she started painting on the wall, drawing figures on the wall, writing names of the different people in her family on the wall and stuff like that. She looked around to see if it was all right and I thought well, she had half the wall already done, she may as well keep going on this section. She did that and then she left the art room and was starting to splotch it around the house and I said, "Let's stick to paper. I don't know if that stuff will come off or not. I think it will, but I'm not sure." There was paper on the walls for painting and I said, "Use the paper." She did except when she was done she also walked into the living room and dumped the whole pan on the carpeting as a finishing thing. She was writing a lot of names of her family. Drawing pictures, like cats and dogs biting and just all of her family and put them in different places, people in the house mixed in with her genealogical family. It came out really good, just an experience to watch that whole thing, to see it both as smearing and a real expression of herself which she hadn't been able to do for a long time.

During the painting, I talked to her about doing it, about the painting, what I saw in it and what she saw in it. I sometimes would ask her, "Who's this? Who's that?" She'd say, "That's the girlfriend I had in high school. That's my younger sister. That's

my mother. That's my uncle." She was writing "cat" and "dog" and "witch" and stuff like that. We just talked about what they were. One of the reasons why it was effective was that it wasn't done in the way of therapy, of me helping her to see what it was. I was curious as to what they were. I didn't know.

A critical difference between our setting and others in which I have participated is that staff at Soteria are trained to acknowledge the person and his crisis. We believe that the crisis may have great meaning for him in the resolution of his life problems and that this experience can be enhanced by the presence of another. The task of the staff, then, is continually to strive to understand him and to remain in active relationship to him. We, as staff members, acknowledge that each person in the house works differently. No one can tell another how to be in a particular situation, for the response must arise out of whatever is happening between the individuals involved. We feel that we make mistakes because of a lack of awareness and that we can learn from these mistakes. Undoubtedly the most difficult part of our work is dealing with the feeling that we don't know what to do. With the exception of one meeting per week, in which individual techniques are discussed, all supervision and training are provided as needed. Like the residents, a staff member may reach out to whomever in the group he feels can best help him, who may or may not be our psychiatrist or myself.

This emphasis on individual responsibility and autonomy allows the staff the freedom and flexibility to deal effectively with all types of "deviant" behavior, with the result that we have been able to avoid disturbances with the surrounding community. During our three years of operation we have had only a few community complaints. It is especially significant that we have had so few abrasive encounters with the surrounding neighborhood when we consider the degree of interaction the staff and residents do have with the community. Residents go to the store, the movies, the barber, the welfare department, night classes, volunteer work, their dentists or medical doctor, or to clinics, alone or with staff, depending on their abilities at that particular moment. Occasionally the staff and the provider of an outside service have had to make special adaptations for our residents, but none that was harmful. Sometimes they are a bit amusing.

Joanie had to have an emergency visit to her orthodontist to have the wires removed from her braces since she often twisted them off. They were scratching the inside of her mouth. The two people closest to her in the house went with her. Before their appointment they

explained to the dentist and his assistant some of the problems which she was experiencing. Arrangements were made for Joanie to have the first appointment of the day so that she would not have to wait and disturb other patients in the waiting room. The two staff people stayed with Joanie while the dental procedure was accomplished, which could well have been a gruesome task, since she was given to biting. This feat completed, two very relieved staff members and Joanie returned to the car. However, for Joanie the episode was not over. She opened the window and pleaded with a passing priest to rescue her from her "captors." A ten-minute discussion followed, which ended with the priest blessing Joanie and our staff for their good work, and the group returned home.

The success with which our staff have been able to resolve almost all of such potentially explosive situations is primarily a function of the degree to which they have been trained and allowed to exercise their individual responsibility. They are aware of Soteria's vulnerability and know that failure to handle adequately critical situations in the community could lead to harassment and even closing of the program. Foremost in the minds of the staff, however, is the awareness that unresolved conflicts with neighbors and other community members could result in the removal of the involved resident from the house. It is out of this strong commitment to continue a relationship with the resident no matter how difficult his or her behavior may be that enables the staff continually to develop new techniques for living in a bewildered and often bewildering community.

As an example of staff involvement I have included an excerpt from a staff journal:

After she had broken one of the big windows, she was just sitting in the living room fairly frightened and way down. I sat next to her on the floor and I said, "You know if you keep on breaking the windows you won't be able to stay here. We can't have the house destroyed." She said, "Ok, I'll leave." I said, "That's not what I'm saying. I don't want you to leave. I want you to stay. I want you to be able to stay, but to be able to stay is not to break windows." At the same time I said, "You're free to leave. It's your choice. I'm not going to keep you here if you want to go." Then she realized she didn't need to leave and said, "But I need to break windows." I said, "When you're going to break a window or when you're going to start a fire or anything like that, just tell me you're going to do it, and I'll take the responsibility from then on in." I said, "Will you do that? Will you tell me?" She said yes,

she would. So we just talked and about an hour later she'd gone upstairs and then came back down and she was just walking by very casually, very fast and said, "I feel like breaking a window." So I got up and went with her right away. She went into the bathroom and took off her shoe, I guess to break a window, and I just held her there and she turned around smiling and said, "Well, you told me to tell you, and I told you." I said, "Well that's all right, now I've got the responsibility for you, and you didn't break it. It's ok." And that worked out. She would be much more explicit and tell me ahead of time. Not way ahead of time; she wouldn't come up to you and say, "Hey, I want to break a window. Stop me." She'd make you pick up on it. She'd throw it out in the middle of a conversation or very casually as she was walking past you. "I feel like breaking a window. I feel like lighting a fire." Even that didn't work forever. It worked for a while.

Still another example from a staff journal follows:

Everyone was up talking until 3:00 or 4:00 A.M. Finally Hope's facade broke down, and she began to be very crazy, again feeling she was the devil and should die. She sobbed and sobbed, was very angry, upset, and nervous. Jeannie and I held her for a long time. Not much was said except to comfort her and support her. Later she went to bed, Jeannie with her. I joined them, sat by the bed, and held her hand. She went into her being the devil. She wanted to die and should be killed because she was so bad. I asked her who in her life was the devil; she responded immediately with "my uncle." "He raised people in a warped way, treated them like flowers and bushes; they should grow straight as he wanted them to." She went on to say how her behavior for the past several years had been her way of showing him that she didn't like his ways, but that then she felt very bad, and she should die. I pointed out that she was wanting to kill her uncle in her. She picked that up and began to focus on how angry she was with him for what he'd done to her, how he had caused her sister's death (with asthma) because Sis no longer cared to live. At that point she began to wheeze and did so as we continued to talk about her sister—how she'd liked her but hadn't really known her. She felt bad she'd been stoned when she found out about her death. She had gone to the funeral but hadn't been to the grave since.

She then focused in a very real way her anger on her uncle: how she ought to tell him she wanted little to do with him. With

this attribution of affect to him her mood lightened, she was much less depressed and could even laugh about some of the things that had gone on. By sunup she was very much together, relaxed and her asthma had gone away. She went to sleep peacefully.

Many residents return to the house after graduation. Some return as volunteers, others just drop by to say "hi." For many of them the house has become a surrogate family, for which they feel much affection. One departing resident described his feelings:

It's a really worthwhile thing, and if it wasn't for this place, I don't know where I'd be right now. I'd have to be on the run if it wasn't for Soteria. Fourteen days they were going to hold me at the hospital. Soteria saved me from a fate worse than death. Food's good too, food's excellent, good cooks, and there's a whole lot of love generated around this place. Caring for each other. More so than any other place I've been.

Still others return for help in dealing with personal problems.

Johanna stayed in touch with the house and came back a couple of times when she got scared. She felt comfortable enough and safe enough to call and say, "Hey, can I come back?" Maybe just for a couple of hours in the evening. Then it went from that to her calling me and saying she needed to talk. I'd go down to Palo Alto, and we'd sit and talk for hours about how she was scared. This was when she was pregnant, in the first stage of her pregnancy, the first couple of months, I think. And talk about how she remembered things that happened at the house. Some things she understood and some things still scared her. She thought about it and wondered what we thought of her when she was spaced out, and stuff like that.

She talked about her pregnancy, and about when she was here and wasn't pregnant. Everybody knew that Johanna wasn't pregnant but everybody went through Johanna's pregnancy with her. She ended up feeling better about it. Part of it was she didn't know how much was in her mind and how much was still fantasy, and it helped to check it out with me, "Yes, it did happen." "Yes, you did do that." "You did know what was going on." That said to her that at least it really happened and she wasn't freaking out again. She went through ups and downs during her pregnancy, a lot of it having to do with her living situation and her husband. I just think she's done amazingly well.

We believe that the inner voyage of the schizophrenic person, which is induced by the environmental crisis, has great potential for natural healing and growth, and we therefore do not attempt to abort, rechannel, or quell it before it has run its natural course. But, though our attitude is one of tolerance for regression, we nonetheless expect (and hope) that the person's inner voyage will eventually bring him back toward the outer world. We believe that this voyage will help him to integrate the psychotic experience into the continuity of his life and that he also will be able to come to grips with experiences of growing up which have long been denied or deliberately kept out of awareness. It is our position that, through the integration of the psychosis and of these heretofore "split-off" fragments of experience, the schizophrenic person can develop the ability to use coping skills previously unavailable to him and can learn new ones. We also believe that the psychosis can act as the individual's rite de passage into adulthood—a ritual which has been noted as lacking in this culture. From this perspective, too, it may do the individual an injustice to deprive him of the spontaneous psychotic experience.

At Soteria House, the staff are to be respectful, tolerant, empathetic, and sensitive to the person's crisis, but they are not to reinforce or perpetuate the regression unnecessarily. Regression is not regarded as an end in itself. The ability to identify the cues given by those who are beginning to emerge from a regression is a delicate clinical skill, but not one which has thus far proved impossible to attain. When recognized, those cues are acknowledged and validated as strongly as the voyage into the depths had been previously. In this way we hope to avoid unnecessary perpetuation of the regressed state, which can only lead to a career as a mental patient.

Our theory is one of crisis and development, but this does not mean that we believe that every person who is admitted to the house will be in such a state of crisis or that the regressive inner voyage is always necessary to recovery; nor does it mean that we have preconceptions about the reasons for a crisis's occurrence. Rather, we attempt to see each crisis as a unique experience which can nonetheless be shared, understood, and put into perspective. How the crisis evolves and is ultimately resolved should be determined by the resident, not by the staff. But we hope our accepting attitude will help him to take seriously, look at, deal with, come to terms with, and learn from his crisis. We hope too that our presence will make him feel less alone and that he will find comfort in our ability to stand by and support him in his turmoil. It seems to us that the family-like intimacy of the setting is particularly well-suited to the development of trust and a willingness

to explore the inner self without fearing punishment for it or being used to meet the needs of others. In addition, the house makes quite clear that it will meet the individual's needs so long as he is unable to do so himself.

There are important differences between Soteria House and other psychotherapeutically oriented settings. (1) The house is a nonauthoritarian, nonhierarchical organization. All staff members are viewed as equal in overall therapeutic potential, and they interact as a group of peers. I act as research and referral coordinator, supervisor, and mother hen but am not viewed as a "special" therapeutic person. Our part-time psychiatrist evaluates each resident, takes care of medical records, and supervises staff but is not a primary therapist in the house. Although we emphasize the need for schizophrenics to feel "successful," we do not mean this in a competitive sense. We want to maximize the possibility of our residents controlling their own destinies, however they wish to define them. In this setting success is defined in strictly individual terms. We believe this view is most congruent with the nonauthoritarian, fraternal orientation of the house. (2) The house has flexibility of response, which is difficult to achieve in hospital-based care. For example, crisis sessions last as long as necessary, because our staff can and will commonly spend six or even up to eighteen hours at a stretch with an individual resident. In addition, the scheduling of the "therapy" is not based on staff needs and routinely takes place in a variety of settings. (3) The staff have sufficient time and energy to allow the issues to be acknowledged and worked through at the height of intense crisis. The individual in crisis is allowed, encouraged, and supported in exploring reasons for whatever "irrational" acts are concomitants of the crisis. They are handled without resorting to such angry rebuffs as "Now, look what you've done" or "What did you think you'd accomplish with that?" (4) We have a flexible role allocation in our approach to crisis. We feel this is both unusual and extremely important in terms of the person's learning to model and imitate behaviors he becomes acquainted with in the setting. (5) There is the absence of the kind of magical expectations which inevitably are attributed to "the therapist" in ordinary psychotherapeutic settings. At Soteria two or three persons, including other patients, may be seen as therapeutically important, thus diluting any "expert," "fixer" role of an individual. This also seems to lessen the effects of one person's absence, decrease the potential for an overexclusive shared dependency, and make countertransference problems less common.

So now back to the beginning, myself, why me? At times I feel that

all my life experiences were preparation for being a part of this house.
I remember well all the other jobs I've had; they were good for me,
and I was good. I learned from them. But I know that I could never
go back. I have learned a better way. I have come very far.

I was born about ten thousand years ago
there ain't nothing in this world that I don't know.

Of course I was the middle daughter, born to my parents about nine
months after they left New York City and came to California for a new
life where my father was to take over an Italian newspaper. My father
had left southern Italy and a promising career as a young lawyer. He
had been an active socialist there and refused to live under Mussolini
and his threatened persecution. Both my parents were members of a
small minority of Italians whose mission was to defeat fascism in their
native country and to improve the lot of working people in the United
States. They were highly individualistic, eschewing organized religion,
anticapitalistic, and blessed with an optimism in the potential of
humanity with reason and technology truly to create a better world,
without war and without want. They set out for California to continue
to work for this end.

Both parents were determined that the children be well-educated.
They taught us their optimism and hope for the future. We believed
that we were indeed citizens of the world and that thought and reason
could save humanity. When I was a small child my mother arranged,
with little money, to have me learn many things. At about age three
I had piano lessons, dancing, and art classes at various neighborhood
houses around San Francisco. These lessons in refinement continued
on through high school.

I look back on my adolescence with extreme sorrow. I was a total
misfit in high school and looked upon my two or three musically talented boyfriends as inadequate misfits also. I got through high school
in three years, missing at least two months of school each year. I read
everything I could—lots of Shaw, Mann, Freud, and music. Music and
art were the only important things in my life. I worried that I was not
talented enough to become a great musician.

I went away to college and shared an apartment with two other girls.
I enjoyed learning but was very concerned about the problem of a
middle-class person attempting to solve problems for individuals in
other social groups. I was convinced and trapped by the idea that I was
just a product of my culture. After a few months away at school I began
to feel that there was something seriously wrong with me. I stayed in
bed for days at a time (while this was not much different from what

I had done in high school, I did not wish it to be happening now). I missed a lot of classes and got a D in my favorite class, cultural anthropology. I applied for treatment at the college mental health clinic and was seen weekly there for about seven months. I like to think that I was a subject for the work that Mary Sarvis did at Berkeley. About that time she did some of the very earliest research on time-limited treatment. At any rate, the treatment there helped me through the separation from the family: I think I experienced a classic identity crisis. When I felt bad I did not know who I was or what I wanted to be; I could not separate myself from what others wanted me to be.

I soon discovered modern dance and was a full member of the national dance sorority. Dance provided a great release and, perhaps even more than music, provided me with greater transcendental experiences. I did fairly well in course work, learning psychological theory from Tolman, Postman, and their group. I liked studying psychology, anthropology, and sociology.

During my third year in college I met my husband. We were very poor students: in the beginning my husband worked weekends as a janitor and taught Hebrew during the week. I worked as a switchboard operator at the Women's Faculty Club and as a food demonstrator giving out samples in markets on Friday and Saturday. It was a good year.

After receiving my B.A. in psychology I got the only job I could that was related to my interest—a secretary to a school psychologist in a near-by school system. The two of us sat in a tiny office (without space enough for him to chase me around the room). I was a terrible typist. I was most unhappy at this job and recall several afternoons spent sobbing alone in the little office. I wanted to be the psychologist; I thought I could do a better job. I had an opportunity to observe the workings of a school system. I had thought that one day I too might finish my studies to be a school psychologist. As a peripheral person in this institution I could watch the mediocrity, the petty jealousies, the bureaucratic and senseless procedures. I resolved never again to work in a school system. So I decided to end it all: I became pregnant. My husband was still in school and while we both wanted to be parents, it certainly was an inconvenient time. However, we did manage— eating horsemeat, sand dabs, and day-old bread. My husband took on more Hebrew lessons. I was at home for most of the pregnancy— enjoyed it thoroughly—the only time in my life that I have been entirely self-indulgent. I gave birth triumphantly.

When my daughter was one year old I took a job as an administrator of a union welfare fund. I didn't know much about the work but

learned fast. The office was a large series of cubicles on the edge of a large hiring hall and pool room. I remember blushing each morning as I entered the building and walked the entire length of the pool hall to my cubicle. The looks and the remarks were standard procedure for any woman transgressing into this man's world. Although I had worked for several other unions, I had never before been so closely involved with the membership. My boss was a huge, Irish, hard-drinking old IWW guy. The members were hard-working men from many parts of the world. I was fascinated by my boss's ability to lead this band of ruffians and to negotiate with employers and insurance companies. I learned a lot about how groups work on that job and look back on it warmly.

My husband completed his Ph.D. Again I became a housewife: my daughter was three and I took on the "career" of co-op nursery school mother.

My son was born four years after my daughter. The birth was another feat—even the right sex! I was a better parent the second time around. I remember realizing that my daughter was teaching me how to be a child—to play like a child, to enjoy like a child.

When my son was one year old I took a job. It was as an organizer for a consumers cooperative. I liked it—arranging consumer education programs, helping people become more involved in the co-op concept, and providing the organizational skills for a variety of grass-roots programs. Again, by watching the leaders and by trying things out for myself, I learned more about how and why groups of people band together to achieve some common goal and how the individual's need for community can be used to achieve those goals. I left this job when my third child was born.

Despite my work during these years of small children, I saw my main task as helping my husband in his career, running an intense social life, raising my children, and, if there was anything left, getting something for myself. I remember often feeling like my husband's child and sometimes like my daughter's child.

I was twenty-nine years old and was just experiencing myself as grown up. I again took up an old dream, long cast aside, to go traveling. I decided to go for an extended visit to Israel. I needed money to finance my trip so I found a job through friends as a technical writer at an electronics firm. I felt myself blooming: I could do anything. I did very well at work and realized that I liked going away from home each day, doing interesting work. I resumed dancing, took courses in existential philosophy, dabbled with meditation, and even found time to play the cello! I decided that I would continue to work even after the

trip but that I needed more training to do something I liked better. Although I was well-paid, I resented working for a profit-making organization. I applied to graduate school in social welfare and planned my trip. Instead of going just to Israel, I, with my three children, set forth on April Fools' Day for a four-month trip around the world. My eldest daughter was nine, my son five, and my little girl two and a half and in diapers. I regard this event as my rite of passage into adulthood. I recall being conscious of my sense of smell: it seemed I went about smelling the world.

When I returned, I felt that all the world is beautiful and that I could live in many places but that this place was my home and quite good enough. I entered grad school, commuting 120 miles daily. I felt being in school was absurd at my age—another feat to complete. I recall amusing myself while running late to class with the thought that school was keeping me out of the pool halls. Although I did very well in schoool, I felt that I was teaching myself and continually making judgments about what was worthwhile learning and what I wanted to know. Sullivan, Erikson, Goffman, and Don Jackson were revelations to me. I became enchanted with crisis theory and concepts of culture and mental illness. I was confused by the varieties of behavior theories we were taught and annoyed by the teachers who said we should be eclectic. I was a student during the Free Speech Movement at Berkeley, when students and faculties were just beginning to discover the notion of relevance. Because of my marginality in this group and my prior education in the school of hard knocks, I was able to get through the course of study discovering my own relevancy. I feel I was well-trained, although during the experience I was angry and complaining all the way. I learned of the history and of the inadequacies of many of the established social institutions, and I was taught to call myself a "change agent," I learned how one intervenes in these social institutions to benefit the client and how change is the result of a confluence of forces. My first internship was as a case worker in the welfare department. I was appalled by the bureaucratic procedures which only impeded the client's efforts to get financial assistance and seemed only to provide jobs for welfare employees to save and carry papers about from place to place. I worked with families oppressed by poverty for generations, who, because of poor health, inadequate housing, inadequate vocational opportunities, and inadequate educational opportunities, were further oppressed and treated as nonpeople by welfare departments, county hospitals, schools, courts, probation departments, money lenders, and public defenders. I recall the first client I had who was psychotic. I did not know that this was her label; my supervisor had

to provide it. I only knew that she was very troubled, that her problems were legion, and that I was supposed to do something about them. Given the problems in her life I did not see how she could be otherwise. I brought her to my teacher and supervisor. She was put in a hospital, and I spent the next two days in my bed wondering why on earth I wanted to be a social worker.

I struggled with this question for the two years of graduate school. My second year internship was at a V.A. hospital, and although I gained skills in dealing with clients and institutions, I became further convinced that the hospital as a social institution was bankrupt. I finished my training resolved never to work with crazy people in crazy hospitals. Yes, institutions are a mess, but I was allowed to learn that they were a mess. And only people who are aware of this can effect changes in the system, and they can at least minimize the damage done to the people they are supposed to serve.

After graduation I took a position at the local state hospital resolved to become part of the movement to empty the hospitals. I did not realize that changes would occur so quickly. During the time I was in the system drastic changes were effected in the rights of the mentally ill in the state of California, and the community mental health systems grew rapidly. The hospital was finally closed. The movement to close hospitals left us with the need to develop other methods to deal with that deviance called schizophrenia.

The three years that I have been a part of Soteria House have been the culmination of all the experiences of my past life. I began as the daughter of humanistic visionaries, believing in their dream for a better world, living long enough to see that in this real world the more things change, the more they remain the same. Because of this belief, my sorties into the educational system, the trade union movement, the cooperative movement, the electronics industry, advanced education, and the established mental health system have been as an on-looker. I understood and learned many things, especially how people can get together to accomplish goals and how institutional structures and histories can sabotage the best efforts of the most well-meaning and ablest of us, sometimes without our being aware of our own impotence.

At least for these three years, the Soteria experiment has managed not to succumb to this danger. Those of us who work at Soteria know experientially how it is a better place than the traditional hospital. It is a place which encourages growth not only for those who come for help, but also for those who help. I know that my own sense of self has changed. I wear my professionalism with more ease. I am less angry. I am more aware of and more comfortable with my own craziness. My

Soterians simply say I'm more disorganized. I am less grandiose. As a child I set out to change the world. At Soteria I have learned, and I delight in the way we *have* changed the world, if only in a small way.

Author's Note

Those of you who wish a more academic presentation of Soteria House and the work we do there may refer to the following professional papers:

Mosher, L. R. "Research Design to Evaluate a Psychosocial Treatment of Schizophrenia," in Rubinstein, D., and Alanen, Y.O., eds. *Psychotherapy of Schizophrenia.* Amsterdam: Excerpta Medica Foundation, 1972, pp. 251–260. Reprinted in *Hospital and Community Psychiatry,* 23:229–234 (1972).

Mosher, L. R., Reifman, A., and Menn, A. "Characteristics of Non-Professionals Serving as Primary Therapists for Acute Schizophrenics," *Hospital and Community Psychiatry,* 24(6):391–396 (1973).

9. Rap Groups

ROBERT JAY LIFTON

One of the main themes of these essays is the effects of one's politics, not of one's political beliefs or the number of causes one has joined, but of one's beliefs about what a fair and just society ought to be on how one practices and defines the task of therapy. In this account, consisting of Chapter 3 and parts of Chapter 14 of his book *Home From the War,* Robert Jay Lifton relates how his political involvement in the Vietnam War led to a new type of healing community and a new professional role for him as helper as well as advocate. To me, this account is important because so many therapists express a sort of helplessness or disconnection between their feelings about society and social institutions and an often highly conventional and even oppressive style of work and institutional identification, which contradicts their sincerely held beliefs. It is my feeling that a therapist who is a radical has to undertake the kind of examination of himself, his personal relationships, and the structure within which he offers help that Bob has begun by his participation in the rap groups and the antiwar movement, which is as inseparable from his research and professional concerns as his therapy, as practiced here, is from his politics.

Bob Lifton is a professor of psychiatry at Yale Medical School. His works concern the connection of personal transformation with social and historical events, to which he applies the term "psychohistory." His books include *History and Human Survival, Death in Life, Thought Reform and the Psychology of Totalism,* and *Boundaries.* He is currently working on a book on a "new" paradigm of death and the continuity of life, and doing research on the "formative" patterns of radical and innovative professionals.

From *Home From the War* (New York: Simon and Schuster, 1973), pp. 75–90, 92, 411–414, 422–426. Copyright © 1973 by Robert Jay Lifton.

Vietnam rap groups came into being because of antiwar veterans' sense that they had more psychological work to do in connection with the war. The groups evolved from correspondence and telephone discussions between Jan Barry, then president of the Vietnam Veterans Against the War, and myself. In his first letter to me (November, 1970) Barry spoke of "two perhaps separate projects which we are trying to bring together as one": the first, doing something about "the severe psychological problems of many Vietnam veterans because of their experiences"; and the second, countering "the military policy of the war which results in war crimes and veterans' nightmares." As part of this second point, he invited me to participate in the Detroit Winter Soldier Investigation (January, 1971), one of the first and certainly the largest of the public meetings at which veterans have given testimony on American atrocities in Vietnam—and I did eventually become a panelist at that memorable gathering.

Barry was less specific about the first matter, a psychological program for veterans. He asked about circulating a statement on the brutalization of GIs I had made earlier that year to a Senate subcommittee, and about the possibility of my preparing further commentaries for, and exchanging ideas with, a number of the veterans. But from the beginning of our discussions, in his mind as well as in my own, the political-ethical and psychological-therapeutic components were inseparable.

I called in Dr. Chaim Shatan, a psychoanalyst at New York University with whom I had worked previously on issues surrounding American war crimes; when he and I sat down with Jan Barry and several others from VVAW, we all met in antiwar colleagueship. The veterans told us how intensely VVAW members "rapped" with one another in the office—about the war, American society, and their own lives—and how they felt they would like to have people around with greater psychological knowledge. I suggested that we form more regular rap groups, which seemed to be what the veterans themselves had in mind. What evolved, then, was initiated by the veterans, and had direct continuity with informal processes already taking place among them.

It also seemed natural for us to schedule meetings at the VVAW office—on the veterans' own turf—where the group I have been part of met regularly for two years. Though the place was modest and its facilities cramped, the occasional suggestion that we meet at some more comfortable place—a university or an office of one of the professionals—was either vaguely rejected ("It's easier to meet here") or ignored. Another group did make such a move, but only after a good

deal of trust and cohesiveness had developed after six months of weekly meetings, and that move could have been a factor in the group's later demise. Otherwise, all meetings have continued to take place at the VVAW office (the rap groups moving with VVAW when it changed its office site) as one of the kinds of personal involvement for veterans made available at that office.

We made plans for weekly two-hour sessions. But the atmosphere in those early groups was so charged and so compelling that nobody left at the appointed time, and we got into the habit of continuing the meetings for three hours or more. The explosion of feeling that occurred, associated as it was with a war whose pain pervaded all of our lives, rendered those first meetings unforgettable in their emotional power and poignancy.

Mostly through Dr. Shatan's efforts, we quickly formed a panel of professionals from psychological and psychiatric colleagues in the New York City area. From the beginning he and I had a sense of groping toward, or perhaps being caught up in, a new group form. Though far from clear about exactly what that form would be, we found ourselves responding to the general atmosphere by stressing informality and avoiding a medical model. Hence, we called ourselves "professionals" rather than "therapists" (the veterans sometimes discarded both and referred to us as "shrinks"), and the meetings "rap groups" (which stuck) rather than "group therapy." The casual, first-name basis on which we had come together extended directly into the groups, as did the fluidity in boundaries between professionals and veterans. Another part of the group's evolving ethos was the requirement, at first unspoken and later discussed, that everyone put a great deal of himself or herself on the line—a process that seemed natural enough to the veterans but was a bit more problematic for the professionals. As people used to interpreting others' motivations, it was at first a bit jarring to be confronted with hard questions about our own, and with challenges about the way we lived. Not only was our willingness to share this kind of involvement crucial to the progress of the group, but in the end many of us among the professionals came to value and enjoy this kind of dialogue.

As in certain parallel experiments taking place, not only in psychological work but throughout American culture, we had a clearer idea of what we opposed (hierarchical distancing, medical mystification, psychological reductionism that undermines political and ethical ideas) than of what we favored as specific guidelines. But before long I came to recognize three principles that seemed important. The first was that of *affinity*, the coming together of people who share a particu-

lar (in this case overwhelming) historical or personal experience, along with a basic perspective on that experience, in order to make some sense of it (the professionals entered into this "affinity," at least to a certain extent, by dint of their political-ethical sympathies and inclination to act and experiment on behalf of them). The second principle was that of *presence*, a kind of being-there or full engagement and openness to mutual impact—no one ever being simply a therapist against whom things are rebounding. The third was that of *self-generation*, the need on the part of those seeking help, change, or insight of any kind, to initiate their own process and conduct it largely on their own terms so that, even when calling in others with expert knowledge, they retain major responsibility for the shape and direction of the enterprise. Affinity, presence, and self-generation seem to be necessary ingredients for making a transition between old and new images and values, particularly when these relate to ultimate concerns, to shifting modes of symbolic immortality.

Things did not always go smoothly. Confusion was greatest at the beginning, but throughout the experience there has been much divergence of opinion on goals and on what was actually happening. For the first few Saturday afternoons we met as one expanding group, consisting not only of veterans (who heard about the project either through office scuttlebutt or notices sent out to VVAW membership) and a few professionals, but also occasional journalists interested in the veterans, who had arranged to be invited by one or more of them. The atmosphere became so informal and the open door policy so open that, as one of the veterans put it a bit later when the door had been closed a bit, "We felt like monkeys in a zoo." This early confusion and experimentation, however, in no way diminished the intensity of these meetings.

The group's first crisis came a month after it was formed, during which its size (fifteen to twenty veterans and three to five professionals) had increased to the point of becoming unwieldy. The idea of dividing into two groups had been mentioned repeatedly and then put aside because of the unwillingness of the veterans to make the separation. Finally a definite decision was made to divide the group, but all efforts to agree just how to do that ended in excruciating impasses. The "old-timers" (men who had been in the rap group from the beginning) insisted upon sticking together, causing the "newcomers" to feel bitterly rejected. The situation was finally resolved by an arbitrary suggestion on the part of one of the professionals that those sitting to his left constitute one group, and those to his right another. Later, in looking back on how painful the division had been, the veterans could

recognize their need to hold onto whatever intimacy they could achieve, and connect that need to the extreme precariousness of all intimacy in Vietnam and to their subsequent difficulty in becoming, or remaining, close to other human beings.[1]

Of the two smaller groups thus formed, one ran for about eight months, and the other (the one I have been associated with) for more than two years (and is still going as of June, 1974). Each of the groups consisted initially of about twelve veterans and three to four professionals. In my group the professionals checked regularly with one another to make sure that at least one or two would be present at each session, but this usually proved quite unnecessary as all of us were profoundly drawn to the group, and on most occasions three or four of us would be there. But the style of the groups, for both veterans and professionals, was one of relatively fluid comings and goings. In my group, for instance, over a two-year period, there have been about thirty-five veterans who have participated intensively, a third of them for a year or more, another third for a minimum of ten to twenty sessions (thirty to sixty hours), and the remainder for a minimum of five sessions (fifteen hours). There have been about eighty additional veterans who came to just one to four sessions (three to twelve hours). We have had six professionals, of whom I have been the only one associated with the group throughout its life, though for periods of time some of the others have been more regularly involved than myself. A veteran-coordinator with some psychological training has had a central part in maintaining the group's continuity.

This fluidity was partly a reflection of the "open door policy" of the rap groups: from the beginning they were open to all Vietnam veterans, and, by practice, to any veteran of the Vietnam era and even to active-duty GIs when they turned up. A newcomer who expressed doubts about eligibility or a sense of belonging was likely to be told by one of the men, "You're our brother." In this sense the rap groups resembled various forms of street-corner psychiatry. Also contributing

1. At that early stage, they had not yet found their individual or collective voices sufficiently to explore and decide upon the matter in a way satisfactory to themselves. Prior to the arbitrary suggestion by the professional, the grumbling over time wasted on the decision and the rising bitterness threatened (in the retrospective opinion of a number of us) to end the rap group experiment almost before it had begun. Yet one might also speculate that, had the professionals been able to interpret more sensitively to the veterans what was happening in a way that could have facilitated their coming to their own decision about the group division, this might have contributed to still greater self-generation on their part throughout the subsequent rap group program.

to their fluidity was the style of life of the veterans—many of them traveled a great deal throughout the country, either working for VVAW or just on the move, very few had regular jobs, and their general sense of restlessness was a constant subject of discussion. Among professionals, fluidity had to do with time available and depth of interest, as well as with the evolving tradition within the groups combining intensity and flux.

But the groups differed from street-corner psychiatry in their second function, important from the beginning, of probing the destructive personal experiences of the Vietnam War for eventual dissemination to the American public. This investigative-publicizing function could come into conflict with the other goal, that of individual healing and change. While there was still just one large group, a television network asked to be permitted to record a rap session. After extensive discussion, the request was refused, but a compromise arrangement was made in which the group gathered round a television camera right after a rap session and, in response to questions, discussed the kinds of concerns and feelings it had just been talking about behind the closed door. The smaller groups then more or less formalized this kind of compromise, specifying that no one, other than veterans and designated professionals, would be permitted to sit in on the rap sessions themselves.

There was, then, a tension between openness and closure, between a bond of brotherhood extending to anyone interested in sharing something about the negative impact of the war and more focused concentration upon individual needs. The sudden appearance of new people could be jarring, and sometimes led to frustrations among regular group members who wanted desperately to talk about their own struggles. The very intrusion, however, could serve to reawaken the group's sense of being part of something much larger than itself. This openness completely disappeared in the other of the two original groups when it moved to the office of a professional, and it continued to function for only a month or two after that. In my own group, the openness was diminished somewhat, though by no means eliminated, when a decision was made (after the group had been in operation about six months) to change the meeting time from Saturday afternoon to Thursday night. The reasons governing the change had to do with scheduling problems on the part of both veterans and professionals and a general feeling that, with the warm weather, people tended not to be around on weekends. But since Saturday afternoon is always a time of more comings and goings in the VVAW office, an element in the decision might well have been the impulse, on the part of some veterans and

professionals, to sequester the group a bit, and achieve sufficient closure to focus in more on intense individual experience. On the whole, that is what happened during the year following the move, though a number of new people came and a certain amount of fluidity was retained.

This issue of openness and closure—really one of boundaries—reflects a fundamental theoretical question about the groups, felt particularly keenly by the professionals, one that has never been and perhaps cannot be resolved. It had to do with two conflicting views of the nature of the groups. Most of the professionals took the position that what we were doing was group therapy: the psychoanalysts, psychiatrists, or psychologists in the group were offering necessary therapy to the veterans who were, in effect, our patients or clients. The minority view, for which I was an active spokesman, was that we were trying to create a new institution, involved in an experiment with a new community, and that although there were definite elements of group therapy, the process could better be described as a dialogue between professionals and veterans, beginning from a common stance of opposition to the war, each drawing upon special knowledge and experience. The first understanding permitted sharp role definitions: the veteran was there to be helped, the professional to help. If we abandoned the group therapy model, the argument went, the veterans would be denied what they most needed, and in a sense cheated. But the second understanding placed greater emphasis upon sharing of roles, upon ethical and political commitments of professionals no less than veterans, and upon a generally open-ended attitude toward group norms and boundaries. This view stressed the uncertainty of the appropriateness of our psychological procedures for what it was the veterans sought, and the need for professionals to open *themselves* to change.

The disagreements, friendly but continuous, were expressed at several special meetings of professionals involved in the program and extended into the rap groups themselves. Some professionals were concerned that, if the second view of the groups were adopted, we would find ourselves prescribing "correct" political opinions as a prerequisite for group acceptance. While agreeing this would be highly undesirable, I found myself arguing that our shared antiwar position was inseparable from our capacity to contribute to the psychological well-being of the veterans and that, since political and ethical views inevitably affect and to some extent define therapeutic encounters, we would do better to examine these relationships openly.

Despite the continuing disagreement, the professionals too tended

to be drawn into the common bond of brotherhood, largely I suspect through identifying with the veterans' death immersion and survival experience. But those of us who held a more radical view of the groups tended to outlast the others in the general program—both because we were more at home with the unorthodoxy and unpredictability of the situation, and also, I suspect, more politically committed to it. Moreover, a number of the more traditionally minded therapists leaned toward the more radical-experimental view, as we all came to recognize that whatever it was we were offering attracted only a limited number of veterans, no more than enough to keep two or three groups going at any one time.

Each of the professionals tended to retain a certain personal and professional style, for which he or she became more or less known. In my group, another male professional had a keen eye for physical-spatial patterns in the group and for immediate group process. A female professional had a particular talent for exposing tendencies to avoid or cover over real feelings, often related to early family experience. Another female professional was sympathetically sensitive to seemingly bizarre behavior, which she could not only make sense of but connect readily with ordinary experience. And a third female professional had an extraordinary capacity to combine keen interpretation with warm involvement at every level. I became known for connecting individual emotions with general social and historical trends, and for my sensitivity to issues of death and survival. I also was thought of as something of a "mediator"—less likely to initiate confrontation than to express understanding for divergent positions.

Most of the veterans came into the experience knowing relatively little about group process. On the whole they tended to favor the more experimental, open-ended idea, but they had no definite collective position about the two competing visions of the group. Their reactions could be complex, however, in ways that revealed the impossibility of attributing absolute "correctness" to either of the two views. For instance, they encouraged one of their number to coordinate group arrangements, as well as referrals for individual therapy when these were sought by a veteran or recommended by a professional. Through him the veterans, in effect, ran their own program. But this same coordinator was occasionally criticized in the group for what one of the men called "training on us": for using the group for his own educational purposes as the aspiring psychologist he in fact was. They were sympathetic to the idea of an experimental community, but not at the expense of their own dignity or psychological needs.

Behind the rap group program was Vietnam, and over the course of

time one could observe an evolution in the relationship between the men and their war. During the first few meetings there was a direct focus on the war and a rush of resentment, horror, and atrocity. At times these meetings had some resemblance to public hearings, the important difference being that the men focused on themselves, upon their own guilt, pain, and rage. Emotions came in a great flood, and the strange rendition of purgatorial corruption, and commitment to growth beyond that corruption, had a profound impact on everyone present. Yet after a while the men themselves detected a tendency to "tell war stories" as a means of *avoiding* personal feelings. And after a few months there was a shift, as one of them put it, "from war stories to ourselves"—with increasing focus on here-and-now psychological struggles. Having achieved that focus the veterans could then return to the war, as they repeatedly did, but in a way that connected it to their immediate lives. Memories and images of the war then became bound up with but also subsumed in a deepening self-exploration— with subtle combinations of "war" and "now" often emerging in the dreams the men described.

Sometimes the war seemed almost forgotten during weeks of explor- ing conflicts in love relationships or jobs, only to reappear suddenly with the entrance of a newcomer who had been attracted to the rap group precisely because of painful preoccupations with things that happened in Vietnam. At the beginning of the meeting the newcomer was usually introduced around by the coordinator and then left alone for an hour or two if he chose to do some listening, as was frequently the case. Then, finally, someone would turn to him and ask him gently about himself and why he had come. He might then talk directly about the war, or about almost anything else—feelings of loneliness, "hassles" with the Veterans Administration, or desperate thoughts of suicide. The group was always solicitous and responsive. The other veterans would, in fact, manifest striking, previously hidden sensitivities. They conveyed the impression that any man who shared their catastrophe had claim on their energies. What is more, a newcomer had special value because (as one of the veterans pointed out after a year of meet- ings) "he brought us back to the war."

The men were not without their ambivalence to this continuous reactivation of war conflicts. But they sensed that repeated reexamina- tion of those conflicts, along with therapeutic help to others less far along, contributed greatly to their own transformation. There are im- portant parallels here to Alcoholics Anonymous and drug addiction programs run by former addicts. But here the habit one is kicking is war, and the commitment includes not only staying off the drug, but

making a basic political and social realignment, becoming a different kind of person.

Discussions moved quickly from present struggles to war experiences to prewar conflicts, but each meeting tended to be dominated by one or two general themes: a pattern of guilt or violence, the struggle for love and intimacy, counterfeit versus authentic situations, the ambiguities and limitations of being an antiwar veteran, the appropriateness of emotion and the capacity to feel. The themes intertwined in endless ways, yet each, in the form it took, was directly bound up with the special kinds of death immersion, survival, and struggle for meaning associated with the Vietnam War.

The combination of ultimate questions and experimental arrangements gave all in our group the feeling that we had to call upon new aspects of ourselves, become something more than we had been before. Central to this process were the changing relationships between veterans and professionals. The veterans who came regularly became increasingly sensitive to currents in the group process and began to assert themselves more and offer forthright judgments on the professionals. For instance, on one occasion several veterans strongly praised one of the professionals for having pressed them toward self-examination and away from "telling war stories." But when that same professional, perhaps partly in response to their praise, continued to assert individual-psychological (and past-oriented) interpretations that diverted a few of the veterans from other immediate issues they were bent on exploring, one of them (with a little background experience in psychological work) angrily rebuked her for insisting upon a narrow perspective under the guise of neutrality and for being too conventional in her psychological approach. True to form, I found myself meditating—agreeing with the veteran and saying so, but also affirming the professional's good faith in seeking to illuminate suppressed conflicts.

Looking back now, I realize that this kind of mediating on my part probably perpetuated some of the ambiguity of the group—I neither rejected her conventional, somewhat reductionist approach out of hand nor insisted upon its complete replacement by the model of a new community. But in mediating in this fashion I was reflecting both the dual feelings of the veterans themselves and my own struggles toward responsible forms of professional and political radicalism and advocacy research.

During that same meeting one of the veterans began to describe, with considerable ambivalence, the images of me he held—that of an eminent professor and writer who sent him a letter on elegant Yale

stationery (implying a mixture of distance, resentment, and admiration), and that of an ordinary fellow named Bob who was regularly in the group and with whom he felt easy. Toward the end of that session, one of the more quiet and self-effacing veterans suddenly came out with a still sharper comment: "You can disagree with her [referring to the conflict with the other professional], but at least she is here in the group with us. What about Bob Lifton—taking all those notes? Is he really in the group?" During earlier discussions of purposes and motivations I had told the group of my efforts to combine investigative, therapeutic, and antiwar commitments, and of my intent to do some writing about the rap group experience, all of which had apparently been well accepted. I had taken some notes in the past, but that day I had been taking particularly extensive notes and was jarred not only by the sudden confrontation but by my immediate feeling that there was much justice in the criticism. I responded by both affirming my intention to write on the subject (which again nobody objected to), and at the same time admitting a certain insensitivity and distancing in taking extensive notes (which is what they *had* objected to).

The professional who had been criticized earlier then complimented the veteran on his "courage" in confronting me—adding that she had felt like saying the same thing on a number of occasions but had not had the nerve to do so. To which I commented that the veterans, lacking professional training, had less to unlearn. At the end of the session, another of the professionals told me, gently but definitely, that she too had been uncomfortable about my taking notes, and offered to sit down with me and pool our memories if I wished to reconstruct exactly what had gone on in a particular meeting.

After thinking about the matter, I decided simply to cease taking any notes at all—which was briefly and favorably noted in a later session. I found I could reconstruct most of what went on—including key phrases used—by jotting down recollections right after the session and dictating a detailed summary a little later. And although I had always felt myself to be actively immersed in the group process, my involvement became a bit more intense and personal. Sometime later I discussed that particular confrontation with a colleague, who was critical of the veterans for what he viewed as the kind of exaggerated demand for concrete, personal encounter so characteristic of young people today, and who thought I should have held to my investigator's prerogative and continued taking notes. But I saw the matter differently. What had been at issue was the veterans' pride and emerging confidence in shaping their own group pattern: they could accept a wide variety of styles, motivations, and conceptual positions on the part of professionals, but demanded full "presence" from them. Aware

that much of what was happening would eventually reach beyond that small room, their sense of dignity nonetheless required that they reject any arrangement that could be construed as making them into mere objects of study.

On the whole the fluidity of boundaries between professionals and veterans encouraged feelings of relaxed camaraderie. Members of the rap group came to see me about plans of one kind or another; I wrote recommendations for a few of them; and on one occassion I prepared a statement relating a veteran's conflicts to his war experience for use in a minor court procedure. On a number of occasions I drove between New York and New Haven with veterans in the rap group, or had meals or drinks or coffee with them, in connection with various psychological and political meetings we participated in together. Yet the boundaries by no means disappeared: what we have been able to do together has depended upon our distinctness and separateness from one another as well as upon intense common concerns.

My impression has been that this dialectic between "presence" and separateness has generally been well understood and mutually comfortable. But not always. At one meeting I did not attend, at which there were only two veterans and two professionals (word had gone out to most of the others that the meeting would be canceled because of an organizational action on that day, but those who came decided to go ahead with a rap group anyway), an issue came up during which a professional, in response to a veteran's prodding, agreed to "get out of my therapist's bag" and "mix it up." Which he did, in the process telling one of the veterans that he very frequently thought him "full of shit." At subsequent meetings the veteran expressed his hurt and anger, and pursued the question of what the whole incident had meant. Reviewing the sequence of the exchange, it became clear that the professional had become irritated with the veteran's attempt to assume a therapeutic stance toward others as a way of avoiding his own emotions. But another important element was the increasing alienation from the group on the part of that professional, who had earlier been central to its function. The meetings had become problematic for him, partly because of their changed time, but also for other reasons that could well have been related to conflicts over roles and boundaries. In any case his little outburst was a kind of parting shot, as he did not again appear. The matter was never fully resolved, but the veteran could readily accept my own comment that professionals, in "getting out of their therapist bags" and "mixing it up," were as capable as anyone else of losing their balance, showing bias, being less than perfectly controlled.

This was the only incident of its kind, and one could probably say

that the veteran and professional concerned expressed rather bluntly the kind of feelings that often exist but remain unsaid in various therapeutic or partly therapeutic situations. Yet much of the veteran's hurt had to do with the degree of mentorship and interpretive power vested in the professionals. Without saying so, the effort on the part of everyone in the group was to avoid classical forms of "transference," in which patients are expected to revive and project onto therapists infantile feelings originally experienced in relationship to parents; and to create instead an atmosphere in which the professionals' undoubted therapeutic authority could coexist with genuine mutuality and individual autonomy. But I do not think that kind of atmosphere can be created without significant tensions from both sides—professionals rendered anxious by less role structuring than they are used to, and veterans touchy about professionals' therapeutic authority, both wanting it to exist (which is why they called professionals in) and resenting any suggestion of infringement upon their own autonomy.[2]

In general, our group was made up of people who would not otherwise have come into ready contact with one another. But for the war and, one suspects, the antiwar movement, most of the veterans would not have sought out professional psychological help—because neither their social-intellectual backgrounds, nor their degree of psychiatric disturbance, would have inclined them toward such help. Nor would the professionals have encountered either the veterans or each other in such intensive group interplay. In this serendipitous mix, everyone's preexisting assumptions were challenged: the veterans' notions of what "shrinks" were like, and how much of self and society had to be examined in order to make a genuine break from the war; and professionals' ideas about neutrality and advocacy, the efficacy of standard psychological practice for unstandard situations, and how to risk a bit more of oneself in one's work than one was accustomed to; and on both sides, about dealing with uncharted situations growing out of catastrophic war and rapid social change.

The rap groups involve people in risk, a stance that came more easily to veterans than to professionals. The whole experience raised questions for me about my own profession and the professions in general —about the extent to which everyday professional function means washing away these struggles around integrity instead of pursuing

2. Descriptions of racial, religious, and other background characteristics of people in the groups—and what has happened to them—can be found on pp. 90–93 of *Home From the War.*

them, the extent to which the special armor of professionals blocks free exchange between them and the people they ostensibly serve.

Part of the excitement a number of us experienced in the rap groups had to do with divesting ourselves of that professional armor. The same was true for me in individual interviews—more dialogues—in which I would at times discuss or answer for my own views and actions concerning the Vietnam War, being a professor at Yale, the psycho-analytic movement, marriage and family, and just about anything else. This in no way meant a merging of my role and the veterans'; they in fact remained quite distinct. As an antiwar psychiatric investigator I was both gathering information and helping with a therapeutic proce-dure; the veteran told of Vietnam experiences in order to contribute both to my investigation and to his own understanding and well-being. This was not my initial foray into unorthodox investigation: I had done idiosyncratic research in Hong Kong and in three cities in Japan, as well as in the United States, all of which involved open dialogue and considerable improvisation. But I felt on this occasion a fuller commit-ment to the entire process—to what I would call my investigative advocacy—than I had in any previous work. This was partly because all of us, veterans and professionals alike, were more or less in the middle of the problem—the war continued and we all had painful emotions about what it was doing, and what we were doing or not doing to combat it.

But I also came to realize that, apart from the war, the work had important bearing upon a sense of long-standing crisis affecting all of us in the psychological professions and the professions in general—a crisis the war in Vietnam both accentuated and illuminated but by no means created. We professionals, in other words, came to the rap groups with our own need for a transformation in many ways parallel to that we sought to enhance in veterans. We too, sometimes with less awareness than they, were in the midst of struggles around living and working that had to do with intactness and wholeness, with what we have been calling integrity.

One source of perspective on that struggle, I found, was a return to the root idea of profession, the idea of what it means to profess. Indeed, an examination of the evolution of these two words could provide something close to a cultural history of the West. The Latin prefix *pro* means "forward," "toward the front," "forth," "out," or "into a public position." *Fess* derives from the Latin *fateri* or *fass*, meaning "to confess, own, acknowledge." To profess (or be professed) then, origi-nally meant a personal form of out-front public acknowledgment. And that which was acknowledged or confessed always (until the sixteenth

century) had to do with religion: with taking the vows of a religious order or declaring one's religious faith. But as society became secularized, the word came to mean "to make claim to have knowledge of an art or science" or "to declare oneself expert or proficient in" an enterprise of any kind. The noun form, "profession," came to suggest not only the act of professing, but also the ordering, collectivization, and transmission of the whole process. The sequence was from "profession" or religious conviction (from the twelfth century) to a particular order of "professed persons," such as monks or nuns (fourteenth century) to "the occupation which one professes to be skilled in and follow," especially "the three learned professions of divinity, law, and medicine" along with "the military profession." So quickly did the connotations of specialization and application take hold that as early as 1605 Francis Bacon could complain: "Amongst so many great foundations of colleges in Europe, I find strange that they are all dedicated to professions, and none left free to Art and Sciences at large."

Thus the poles of meaning around the image of profession shifted from the proclamation of personal dedication to transcendent principles to membership in and mastery of a specialized form of socially applicable knowledge and skill. In either case the profession is immortalizing—the one through the religious mode, the other through works and social-intellectual tradition. And the principles of public proclamation and personal discipline carry over from the one meaning to the other—the former taking the shape of examination and licensing, the latter of study, training, and dedication. Overall, the change was from advocacy based on faith to technique devoid of advocacy.[3]

To be sure, contemporary professions do contain general forms of advocacy: in law, of a body of supra-personal rules applicable to every-

3. One can observe this process in the modern separation of "profession" from "vocation." Vocation also has a religious origin in the sense of being "called by God" to a "particular function or station." The secular equivalent became the idea of a personal "calling" in the sense of overwhelming inclination, commitment, and even destiny. But the Latin root of vocation, *vocā, re*, to call, includes among its meanings and derivatives: vocable, vocation, vouch; advocate, advocation, convoke, evoke, invoke, provoke, and revoke. Advocacy is thus built into the original root and continuing feel of the word vocation; and vocation in turn is increasingly less employed in connection with the work a man or woman does. If we do not say profession, we say "occupation," which implies seizing, holding, or simply filling in space in an area of in time; or else "job," a word of unclear origin that implies a task, activity, or assignment that is, by implication, self-limited or possibly part of a larger structure including many related jobs, but not, in essence, related to an immortalizing tradition or principle.

one; in medicine, of healing; and in psychiatry, of humane principles of psychological well-being and growth. But immediate issues of value-centered advocacy and choice (involving groups and causes served and consequences thereof) are mostly ignored. In breaking out of the pre-modern trap of immortalization by personal surrender to faith, the "professional" has fallen into the modern trap of pseudo-neutrality and covert immortalization of technique. As a result, our professions are all too ready to offer their techniques to anyone and anything.

Large numbers of American psychiatrists, in the midst of their considerable success, are experiencing profound uneasiness bordering on despair. One feels that despair in the anxious defensiveness of the psychiatric and psychoanalytic older generation, as well as in the confused eclecticism of younger professionals. Allen Wheelis, one of the first to point out this recent wave of despair, attributed it to the mature psychoanalyst's inner division between continuing to profess publicly the truth of the elaborate conceptual scheme he inherited while privately losing faith in it and denying and violating it. Leslie Farber's description of "therapeutic despair" in many who treat schizophrenic patients involves a similar division between proclamation of special "meanings" in therapeutic transactions that endow first patient and then therapist with "oracular powers"—and the actual "emptiness, meaninglessness, and lack of confirmation" in the work. These legacies operate in many of the psychiatrists-in-training I regularly teach, who express in varied combinations: disbelief in most received theory (sometimes taking the form of a desperate embrace of that theory), criticism bordering on contempt for the morality (or immorality) of the profession, and a sensitive openness to a variety of currents consistent with what I have described as the Protean style. They often strike me as young men and women awaiting a transformation of their profession and of themselves, a transformation that seems always in the offing but never quite accessible.

I believe that parallel dilemmas exist throughout the professions, and are part of a broader psychohistorical dislocation. I focus on my own profession both because it is my own and because its particular ethical-psychological struggles are especially well-illuminated by encounters with Vietnam veterans. I believe that psychiatric stasis and despair have to do with a shared sense of breakdown in integrity and wholeness around two untenable self images: that of the master psychological scientist-technician and that of the omniscient spiritual guide. Put simply, American culture has so technicized the idea of psychiatric illness and cure that the psychiatrist or psychoanalyst is

thrust into a stance of scientifically based spiritual omniscience—a stance he is likely to find much too seductive to refuse entirely. Anointed with both omniscience and objectivity, and working within a market economy, his allegedly neutral talents become available to the highest bidder. In a militarized society they are equally available to the war makers.

The technicist model in psychiatry works something like this: A machine, the mind-body function of the patient, has broken down; another machine, more scientifically sophisticated—the psychiatrist— is called upon to "treat" the first machine; and the treatment process itself, being technical, has nothing to do with place, time, or individual idiosyncrasy. It is merely a matter of being a technical-medical antago- nist of a "syndrome" or "disease." Nor is this medical-technical model limited to physicians—nonmedical psychoanalysts and psychother- apists can be significantly affected by it. And the problem is not so much the medical model as such as it is the technicism operating within that model. The technicism in turn feeds (and is fed by) a denial of acting within and upon history.

To be sure no psychiatrist sees himself as functioning within this admittedly overdrawn model. But its lingering technicism is very much with us and can have the catastrophic results we have observed. Even psychological groups bent on breaking out of this technicism, such as some within the humanistic psychology movement (or "third force"), can be rendered dependent upon it by their very opposition, to the point of being unable to evolve an adequate body of theory and practice of their own.

An alternative perspective, in my judgment, must be not only psy- chohistorical, but also psychoformative. By the latter I mean a stress upon the evolution of inner forms and upon the specifically human mental process of inwardly re-creating all that is perceived or encoun- tered. My stress is upon what can be called a formative-symbolic *pro- cess,* upon symbolization rather than any particular symbol (in the sense of one thing standing for another). The approach connects with much in twentieth-century thought, and seeks to overcome the nine- teenth-century emphasis upon mechanism, with its stress upon break- down of elements into component parts—an emphasis inherited, at least in large part, by psycho*analysis,* as the word itself suggests. Twentieth-century technicism could be described as an aberrant (and in a sense nostalgic) re-creation of nineteenth-century mechanism. In contrast, a focus upon images and forms (the latter more structured and more enduring than the former) and upon their continuous devel-

opment and re-creation gives the psychiatrist a way of addressing historical forces without neglecting intrapsychic concerns.

The antiwar passions of a particular Vietnam veteran, for instance, had to be understood as a combined expression of many different psychic images and forms: the Vietnam environment and the forces shaping it; past individual history; the post-Vietnam American experience, including VVAW and the rap groups and the historical forces shaping these; and the various emanations of guilt, rage, and altered self-process that could and did take shape. Moreover, professionals, like myself, who entered into the lives of these veterans—with our own personal and professional histories, personal struggles involving the war, and much else—became very much a part of the overall image-form constellation.

Applied to more routine situations, this perspective would view people undergoing discomfort or incapacity, and the "healers" or "professionals" of any kind from whom they sought assistance, as coming together at a particular historical moment during which a culture tends to promote certain styles of disturbance (or deformation) and certain kinds of "treatment" (or resymbolization). The understanding that their approach is only one among many socio-historical possibilities could foster, among "healers" (not only psychiatrists and psychoanalysts but teachers, clergymen, and in many cases social and political activists) crucial restraints against technicism and claim to omniscience. With that knowledge also conveyed to those who seek help or change, choices are possible for everyone: "seekers" may select healers sympathetic to the forms they wish to cultivate (whether having to do with religious mysticism, political radicalism, or personal openness); and even if their quest for integrity and new integration should lead them to modify or abandon these forms, they would be active agents in those decisions rather than becoming passively entrapped in someone else's (often counterfeit) expertise. The healer, in turn, would make conscious decisions about where he wishes to apply his capacities, according to the personal and professional forms he seeks to investigate or cultivate. He would thus combine the technical knowledge and skill associated with his profession with ethical and political decisions concerning what he does, to what effect, and for whose benefit. And these decisions would involve not only people he seeks to work with but institutions and groups with whom he becomes affiliated and the overall question of the extent to which he lends his talents to perpetuating—as opposed to significantly changing—existing social and political arrangements. What I am

suggesting is that the healer, no less than the seeker, functions intellectually and ethically from a particular formative place, from a particular relationship to history.

The rap groups have represented a struggle on the part of veterans and psychological professionals to give form to what is, more than most realize, a common survival—for the veterans of a terrible death immersion, for the professionals of their own dislocations in relationship to the war and beyond. During our most honest moments, we professionals have admitted that the experience has been as important for our souls as for theirs.

10. Notes on the Tao of the Body Politic

MICHAEL ROSSMAN

I invited Michael Rossman to contribute to this volume (though he does not identify his work as therapy) because he is involved with learning and personal change, and the interrelationship of these processes with social change. His work develops a theme common not only to radical therapists, but also to the more conventional work of Carl Rogers and humanistic therapists: that there is a convergence between the process of education and of therapy, and between the roles of educator and therapist. As Michael does, I would add to this equation the role of community organizer. Like Bob Lifton, Michael is trying to make sense of his personal experience and outrage at our social system in a time of profound dislocation and breakdown, and trying to act on new concepts of human interaction and development. That is why I would call his practice therapy, and why I see his insights as relevant for the choices that professional therapists have to make in less troubled times. Another reason for his inclusion and the inclusion of Don Johnson's essay next is that through his political work he became engaged therapeutically with the human body—not in the usual limited way of the physician healing disease, but in comprehending the personal implications of the ways that forces of social development shape one's physical character.

Michael's books, *The Wedding within the War* and *On Learning and Social Change*, reflect his development from a student at Berkeley during the first stirrings of the student movement through some years of work in organizing alternative educational ventures. His writings have appeared in *The Village Voice, New American Review, Saturday Review, Intellectual Digest, Change,* and *Rolling Stone.*

Let me try to explain how I find myself in a book of therapists. When I think of "therapy," I think of human pain and its relief or, more generally, of dysfunction (in terms of some notion about what it means to be human, healthy, whole) and its remedy. When I started practice in the late fifties, the dimension of therapy I chose was social, and its mode was political action. I saw little reason for making arbitrary separations between the practices of social therapy, personal psychological therapy, and bodily therapy. Each dimension of therapy opens into the others, and as my work evolved, it came to include elements of all. Every ill has a private and a public root, a material and a psychical expression. I now see no reason to continue thinking of these dimensions as independent; we must face their conjugacy. Indeed, the key task of therapy today may be to arrive at an understanding and create a practice that treat the human spirit embodied in society as an integral organism.

But at a deeper level, though I often violate it, I am pledged to the view that "therapist" is a dysfunctionalizing category deepening some of the problems with which it deals. I want to melt down all the concepts and practices which perpetuate the *specialist* culture of our bureaucratoindustrial age, for they guarantee our general disenfranchisement from power over our daily life. Therapy may remain as a perspective, and skill surely will. But we must learn to be responsible for the fact that we are all therapists and that our every action has a therapeutic face, and we must make a language of some sort which reflects this, and a way of life too. I feel this as strongly about the therapeutic function of citizenship as I do about tinkering with individual psyches.

Two things strike me about therapy. One is how complex and intimate is the interplay of social and personal factors, not only in the origin of distress but in the act of its remedy and in the life of the therapist. The other is how the practice of therapy, social or personal, changes the therapist, leads her (if she will go) through personal transformations which in turn transform her practice, in a slow and integral cycling.

I hope these two themes unify the fragmentary snapshots which follow, in which I try to see myself as a therapist-person in the process of a particular transformation of work at a particular time in history. Since the late sixties a growing number of political activists, veterans of the New Left, have been turning to disciplines of the body/mind/ spirit for various reasons: some say to retreat from politics, some say to transcend it. I'm not sure how representative I am, since I see my

present turn of work as continuing my past. I think my experience as a member of this class may be more interesting for the way it illustrates the interplay of the social and the personal, which may be recognized in more conventional therapeutic life. So I focus on this aspect of my changes, rather than on more strictly intimate details.

How I Got Back into My Body, in Good Company

So how did this former sit-in leader come to find himself in a yoga posture? Human pain led me to politics young; I grew up in the New Left before it was named and worked in the Movement all through my twenties. My experiences there led me to focus on education as a crucible of political citizenship, and since 1964 most of my work, insofar as it's categorizable, has been in this domain. Attempts to remake educational institutions led me to concentrate on the *process* of institutional education, which so determines the nature of our therapeutic efforts. This concern with process led me, with others, to develop new learning forms, whose key features included the acting out of cognitive investigations by means of theater, through our bodies. This work led us to recognize the importance of the proposition that it's not simply the "whole person" who learns, but that learning is done in and with the whole body. This has led me in turn, during the past four years, to empirical research on what it's like to live in and learn in and tend a body.

This is the dry pedigree of my professional interest in the body. How I came to it as a man is richer.

In 1969 nine of us formed the Troupe. We had come to know and care for each other through the Movement. High on sixties momentum, we came together to integrate and extend our work in education, and to grow toward family. But the Troupe lasted less than a year. Perhaps we weren't committed enough to handle all the energy; certainly all our professional smarts about how to help healthy groups grow proved inadequate in the end, for we could not help ourselves, or else we chose not to. I omit the complex, painful details, but after this venture's failure I endured a paralyzed depression for two years. Many people were going through similar depression around that time, perhaps as much from having tried to do too much too soon as in response to the grim theater of Kent State.

The memory of that mixed time with people I love is still precious, and in one way the Troupe was a pure and lasting success. For the vehicle we chose for our first work was theater, and its medium was

our bodies. In training we worked with Jerzy Grotowski's exercises and our own, and with Ann Halprin, a fine movement teacher. We each had messed a bit with yoga and whatall before on our own, but working together for months was different. It broke each of us through to some new space, a different kind of connection with our bodies. And a new line of cooperative work opened. Doing improvisation postures, we observed that we had idiosyncratic forms. We speculated about them, tried to adjust their imbalances by motion, then by walking on our chests, finally got around to touching each other with our own hands in deep exploration. By the time the Troupe blew up we had developed the rudiments of a praxis of body therapy.

I worked at it alone thereafter, in odd hours stolen from my other life as an intellectual, using improvised yogas, medical texts, and psychedelics to feel out a slow program of undoing the warps and blockages I could recognize in my flesh. As my body changed, how I am who I am changed, and I found some connections, as when I unraveled the defensive hunching of my shoulders and the supermanly tightness of my diaphragm and belly. Since lazy mornings with my mother I had always been into backrubs; now I gave them with a new and increasingly clinical eye. All this body work turned out to be a form of meditation, though I did not seek it as such. It affected me slowly beyond my awareness and drifted me into a subtler consciousness of the body and its processes.

Meanwhile life went on. I finished two books; my kid learned to argue; my erstwhile comrades went though their own cycles. Some had also found themselves committed to major programs of body reinhabitation and to plumbing "the mysteries of the organism." Two years after the Troupe exploded, three of us trickled back together to form a nucleus for the Body Group, to carry on this work that had become important in our lives. At this time Body Group has been meeting for eighteen months. We have completed one cycle of exploration, in which we came to know each others' bodies and used them as a laboratory to develop and test out a common practice of body therapy. Now we begin a more public cycle, finding ways to share our learning. From one angle we are just a group of friends who hang out together once a week, poking at each other's bodies with lazy laughter, a bit stoned. From another, we are a political cadre. For the repression of bodily energies is key to the functioning of authoritarian social systems, and the freeing and rebalancing of our body vitality is perhaps essential in the struggle against them.

We are a political cadre in another, more immediate sense: The processes by which therapy is learned and transmitted and developed

are political, and we are trying to change them. In our innocent re-search we find ourselves in the milieu of "your wallet or your soul." Abroad now are at least two dozen disciplines, from Rolfing to mind control, which deal with the mind-body interface. We study in a welter of partial bodies of practical knowledge, on a wide front of break-through whose connection with the broader culture has not yet begun to be articulated. It's rich new terrain to explore, but the entrance lies through old portals. To get training, either you have to pay a price only the affluent alienation of the middle class can afford, or you must turn the better part of your life into service in someone's brand-name en-tourage, becoming an Inner Groupie. I resent both these options bit-terly, because the effect is to reproduce the worst aspects of therapy —psychological, medical, political—in our society, in which therapeu-tic skills and goals become, as commodities, the private property of specialist, upper-middle-class elites; the people's capacity for exercis-ing therapeutic power in their lives withers undeveloped; and therapy itself, as received by those with no means to integrate its practice in their everyday lives, becomes an expensive entertainment, oppressive in its cruel delusion.

Our bumbling casual group is one of many now trying to model different ways of learning and sharing power. As a learning collective (a name we have never formally spoken), we have learned how to move democratically on a frontier, together enough for support, loosely bound enough for each to pursue his or her idiosyncratic ex-ploration. To this home base we bring back the fragments of learning that we discover or buy on the expensive market. With no leader but each teaching when ready, we share them, take them apart, puzzle them into new combinations. We find that the pressure points of polarity therapy can be understood in terms of the acupuncture meridian net and used to deepen the effect of bioenergetic release exercises. We try to package the theory, design simple dances that two people can help each other through, whose habitual practice will open and harmonize their energy flows. Beyond our particular knowledge, we can teach the *processes* of learning to take care of our bodies and of learning collectively, and now each of the five who have been Body Group's steady core move in some way to do so. We begin to share our developing praxis with our children; we take first steps with friends and peers to pass on what we have learned free or for trade. We are very low-key proselytizers; still we think in terms of power to the people.

So much for the political sermon; we do what we do more naturally than it may suggest. Meanwhile, most of all, it is good to be among

friends. The group has been the best ongoing cooperation I've had in many years, warm and intimate without being mushy, strengthening us each and all as we move slowly into the unknown waters of our being.

A Little Bit Strange

1970, Cambodia, the Troupe is coming apart at the seams, my child is about to be born, the streets are full of tear gas, and four are dead at Kent State. In this instant I sit writing, bawling like a kid, about all this and a decade of the Movement, and about the holy language of Energy we are investigating, which manifests in saints and social fire. I write of how the currents of transformation flow strongly through Berkeley and out across America, and how, if you stay open to them, "you are transformed into an active conduit for the common sea of our Energy, lines of its organizing come to flow through you. I think I am learning to feel them in my body. It is frightening not to have a language in which to wrap the nakedness of your experience. . . ."

The kicker is, what I wrote wasn't true, at least not yet. In retrospect it seems clear that years spent as a political therapist, opening myself to intense flows of social energy in crisis and in intimacy, did indeed have much to do with what I came to experience in my body. But at the time I thought I was only making a metaphor. I couldn't begin actually to *feel* those lines of energy and had no intent of trying to nor real consciousness of what it would be like: all this started to emerge only a year and a half later. Who was writing through me, in that torn-open instant, and what did he know?

This uncanniness continued, through my hands. The next year, at a new school in the desert of Los Angeles, I lived through again in weary, vicious five-month miniature, the whole cycle of founding an institution and seeing its progressive essence destroyed by inability and repression. Too much! Twelve years of organizing experience was useless, I could do nothing but suffer: We were all too weary or innocent, and there was no real base to withstand the purge. I had come to teach the politics of institution building, but in the context of the Disney millions, all I could do that was useful, besides be a friend, was give people backrubs to ease the pain. I found myself doing this a lot, before I realized what was happening; when I did, what surprised me wasn't the completeness of my political importance there, but this weird pursuit of touch.

For I noticed that my hands had acquired a life of their own or, at

least, a sense. Like blind snakes seeking warmth they nuzzled unerr-
ingly to the piled blockages of energy in whatever frame I touched.
Since then it has grown to be somewhat embarrassing: I touch a friend
casually in conversation or greeting, or am deep in sexual interplay,
when suddenly I realize that my hands are actively poking into the
secret pain buried in the other's body, intent on knowing and easing
it. The habit has grown less obtrusive but more vivid as my awareness
and action have begun moving from naïve, material poking toward
pure energy manipulation.

One cusp in this unfolding came two years after I started serious
body work, some six months before I organized Body Group for the
comfort of company in the Mysteries. On a night of full moon and
transcendent community, I broke through to feeling the energy centers in the feet. (It was actually a relearning, for passing on the knowledge later reminded me of the precise incident when I forgot or
repressed it at nine years old, through having no language and no
sanction for it.) Through a little diligent work, the feeling quickly grew
into a sense of having eyes in my hands, and certain unfamiliar modali-
ties of sensing apparently centered in my head. I learned to feel the
ch'i flow in the acupuncture meridans, in others' bodies and my own,
and am learning to direct energy flow into and along the meridian
system, with body force or by mind alone. All this sounds much more
grandiose than is the case; with regard to these senses I feel like the
first organism to develop a rudimentary light-spot, barely able to dif-
ferentiate between day and night, but trying for dusk.

Now I teeter on a thin edge. If I have been away from the public
front lines of political action for the past few years, after a decade
there, perhaps it's not only from broader circumstance but because
much of my energy of daring is committed internally. For I ask myself,
what manner of creature am I? I have had experiences, which now are
sufficiently reinforced and verified by others peoples', that cut totally
across my Western concept of being human and being in a body. I start
to feel like some astral starfish, a creature of vivid filmy lines, lumines-
cent in the dark waters, flowing through this meat and able to leave
it. Meanwhile, I wash the dishes and drive carefully, having learned
from acid a decade ago how to endure the dissonance between the
transcendant and the mundane. If I allow myself to feel mainly the
wonder and not the terror of this opening of my frames, it ain't because
I'm not scared. Indeed, I think a thin layer of terror is beneath all my
consciousness these days on this account. Lord knows, my progress
seems so tentative and slow, reluctantly trying to move on through
chest-deep mud and constantly lapsing.

But it is the quality of this motion that is surprising, to a political man accustomed to being a conscious swimmer in history, making my own choices about direction, if not destination. I mean, it's hard to evoke this sense of my hands having a life of their own. It's not as if they were detached from me, alienated; but as if I were a part of them, like, say, their ass, facing backward to what was. If I judge the displacement accurately, it seems that my hands are leading me into experience that becomes comprehensible to my conscious mind only a year or so later. It's like working for a big corporation that moves slowly, so that decisions at the top filter down to the lower echelons only a long time later. Weird! Sometimes it seems that this whole body excursion is like the hands part, leading me on in a fashion not independent of my will, but anticipating it.

The Politics of the Body

Much fell away as the sixties turned seventies, many illusions and some hopes. Emblems of death had been in the air since Chicago, the ideological chaos and disorganization of the Movement was mirrored in people's lives and skulls. If we in the Troupe turned to body to go on, it was perhaps an attempt to ground ourselves in something essential and unalienable. I really felt it this way, that I had chosen to cast myself back on the original solid ground of being. A retreat, perhaps, from inclement clime? But it came at a high point of venture and was more an entrance into Mystery.

For we had come to a curious place together, all of us. As politics grew cultural we realized the deeper forces were involved than had yet been named or tended deliberately. We were adrift in questions and potentials: the organizational disintegration of the Movement as a political body was an outer emblem of conceptual incoherence, the inability to synthesize an adequate frame of understanding (and program) to embody all that we had come to realize was essential for transformational harmony. It left us free to roll our own, from the materials available.

So turning to body, I did so also as a political man seeking, not only solace and diversion, but essential tool and program. We are a long way yet from making actual the fancy potentials of this perspective. But I approach the body seeing, in the tangible dear flesh of my friends, the imprint of antifaggot conditioning that leaves us men tight-pelvised and stiff-wristed, the constricted breath the goes with emotional repression and is taught for the sake of industrial homeostatis, the

numbness that permits us to ignore what our bodies are telling us about the environments and the way we live and the orders we obey, and so much more that follows the thesis that our social condition is mirrored in our bodies and might be approached through them as well.

More broadly, I think the politics of repression which maintains our culture's inequities have dictated that we cut ourselves off from awareness of the many ways in which we so intimately intermesh with each other. The barriers seem thick, yet we can see through them: as we are finding through such primitive disciplines as Mind Control, a mere twenty hours of gentle deconditioning, via practice in forming images while in the alpha state, is sufficient to enable most people to sense in some beginning detail the inner condition of a given stranger's organism and moods and to work on them as well, move him toward health. It is impossible not to recognize what this means about the totalness of how we do co-inhabit the universe.

So when I come this year to ask certain old questions—How do authoritarian structures work, and at what level do they breed? How does the middle class manage to remain insensitive to the suffering of others which secures its privileges? How can people be led to that opening of self-awareness in which any real politics involving them must be grounded? How can we construct participant-democratic groups and organizations in which information and decision making are truly shared? How can we devise a "political" process which pays harmonious attention to the inner and the outer aspects of being and change?—when I come to ask these again, I have some "new" material to put into the search for experimentally verifiable answers. For if telepathy-telempathy, for example, is as basic a human power as I'm now coming to understand it to be, its repression or deliberate cultivation is a political matter, bearing importantly on all of these questions.

I speak of body and psychic stuff together, for one leads to the other if you don't stop it. In this day of Wilhelm Reich's belated popularity, it may be faintly credible that living in touch with our vitality in reawakened bodies is integral to the pursuit of the revolution we dream is necessary. But no one I know in the political branch of the Movement has argued that we must take the matter of the "vibes" between people more seriously, to the point of realizing ourselves in strange dimensions of being in this pursuit. Yet such might be the case. Sometimes when I see all the Nixonian ugliness perpetrated in my name I feel impotent and guilty and long again, despite the guns, at least to be throwing tangible wrenches into the machinery to cry it stop. But confronted with a legion of imaginary Movement brethren who accuse me of pursuing an idle bourgeois indulgence in experi-

ence, entertainment, while the Empire triumphs and crumbles, I reply that no such stupendous change in our conception of people and reality can be, without the most profound social and political ramifications, though for the moment it appears confined to Uri Geller doing parlor tricks on the telly.

Meanwhile we pursue a modestly social aim, banding together in Body Group to make a nonexploitive model of sharing the knowledge of healing. For here is the political core of therapy: Is fixing body-minds, like fixing cars, to continue to be a specialist matter, or is power to pass to the people? "As long as there are doctors," said Lao-tzu or Ché, "the people will be sick." The truth of this is measured by how unable we are to maintain our own health. And so beyond Body Group's humble backyard molehill of mutual learning looms a mountainous sector of the capitalist economy, the $80-billion-a-year medical industry. Liberation here means first, for all people, power over our own lives: if not yet a noncarcinogenic environment, at least good nutrition and new access to the knowledge and internal powers of maintaining our own bodies in health and the bodies of our loved ones.

For me even the modest goal of taking adequate care of my family seems many years off, but already I feel the broad power behind an integral praxis of health that can be learned and passed on by its users. With a clarity of potential I see in few other fantasies, I can see changing our culture's consciousness, person by person, and just wiping out one indelibly exploitive way of handling precious health. And I see that to do true transformation of medicine as a power institution, rather than just redistribute its fruits more equitably, will require measures of no less depth and magnitude.

Life is slower than dreams. At present friends are starting now and then to come to me for relief from some minor distress; and I try, as in organizing, to learn to teach what healing I can catalyze. In precious irreversible experiment, which I handle casually for fear I botch it, I pass colored flows of energy back and forth with my three-year-old son as we lie in long wordlessness on the summer bed. I fumble for a way to help him find validation and language and exercise for realities and skills he has not yet learned to disbelieve; I wonder how much I'll be able to help him avoid the long blindness and miniscule rediscovery that has been my experience. I see already some minor but real integration of these mysteries in my everyday urban experience and wonder what kind of cognitive climate that will create for him, what sorts of political and therapeutic sensibilities might grow up in such soil.

The Cycling of Personal and Social Change

The Movement gave me occasion to see how healthier social conditions, often no more than a mist around our collective action (or a perspiration generated by it), freed people's energy for therapeutic personal change, often in directions outlined by collective analysis but still inalienably private, which in turn freed energy and pointed directions for action to make the society healthier. As I grew from a brash kid of seventeen in the New Left through a struggle that kept evolving to a weary warrior of thirty-three in some confusion, I lived through enough of these cycles of private-public therapy and saw them enough in the lives of my friends to recognize them as such, to chart their periods and grow familiar with their rhythms . . . and with what happened to individuals and to movements when these rhythms and the needs beneath them were not honored. I came to believe that we must know these cycles, go with them, tend them; and to believe that this in itself is as important as the pursuit of either of the two great conjugate streams of therapy which are the cycles' ground.

Much effort is spent now on finding ways to make our society healthier; much effort explores ways for people to realize their wholeness individually. We are coming slowly to realize that these processes are interwoven vitally; but our consciousness of *how* is pretty dim and rhetorical, and we nourish the cycles mostly by happenstance. Ideologically and practically, it seems to me more important to construct the connections between personal therapy and social therapy than to seek to extend either for its own sake; for attention to their cycling will itself give rise to their extension.

Under their grand face these abstractions reduce to the rhythms of my life, as I go on striving to be a healthy person in a healthy society. Fourteen years, an adulthood, in the Movement kept alive a part of my soul, gave me a program for personal reconstruction that I shall not accomplish in this life, even with the thin, dear help of my friends: to be open in my emotions and present in my experience, accepting of my spectral sexuality and nonoppressive in all my relations, capable of deep commitment and ultimate flexibility, empathetic with human and plant alike and connected to the infinite. All this and more was outlined by the thrust of the various streams of our collective movement for liberation and justice. And I am somewhere following this program, more alone than I would be, struggling and indifferently successful.

The summer of a fallow year. Rain will reveal how much the soil has been nourished. My last tour of active duty—running around America trying to organize change—lasted six years. By the time I understood the cycle it was clear that I was running too long and would pay in down time; but work has its own momentums, and it took two years to disengage. I was off-rhythmed by the general contagions of energy in the late sixties: so much was opening, so much needed to be done. When I turned inward, literally, it was partly because I needed a change of pace, a time and way to integrate the inner implications of what was going down in public. (I may be wrong in assuming that only in our time have social therapists begun broadly to be aware of such needs, but it seems clear that personal therapists rarely face their complementary need to explore periodically the implications of their work in the world which surrounds it.)

Part of growing up is coming to see the cycles in longer perspective. Turning thirty, I grew able to see them in years instead of months and plan for them somewhat. When I finished the two books which brought to closure a phase of my work in the Movement, I knew I should need some long term of R-and-R before I could engage so actively again. Though I kept a professional toe in education, I mostly drew back to savor my son's first years, tend my love for my lady, and write privately in my journal about being a father and a son, about death, about the body. This time of tending private gardens has stretched two years and may another, though it seems to be passing as my son's life leads me into deeper perspectives on education and my hands lead me on at their own pace. At times I think of my excursion into body and psychic domains in this light: that six years of heavy-duty service on the social change line, with only partial rhythms of rest and recuperation, built up in me a charge, a potential for personal change which, when I let up, might have spun me in any of a number of intense directions, but spun me in this one, for reasons dynamic in my work and in who I was, and perhaps toward an intimate breaking and re-creation that is quite as radical as anything I propose for society.

I use this perspective to counsel myself when it seems, as it often does, that I have abandoned a struggle faint-heartedly, lapsed into a safe (if not entirely comfy) privacy whose social relevance I only rationalize. The daily and chronic atrocities of the System confront me, call to be dealt with while I consider how memory is cramped in muscle. I observe how minimal my progress is, seemingly with a tenth of my will, and energy sapped from the days to I don't know where. I know now how slow something new grows, while old projects uncompleted beg me to attend them. But the matter of values seems constant to me:

even in the context of occult and spiritual knowledge, it seems right, *just*, to use power to better the material aspects of the lives my own is intertwined with. And doing massage, by itself, is not enough to satisfy my need for political engagement and my sense of social purpose.

The line that distinguishes radical politics from vague goodwill is drawn, I think, by the deliberate choice to work to reconstruct the collective structures of power which determine our lives. I mourn somewhat for my father's day, when it was still possible to believe that an informed electorate and workers' control of GM were a sufficient program. Now a sufficient politics must root itself more deeply, in educational processes and in the body, among other places. It wasn't hard for me to see and justify the consequences for social action of education's reconstruction. But the body is a stranger ground; and though I already see in its lessons applications to the process of social action and the re-creation of the medical industry, I imagine that the full integration of its mysteries with politics will take a long time and unfold in ways for which we have as yet no adequate language.

An Anecdote about the Interplay of Personal/Social Therapy

When I finished my second book[1] a chapter of theory about decentralized educational institutions was missing. The book implied it; I knew its demonstration was already present in the counterculture's learning experience; but strain as I would I couldn't get my mind around its concepts. For a year more they brooded in me, while around me grew the funky subinstitutional structure which embodied them, and I worked on body. Shortly after I first felt clearly the *ch'i* flow in someone's meridians, I went on business to New York. For nights before my trip I was inhabited by vivid dreams. I saw my body as a space of fiery points, dark and vast as a galaxy; and among them tendrils and webs of energy arching, flowing through strange colors, constantly changing, as if the aurora borealis were strung on the stars and gone wild, I think now. At the time it seemed like the mysteriously ordered flickering of lights on the face of a vast computer, but with sensate shimmers and washes of color, like the skin of an octopus flushing with emotion.

When I got home, with a dozen things on my mind to write about,

1. *On Learning and Social Change* (New York: Random House, 1972).

I sat down at the typewriter. What came out was unplanned: an essay[2] sketching the structure and process of a decentralized institution of alternative education (or therapy, if you will)—10,000 working nodes, small groups alive with energy and interlinked in mutating connection, networks of seasonal flushes, fields of radiance. And I was illuminated with more than the pleasure of having got my mind at last around these few simple concepts which extended an old line of thought. For pretty clearly, it was my body experience, which fed into the dreams, that set my mind free to conceive.

I suppose the process ran something like this: We see the world outside ourselves as our extension (though not only this), imagine it shaped in our image, imagine ourselves in the image it reflects back to us. In particular, we see the social body as we see our own, with sharply differentiated heads, stomaches, nerves, and so on; and so our images of change in it are cast in terms of bodily mechanics and metabolisms. In coming to see, simply but profoundly, my own body differently, in terms of different governing metaphors (not replacing but extending my culture's set), I was establishing a ground from which to begin to revision those matters for which we use body as metaphor, in particular the structure, metabolism, energetics, and health of the social body.

I have no idea how deep this revisioning will go, or at what speed. What made it visible to me as a process was the fortunate coincidence of a problem on my mind, which let a radical shift of internal perception be reflected directly in external analysis. Here personal therapy and social therapy feed back and forth through one man, a Movement writer in a body: for equally it was my experience of years of trying to organize decentralized learning forms which opened my mind to accept the reflection of metaphor and see myself vividly as a decentralized learning form. If I had not had around me a social environment which was, at an archetypal level, already somewhat harmonious with the image of self dawning in me, would I have had so readily, or at all, the experiences which prompted me to accept this new image and explore its promises and considerable fears?

The Broader Perspective of Therapy

I started out oppressed by social wrongs, tried to oppose them; learned that we had to clean up the operations of social power, tried

2. "How We Learn Today in America," *Saturday Review*, August 19, 1972.

to do this; learned that for this we had to reform the processes of power among ourselves, as radical political actors and as citizens, which meant to reform ourselves as human beings, not independently of the other projects, but in and by their processes and as their ground. I shared what I see as a key development of Movement consciousness in the white middle class: from action on behalf of unknown others who were wronged, to action on my own behalf, as well and first, through coming to recognize myself as victimized and oppressed in ways which ultimately were key to the oppression of those others. A parallel development in the psychology of radical political process took place during this time (1958 to 1970). The belief that the cutting edge of radical action was change in (political) institutions was faced with competition from the belief that the vanguard action was to lead personal lives which as far as possible embodied the conditions of society we wished to bring about.

The potentials for active harmony between these thrusts were rarely sought, or, I believe, understood. Instead a conflict ensued; the streams of our action divided all too much between the pursuit of traditional political goals by traditional means and the attempt *to live differently*. I found myself often isolated and lonely on the tangled ground between these streams. My late sixties were marked by fruitless visits to the SDS National Office trying to convince people that educational process was important, that the way we learn affects how we are able to function in political action, and by equally fruitless attempts to talk usefully, in country communes, about the relevance of the war and racism. Often enough I felt like a freak, unable to be at home in either stream of action save by denying half of who I was. If therapy is to heal, make whole, what therapy was there for me, except to try to remake my surroundings?

You are the tool you make yourself, as well as more. If I had pursued radical politics in an era when its strategies seemed clearly determined and their tactics engaged fewer dimensions of life, I might have grown into an adulthood and professionalism each as stable, in its way, as those of the normal bourgeois. But I pursued politics (therapy) in a time when its nature was changing radically. What is wrong, what needs to be re-formed, what constitutes political (therapeutic) action—all these questions have opened up drastically, in my mind and in the minds of many others. In trying to keep on dealing with them, the law that "making change changes the changer" has led me through evolutions of work and, more slowly, of personality, which might well have been less variegated in a stabler climate.

Once it had been established in many minds—I believe for the first

time in history—that members of the "privileged" class could think genuinely of revolution as a response to the pain of their own lives, rather than only the pain others felt; and once the American mystification which restricted the adjective "political" to describing the electoral process had broken for many, admitting even sex and the biochemistry of madness to its domain, then a great wilderness opened to us, and we are not even recovered from the shock, let alone finding our way.

In politics is reflected our culture's general state of confusion. Here it can be seen that the visionary task is no longer "simply" to distribute equitably the material privilege and power of the few among all, itself a task we are losing ground in, but rather to reform even those conditions of life which recently we offered to the world as model, in view of the stifling of life and freedom we now can recognize in them. The Soviet bureaucratic state tells us about revolution too narrowly conceived; China tells us each culture must find its own way. And we are here, with all the colors and sexes and ages and occupations learning to demand familiar rights: just at a time when technology forces us to recognize the gestalt organism we have become through it and the many varieties of general death we have set ourselves up for; just when our concept of human nature is breaking open radically; just when the handwriting on the sky says that we must change our middleclass-american way of life, change it more deeply and abruptly than any civilization has been called upon before to do.

In this circumstance I think it is no wonder that the positive function of ideology has disintegrated, leaving adrift citizenry and radicals alike. No one, no group, has been able to grasp the needs and implications of what has opened and offer us a formulation of goal and strategy which embodies them enough to attract allegience. We are left to formulate from the morass, each alone, some sense to apply to the tiny patch of turf on which she labors. We are in a chaos. It has some healthy aspects, for from the rich, bewildering drift of old and new input many different patterns of dealing with reality are emerging. But too many are adrift and paralyzed by the overall lack of sense, and the rest cling overtight against this to what they think they understand.

A Reprise on a Related Theme

I came to the psychedelics in 1963, in personal exploration during a political lull; I think active social disconformity as expressed in political action had prepared me privately to dare such unsanctioned un-

knowns. I found that their use modified my propensity to political activism but on the whole increased it, at least in the context of the time. This question of the relation of psychedelics to activism became of general importance as their use spread and was debated in Movement circles, superficially and at first unfavorably: Their use was held to be hedonistic and sinfully disengaging. A temporary reversal of this attitude was symbolized by the advent of the Yippies in Chicago in 1968.

By then, moved equally by the psychedelics' deep impact upon my own perceptions and by my sense of their relevance to the key processes of *radicalization* with which I was concerned, I had studied in some detail the spread of their uses through the college campuses and developing countercommunities of America, recognized the remarkable correlation of this spread with the spread and stylistic evolution of activism's manifestation, and constructed some elements of theory to account for this.

As a political man concerned with the education and mobilization of a revolutionary movement, I was called upon to consider seriously the uses of these drugs, not only by others but by myself, with all that this implied. The situation was comic and cosmic. I imagine a cartoon: Ché Guevara in the urban wilderness, checking out personally this new little bit of technology, assessing its usefulness for the spread of spirit and precision among the people: drops pill, meets (or becomes) God. *@*#*%*¢**&**$! When I came back to my responsibilities as a radical intellectual, I sought to include, among elements of a liberatory theory of learning, some account of the psychedelics as tools of learning and social change.[3]

In this area my efforts and those of a few better-known others have been completely inadequate. On the whole psychedelics are sold as commodities and used for escape, with little lore about or exploitation of their peculiar potentials for facilitating broad spectra of learning, and with the double-edged consequence that in this manner they ultimately confine rather than enlarge our lives. Still there exists a community of radical inquiry and action which seeks their use in fuller consciousness; and with others I am joined thereby in the rituals of our subculture and lives. Some of these rituals are technical: In Body Group we use grass and subliminal doses of acid to make accessible to conscious control certain phenomena of energy which are in some respects an inner image of the condition of society we would further,

---

3. See *On Learning and Social Change*, chapter 4, and my essay in H. Hart, ed., *Drugs: For and Against* (New York: Hart, 1970).

and which may be practically connected to its furtherance.

In sum, the radicalizing thrust of psychedelics was two-fold. *Socially,* their use made the young criminals, increasing and sharpening their alienation from the state, and bringing with it a cluster of cultural and political attitudes which induced a deviant community. *Privately,* their use opened states of consciousness and powers of being which, for broadly political reasons, had been repressed in our culture. Using the drugs as a citizen opened me to these influences, investigating their uses as an organizer meant to decipher and invent their applications, which were new; together these exposed me to powerful forces of personal and professional change. All this runs parallel to my later experience with body (and indeed led into that), and therapists may recognize parallels to their own experiences with new therapeutic slants. For me, beyond the psychedelic particulars, this example testifies to how strange and open-ended is the pursuit of political liberation these days.

Cycle Back to Community

From the start in 1958, picketing for justice in the New Left accomplished more than the occasional victory. We were marching as much for ourselves as for others: not just in the indirect sense of feeling morally healthy, but for the much richer existential rewards of community. This was hard to recognize at first, since what we had inherited after the postwar purges of the Old Left's ideology and experience did not begin to bespeak the importance of this aspect of struggle. But slowly we came to see that what we were creating was a community not limited to rhetoric. By 1965 the first campus sit-ins had revealed a compact, ephemeral image of full community—political/educational/therapeutic/social/sexual. The subsequent development of the counterculture can be seen as the attempt by many to make this image real, on a mass and enduring scale, rather than a transient artifact of crisis.

In and out of the counterculture, I think the most substantive political work that is being done these years is in the re-creation of local community, in whose patriotic traditions and education must be based any coherent and sustained effort to reform our society's broader structures of power. Real roots is what it's about, the more so in a swirling time; and the efforts of the New Left to mobilize usefully even its adherents, let alone the general citizenry, fell apart wherever they were not so rooted. But during the early seventies, despite the media

myth of the Movement's disappearance, I believe that the sentiment of community planted so fragily at first has taken hold and that in many middling cities and rural areas this evolution of the Movement is expanding beyond its initial defensive ghettoization to involve a broader mix of ages, races, nominal political sentiments, and cultural backgrounds. This reduction of broader political schemes to the slow growth of local community is a version of the shift described above, from reforming institutions to living new lives as key to social change. Here what is being pursued are vanguard examples small enough to be feasible, large and complex enough to feel real and be relevant to the full social context.[4]

What this trend of political impulse meant for me was in one sense simple: it directed my primary attention away from abstract causes and national action, and toward the bread-and-butter of community building. I don't think I did this very well, perhaps not even very much, not only because my work had other, even slower primary emphases, but also because I was confused about my own role and what to do. On what level and through what means was community to be pursued—neighborhood food conspiracies? city charter revision? generating culture and legend?

Fadeout on Therapy

Perhaps the problem I found myself in will be clearer if I phrase it personally, in terms of the stripping away or radical transformation of my definition of myself as political actor. At first I saw as political only my actions of social protest and electoral citizenship. Fifteen years later I see as political every use and limitation of my consciousness, how and where I shit and touch my lover and repair my car. Do I retreat from my Marxist forebears or go beyond them in seeing not a single prime determinant of our condition, like productive relationships, but a total web of factors which will not permit the mechanisms of homeostasis and change to be single-mindedly approached or explained in terms of linear causality? Talking with the other parents about playgroup sexuality seems as profound politically as piling another brick on Watergate, planting a garden and hugging people as essential as wildcat strikes. After ten years of mulling them over, the connections among all these matters have become familiar, I can hardly recall what it was like not to see them.

4. See "Education at Sanctum," *Change*, March 1974.

This collapse of traditional categories—for that's what I'm talking about—didn't just happen to me while I was standing in the crumbling mind of the time. I sought it actively, as a consequence both of my own psychological proclivities and of the understandings I was reaching through my work about education, authority, specialization, and the very process of Western thought, in general about what was dawning in our culture and what was to be desired. And having somewhat in my mind smashed the barriers which divided an integral society into fragmentary processes, I find myself in the odd experience of seeing everything with almost equal vividness through the lens of ultimate politics. On one extreme this invokes in me a deep terror: not being able to define political actions as those which are so primarily in themselves leaves me unable to continue defining myself as political man in any familiar way, and my sense of who I am falls apart in an area quite important to me. On the other extreme there is a modest but transcendent bliss involved in coming to experience myself no longer in fragments, but with my political man and my learner and my lover and my parent and my technical man and all those folks somewhat inescapably one.

"Political" is still a useful term for me, though beyond a small circle I feel like a relativist among Newtonians, making sense only in limiting cases. When I look through the politics lens now, I see that all that I do is an essential test of holiness, politically speaking. And I begin to think of myself as political man now as I did of the Taoists who, I used to imagine, finally pursued the Way intensely enough to disappear from what they were doing, and came back later to resume those same lives, outwardly indistinguishable but transfigured and transforming.

11. The Body, the Cathedral, and the Kiva

DON JOHNSON

No essay so far has held quite the breadth or emotional intensity of Don Johnson's account of how he grew from being a Jesuit priest and professor to intellectual student of the body to being a full inhabitant in his body and taking up the profession of helping others to that state. Although I have avoided asking people who associate themselves with a particular school or style of therapy to contribute to this anthology, in Don's case I feel that the particular style of therapy he engages in, structural integration, has such tremendous implications for the practice of therapy that it has to be included. In fact, the idea for this book came when he and I were walking near his home in Santa Fe, and he was telling me of the insights that he had come to about certain forms of neurosis and psychosis and the way in which they were physically manifest. I began to think that there must be a way to convey to the more verbal members of the profession the knowledge he had gained, as well as the struggle he had been through on the way to it. I also felt that nothing I had read about the new, body-related styles of therapy had been able to convey the experience of working with people on a direct physical level to an audience that was not physically oriented nor predisposed to believe in them. I hope this account of Don's life experiences, dispels the erroneous impression that physical therapies are antiintellectual or dangerously one-sided. Indeed, their aim is to redress a balance that has already been broken, not create a new one.

In addition to his Jesuit training and several years of teaching, Don recently completed a Ph.D. in philosophy at Yale. He then received training in structural integration and has been doing that for the past three years in New Mexico. He has also written a book (currently in press) with two other former Jesuits, concerning their various personal changes in the nearly twenty years since they joined the order.

The night before I began training in Rolfing in the summer of 1971, I had a dream in which I was presented with a large leather-covered folio entitled *The Design of the Temple*. The first pages were opened to reveal line drawings of a Mayan-like temple. The following page consisted of my being transported to what I perceived to be the Yucatán peninsula and being placed in front of what seemed to be two temples, one in front of the other. The closer was like the classic Mayan temples: many stairs leading to a flat top. The rear one was pyramidal. All of a sudden, an immense gray-haired woman arose from behind the second temple and moved it so now it appeared that there was only one temple, a pyramid.

My relation to the body is probably somewhat unique. I came to it only in my mid-thirties. It was an apocalyptic meeting. My views of the body and of Rolfing are colored with an apocalyptic hue.

Dr. Ida Rolf, now in her eighties, received her Ph.D. from Columbia in 1920. She was a research biochemist at the Rockefeller Institute for about twenty years. She was also a practitioner of hatha yoga. Over years of working with herself and her family, who had ills buried in an obscure past, she developed the method of body therapy called "structural integration," popularly known as "Rolfing." Although she occasionally gave workshops for chiropractors and osteopaths, it was not until the mid-sixties, after Fritz Perls invited her to Esalen Institute, that she developed an organized method for communicating her knowledge to an ever-increasing number of professional disciples.

I was an only child raised in a home where there was almost no touching. I never saw my parents naked, with the rare exception of my father the few times we swam at the Elks' Club. My sex life was limited to kissing and light caressing since, as a Roman Catholic, I believed anything more would lead to eternal damnation (or at least an unwanted baby). At age twenty-two I entered the Jesuits, who had a rule that "Jesuits shall not touch one another, not even in jest, but only to greet one another as custom may allow." And, by God, during my twenties and early thirties, I didn't touch others, nor myself. I didn't even look at my naked body. There was another rule that there needn't be any rules about chastity except that "our chastity should be like that of the angels."

Rolfing is a method of restructuring the body so that one can float downstream in the upright posture.

Paul Hilsdale was a child prodigy. Even after taking some years off to travel, he graduated from Georgetown University at age nineteen. He then entered the Jesuits, where he devoted his efforts to social activism. He had a very large head sitting on a tiny body with a sunken chest and locked pelvis. At age forty-five he was invited by Ed Maupin, then director of the Esalen resident program, to participate in the 1967–1968 program at Ed's expense. After a lifetime of celibacy, Paul entered the sexual center of the new age. The first months were hard for him. He was under constant pressure to hop into bed and end it all. As he became more discouraged about his body's strength in keeping him a prisoner of his past, Alexander Lowen came and gave Paul some bioenergetic hope of breaking the walls of the prison. Shortly thereafter, Paul, worn out by the battles with himself, contracted hepatitis. Ida Rolf appeared at Esalen in the winter. Paul came for a visit to Alma College in Los Gatos, where I was studying theology. After two sessions with Ida the hepatitis was gone. His drooping head had emerged dramatically from his body and his chest had opened wide. In the course of the next few weeks he was metamorphosed from an effete intellectual snob into a powerful sexual man. From that time until I began being Rolfed by Ed Maupin three years later, I knew that Rolfing would somehow be a path for me.

Norman O. Brown writes that the awakening of the new man, the resurrection of the body, is an apocalyptic event brought about by warfare: not the surrogate warfare men have mistakenly pursued throughout history, but the struggle to break down the barriers of the body which encase us. Love's body is not just a reality we grow into. The blockades are too ancient and strong. They must be blown apart.

I read *Life Against Death* in the spring of 1967, weeks before I first took LSD. Brown's reduction of the illusions of language and history to the bathroom and the bedroom and his solution to the absurdities of history by a return to the body seemed insane to me. But in my first trip, as I plunged into my absolute isolation, clutching out (in a friend's bathroom) for some feeling of contact but finding only plastic and metal surfaces, I discovered Brown's genius. That experience began to bring me into touch with the sweat and dirt and smells I had successfully avoided all my life. I reveled in my stinking body.

There is really no *thing* new about Ida Rolf's method. Almost every *thing* that goes on in Rolfing can be found elsewhere: in Bess Mensendyck, Andrew Still, Wilhelm Reich, Emanuel Swendenborg, F.

Matthias Alexander, the cranial osteopaths, hatha yoga. Her genius, like that of my philosophical mentors, Aristotle and Aquinas, is in putting it all together—putting the body together.

The principles of her synthesis are two: the plasticity of the body and the relation of the body to gravity. In her experimental work with bodies over the years, Ida discovered that the structure of the body can be altered far beyond what is ordinarily expected. The alteration occurs primarily by working with the myofascial system—by stretching it, unsticking it, repositioning it.

The manipulation of the body is aimed at changing its relation to gravity. If one visualizes the body as an aggregate of large segments —head, torso, pelvis, upper and lower legs, feet—it is easy to see that the displacement of one of these segments from a vertical midline through the body will cause stress and a compensating displacement of other segments. The common forward tilt of the head and backward tilt of the pelvis, for example, require deep tensions to keep these segments united to the body. Over the years, these tensions become part of one's being-in-the-world. They are manifest in one's bodily, emotional, and spiritual behavior. Rolfing attempts to align head, torso, pelvis, legs, and feet so that the movement of the body through life involves the minimum amount of effort and blocking. It is a system for maximizing the energy available to any person.

Catholic sacramental theology prepared me to meet my body as an old but neglected friend. The meaning of God's becoming man in Jesus is, according to this ancient tradition, the divinization of matter. In the early centuries of the church there were violent disputes about this doctrine. It was especially hard for intellectuals in the Platonic tradition to accept that matter, especially the human body, could be divine. But those who defended the conjoined humanity and divinity of Jesus, and thereby the cosmos, won out. The ritual of the church, its sacraments, are merely extensions of this theology. Matter—bread, wine, incense, water, kneeling, singing—is not just matter; it is the revelation of the divine. The central image in the Pauline epistles which explains the meaning of Christianity is the Body of Christ, the reality in which we all share.

In spite of the intellectualism of my life, there was always an undercurrent, arising from my participation in Christian ritual, that the body is more than just a body.

Rolfing is an evolutionary therapy in its adjusting the human body to a fully upright posture. In the early weeks of childhood, the baby's

looking up from a crawling position to explore its world is the beginning of the cervical curve which physiologically (and psychologically) separates the head from the rest of the body. During its first year of crawling, the soft tissue in the lower belly, particularly the psoas muscle, is not lengthened in proportion to the rest of its body. By the time the baby begins to walk, it has already developed the characteristics of the human form at this stage of its evolution: the head slightly forward of the shoulders and the tilted pelvis. Since the child is in a world of adults whose movement patterns cater to these stress points instead of modifying them, it too grows up with gravity continually accentuating these blocks. A major task of the Rolf work is to lengthen and restructure the soft tissue so that the head moves directly on top of the lower body, and the pelvis is turned underneath, the pelvic floor thus forming a solid base for what is above.

I always conceived of myself as incapable of doing anything skillful with my body. I never had much interest in sports. Acute asthma during my first eighteen years kept me from doing much that required intense exertion. I always felt clumsy and angry when attempting to do anything that required fine and patient work, like building model airplanes. My father, his father and grandfather, and my mother's father were all excellent craftsmen. I've often thought that my self-imposed incompetence during those early years was in part rebellion against them. The asthma, added to other illnesses and my moderate body structure, conspired to make me think of myself as physically weak.

The same was true of my concept of my artistic abilities. My artistic career was over by the time I was six. In a preschool art class I was put in the corner several times for making snakes out of clay, much to the embarrassment of my mother, who finally withdrew me from the class. I had great envy for kids who were drawing trees and elephants, but all I could make were clay snakes. After similar experiences with dance, violin, and piano classes, I entered grammar school where my inability to draw or make real looking objects literally made me sick. I often had to be sent home when we had art class. It wasn't until thirty years later, when I took LSD, that I recovered my artistic sense.

So I passed the first thirty-five years of my life thinking of myself as incapable of bodily things and competent only in the field of thought.

The encounter group movement, particularly as inspired by Carl Rogers, was warmly received among progressive Catholics. I participated in such groups throughout the 1960s. In 1967 the entire Alma

College community (108 persons ranging in age from twenty-five to eighty-five) engaged in a three-day marathon conducted by Carl Rogers and his staff. I began to realize that my verbal skills made it easy for me to protect the really deep walls of my ego from the assaults of these groups and from the power of individual psychotherapy. Something else was needed.

From the early part of the Christian era until around 1400, the Southwest was inhabited by the Anasazi culture, the precursors of the Hopi and the Pueblo Indians of today. The Anasazi religion was focused in the kiva, a circular structure dug underground. In the kiva is the sipapu, a hole into the earth. The structure of the kiva and the sipapu represent the Anasazi belief that the gods dwell in the earth from which we all emerge. Ritual involves establishing a link with this source.

The high point of Anasazi culture occurred in the thirteenth century, the same time as the high point of medieval culture. On a visit to Chaco Canyon, one of the Anasazi centers, I realized how my life had traversed what is represented by the two poles of the best of these cultures. Thirteenth-century Europe manifested its genius in the refinement of Gothic architecture and scholastic philosophy. It was the age of reaching up to God in the heavens by way of the Platonic dialectic of intellect. That was the path of my life until my early thirties. My fantasies of the direction of my life were grandiose and high-soaring: childhood fantasies of being a king transforming into college dreams of being a captain of industry changing into fantasies of being a great preacher converting thousands and finally into being a latter-day Aquinas whose synthesis of all knowledge would transform a disintegrated culture into a new community.

I now feel more at home in the kiva than in the cathedral. The downward movement into the kiva and the sipapu are outward forms more consonant with my feelings about myself and my work.

Since it seems demonstrable that man's outer world is a projection of that which is within, is it not possible that some of the problems of our times might be resolved by examining the man himself, his physical being, his body. Could it be logical to suppose that if a way were found to organize better the actual physical structures of men, their other confusions, mental and cultural, might lessen?[1]

1. Ida Rolf, "Structural Integration."

Every day I hear manifestations in ordinary language and thought of the Platonic-Cartesian heritage: "Since you work only with the body, you really don't deal with the emotional and spiritual levels of life." Is stretching a complex of tendons and fascia that for years have bound one's chest in a vice less psychologically significant than talking with an analyst about parental conflicts? The thought forms of contemporary physics and philosophy have transcended the old dualisms between mind and body, but ordinary language and behavior lag.

One sunset, during my Rolfing training at Pigeon Key in Florida in the fall of 1971, I walked out onto the pier. Ida had just finished working on the backs of my knees and my sacrum. As I stood watching the pink thunderheads massing over the gulf, all sense of identity vanished. There was just a vast intricate web of energy with no boundaries between myself the ocean the air the sounds of the gulls the dock the island. Though like ego loss experiences on LSD, it was more rooted in *this* body, *this* air, *this* water. It was less an experience of the mind. It was not a particularly blissful experience since I had no feeling for who *I* was, no feelings which were familiar, which were like past feelings. This experience has remained with me. I have very little body memory of my past—of how I used to feel, of how I used to react.

The ego is embedded in the flesh. It isn't some atomic thing, lurking behind a bodily façade. When the hands of the Rolfer (or elbow or knuckle) release the hangups in the flesh, the ego is partially broken. The mechanical responses to life which constitute the ego are gradually worn away until there remains a fully living and responsive organism.

Rolfing is a political activity—or metapolitical. It destroys the roots of the forces of death in our society: the tight ass, the constricted chest, the drooping head, the twisted spine. These are blocks in the body which keep it from perceiving that there is only one body.

Logos seeks unification; and the fact it faces is Division
Alienation, in the old Marxist vocabulary
the rents, the splits, in the newer Freudian vocabulary
the schisms
the schizophrenia.
Now — if I may make a Great Leap Forward —
alienation is schizophrenia
the outcome of the collision between Marx and Freud is their
                                                    unification
the perception of the analogy between the two

the analogy between   social and psychic
                           society and soul
                           body and body politic.
The disintegration of the boundary-line between inner and outer
                                            self and other
is the disintegration of the ego
the disintegration of the ego of the ego-psychologists
in Marxist terms, the disintegration of the bourgeois ego
                                of bourgeois individualism
or, alienation overcome — — [2]

The "psychological" and the "physical" are in continual interaction. An infant with a tilted pelvis begins to imitate the movement patterns of his father, who has an extremely tilted pelvis and moves according to patterns which make it comfortable for him to live with the tilt. His grandfather did the same. But a tilted pelvis cuts off sexual feeling. Like his father, the infant grows up with sexual fears. The fears and the pelvic structure constitute one problem.

The old structure has to be destroyed radically. But this is only half the story. The destruction of the old world is only the *rite de passage* to a new mode of seeing. The real genius of Ida Rolf consists of her ability to bring the body-person into a new structure, a new balance. Breaking up fascial buildups, separating muscle groups, cleaning attachments of tendons to bones—these are only the preparation. The crucial work of Rolfing consists in attaining a balance in the body between right and left sides, front and back, intrinsic and extrinsic muslces, above and below.

Norman O. Brown once said that his readers mistakenly think he advocates the end of structure and order. But what he advocates is the end of the structures based on ego, on the separation of body and soul, self and others. There is, however, a postapocalyptic order.

Ida Rolf is like Don Juan Matus. I went to her with the expectation that she would teach me how to do the work which I had experienced as so powerful in my own life. I discovered that to learn the method meant that I had to be stripped of my ego, my old world, and my ways of seeing. I would often find myself stripped bare by her piercing eyes,

2. Norman O. Brown, "From Politics to Metapolitics," in *A Caterpillar Anthology*, ed. Clayton Eshelman (New York: Anchor Books, 1971), pp. 8, 9.

naked in front of my peers. She saw all those sides of me which I had seen but not dealt with and which others would always pass by. For example, I had often thought of myself as lazy. On bringing this complaint to various teachers and spiritual directors, I was always met with the obvious, "But look at how much you do." This was the confusing truth: I did do a lot with my time, even though I felt lazy. Ida saw that there was much more energy locked up inside me that I (or my history) would not let emerge.

I found to my surprise that being a Rolfer is pursuing a way. It involves parting with past ways of seeing and being. In involves a discipline consonant with a new way of seeing. This is the first time in my life, in spite of external appearances, that I have pursued anything with diligence and care.

"The human body is not a thing or substance, given, but a continuous creation. The human body is an energy system, Schilder's postural model, which is never a complete structure, never static, is in perpetual inner self-construction and self-destruction; we destroy in order to make it new."[3]

The human body is the living sipapu. We descend into it and find not just sinew and bone, but Everybody.

At Alma College, where I was completing my theological studies for the priesthood in the late sixties, several of us "progressives" gathered for a day of encounter to determine whether or not our chosen way of life was indeed viable for us. It was a day of heavy verbal interaction with much negativity. In the evening walking down to Alma from the mountain cabin where we met, I met a group of stoned hippies. They gathered round and hugged me. I was overwhelmed with new feeling, after some thirty years of not being touched, to be smothered with bodies. It contrasted with the harshness and distance of the day's encounter experience.

Some weeks later, there was a meeting with three other Jesuit friends to discuss Stendahl's *The Red and the Black*. The evening turned into a long attack on my game playing and hollowness by two of my friends. We were seated at four corners of a large room. I remember having the feeling of these distant people throwing rocks at me. The next day I went to see my friend Anita and made love for the first time.

3. Norman O. Brown, *Love's Body* (New York: Alfred A. Knopf, 1966), p. 155.

There is a functional distinction in Rolfing between the extrinsic muscles of the body and the intrinsics. The extrinsics are those with which most people are familiar—the pectorals, the biceps, the recti, and so on. They are familiar because they are used most frequently; they are overused. In children they are used almost exclusively. Because of the patterns of movement in Western culture and the forms of exercise that are rooted in these patterns, these muscles. are developed at the expense of the intrinsics, a deeper set of muscles constituting an inner body which is beyond ordinary experience. These muscles run deep along the spine, through the pelvis, along the arms and legs.

A central aim of Rolfing is to bring the intrinsics to life, evoking a new form of bodily behavior which comes from a balanced use of both the inner and outer body. The overdevelopment of the extrinsics is what constitutes body armor: a hard, fast-moving shell, designed to protect the body from attack. If one presumes an evolution toward a more peaceful culture, this armored body becomes an anachronism which will die out because of its inability to adapt to change.

Rolfing is a growth therapy. It is one of the many factors leading to a fuller appropriation of the energy present in the world, in ourselves.

Encounter groups, LSD, Anita—these were major factors that broke down my old world, my old ways of seeing. I left California for Yale in 1968 to complete my Ph.D. in philosophy disoriented, trying to be a priest, a hippie, a lover, a philosopher, but not really making it at any of them. The fantasies I had during this period, particularly during my occasional psychedelic trips, were often of a world torn by war, bombed-out cities, atomic explosions. They were not experienced as bad but even as ecstatic. I was playing all kinds of games and none of them seemed to go together in me. I had blown my mind and fallen apart.

Ida Rolf often says in exasperation: "Many can take the body apart; hardly anyone can put it together again."

While at Yale, I decided to try to put together some of the fragments of my newly emerging world by doing my dissertation on Norman O. Brown, particularly on his thesis that changing a culture's body image changes the structures of the culture itself. I went to visit Brown at Middletown. He was another refugee, unable to sleep since writing *Life Against Death*, afraid that psychedelic drugs or meditation would

remove his little remaining ability to cope with his academic profession. I went away feeling deeper respect for him both as a person and for his work. He, more than anyone I knew, understood the true nature of radical change in culture. From his perspective I could articulate what I had experienced about the revolutionary aspect of the human potentials movement and the psychedelic movement. This I attempted in my dissertation. But I also came away realizing that Brown was no longer my teacher. He didn't know any better than I how to move beyond the apocalypse to the new world.

Dan Berrigan was another side of my life. He symbolized why I remained in the Jesuits during those latter years. He was a poet, a mystic, a compassionate human being, an exciting revolutionary, and very much a Jesuit. My pre-Brown, pre-LSD direction was his way: religious, political, radical change. But I couldn't give myself fully to this path: It sapped me of energy and seemed at times frantic and showman-like. Berrigan stayed at my apartment in New Haven shortly before he went underground. He put to me the decision whether or not finally to commit myself to his movement by organizing the burning of the New Haven draft files. I decided against it, not clearly knowing then what I was deciding in favor of.

> What to do with madness
> The political solution to the problem of madness is
>> divide and conquer
>> segregation and repression
>> (like in asylums)
>> perpetual conflict
> the political revolution is a temporary break-down followed by
>> the reinstitution of repression
> a cycle of explosion and repression
>> activity and passivity
>>> in eternal reoccurrence
> Perpetual conflict is the rule of politics
>> the reality principle
>> the world as we know it
> Is there any alternative?[4]

Carlos Castaneda tells of taking Don Juan to a meeting of radicals at Earth Day in Tucson. Don Juan said of the speakers who were drooped over the table, smoking heavily: "They don't even care about their own bodies."

---

4. From Brown, "Politics to Metapolitics," pp. 11–12.

The change of one body or several bodies is irrelevant to a change in the culture. You and I may feel better and operate better in our semiprivate spheres. It is the change in Everybody that changes the culture. To change the way vast numbers of people experience their bodies, the way they exercise, what they eat, what they do with their bodies in their work, what they permit to happen to the bodies of their children (visualize what happens to the body of a seven-year-old sitting at an aberrant desk for six hours a day, looking straight forward, straining to see and hear a boring teacher whose own body is effectively dead), to change the character of sport, the image of male and female beauty.

The way out of my adulthood crisis began to clarify with two events that happened the same week in the fall of 1969: I began seeing Elissa, whom I later married, and Ed Maupin did my first hour of Rolfing. At that time I was chaplain of the graduate school at Yale and William Sloan Coffin's assistant pastor of the university chapel. It was a last try at a meaningful priestly work. I invited Ed to do a workshop in body movement for graduate students. Elissa was a friend who, like myself, was in that never-never-land drifting between worlds. A dancer and an artist, she had recently divorced her husband, a professor of psychiatry in the Yale Medical School.

The completion of my first ten hours of Rolfing with Ed took over a year and several thousand miles. I was a trustee of Loyola University in Los Angeles. I would fly to a meeting, drive rapidly up the coast to Ed's home in Big Sur for a session, and fly back to New Haven. It had the feeling of a warrior's journey in search of a legendary city. During this time I was writing my dissertation, which carried me further in the direction of feeling that what I really wanted to do was devote myself to changes in the body. There seemed to be something mad about my mind trips, both philosophical and political. Being a Rolfer, however, never entered my mind since I had never thought of myself as capable of skillful physical work.

Ida Rolf developed a system of working with the body which involved a basic therapy of ten sessions, each lasting about one hour. During the first seven hours the old structure of the body is taken apart, muscle groups are separated, fascial adhesions are broken up, attachments are clarified. During the final three hours a new structure is introduced into the body. After the ten hours this new structure too can be opened up again to leave room for a still more refined one. The body is infinitely complex and capable of unlimited refinement.

Coping with the notion of structure was an important part of my transition from philosophy-theology to Rolfing. That day at Chaco Canyon I recognized more clearly what had happened to my relation to structures in those years between 1965 and 1971. The structures blasted apart by LSD were the structures of the medieval synthesis. They were highly abstract, heaven bound, and unrelated to the body. I don't believe that the Aristotelian-Thomistic tradition is liable for all the caricatures heaped on it. It was based on the solid reality of perception. But given my family and churchly history, these systems fed a tendency in me to use concepts to protect myself from the hurly-burly of life and the horrors of intimacy. In my post-LSD period I identified the inhibiting structures of my past world with all structures. My thought was that no structure was desirable: neither educational, marital, vocational, nor moral.

What I came to realize, largely through my experience of being Rolfed and my training as a Rolfer by Ida, is that there is a structure inherent in things, us, the world, which maximizes energy. It's not a structure imposed from without but one which emerges from within when the blocks are removed. (Aristotle knew this. It was the crux of his break with Plato.) Rolfing is highly structured, as was the Anasazi culture. But the structure comes from opening up the lines of energy in the body, just as the Anasazi structures came from the earth in harmony with the changes in the seasons and shifts in the stars.

When I was in grade school and high school, I used to spend hours lying on my bed, tossing in the air and catching a solid rubber version of one of the seven dwarfs, dreaming endless fantasies. Most everyone else my age was out playing or working.

As my time at Yale drew to a close, I found myself increasingly dissatisfied with the prospect of going just anywhere there happened to be a good job and, when there, teaching philosophy. The then far-out prospect of becoming a Rolfer occurred to me. I was able to meet with Ida in one of her few visits to New York and was accepted for preliminary training. About the only specific things she liked about my past were that I had spent my high school and college summers on construction jobs and that I had been a Jesuit and friend of Paul Hilsdale.

That was a stormy afternoon in January 1971. From then until the following November, when I completed my training, was a time of intense fear and uncertainty. All of my insecurity about using my body

came to the fore. I was giving up all the intellectual skills I had accumulated over the past fifteen years to undertake an extremely strenuous work requiring great manual skill. At Pigeon Key in October I discovered, working for the first time under Ida's watchful eye, not only that I was capable of doing physical work, but that I could do it well.

I dreamed that another Rolfer and I drove to see Ida who was living in an immense Victorian mansion. When we went in, she seated me, told me to let the top of my head go up while she placed her knuckle on one of my neck muscles. I went into a state of cosmic consciousness.

> Tiger got to hunt,
> Bird got to fly;
> Man got to sit and wonder, "Why, why, why?"
> Tiger got to sleep,
> Bird got to land;
> Man got to tell himself he understand.[5]

I came to Ida after four years of working with the linguistic analysts, particularly with Ludwig Wittgenstein. This method of doing philosophy is a rigorous therapy whose aim is to remove from mankind the madness which comes from plaguing itself with false questions, with questions which admit of no answer or which are cast in such a way that they can't be answered. I had spent a good deal of my life anguishing over cosmic why's. Wittgenstein was a major step in drawing my awareness to the more specific and worldly. Meeting Ida continued this process. Her constant retort to the troubled brow asking questions about why is the right side of this body bigger than the left, why did the work on this person's ankle release old rage, was, "I don't know why, I just know that!" It was clear to her, as it was becoming clear to me, that the "causes" which have brought us to where we are now are so various and complex, some going back centuries, that being concerned about the specific cause of a specific phenomenon is to misdirect our energies.

After my first training session at Esalen in the summer of 1971, Elissa, my three step-children, and I moved to a nine-acre place just outside of Santa Fe. We live in an old adobe house which grows right out of the ground. Elissa, some friends, and I built a bedroom for

5. Kurt Vonnegut, Jr., *Cat's Cradle* (New York: Holt, Rinehart and Winston, 1963), p. 124.

ourselves, also of mud. Our life here has been more in contact with the earth, the seasons, and bodily work. We don't live the primitive life that many of our friends do. We have most of the modern conveniences. But things are simpler than before, more difficult in an immediate bodily way, and more in keeping with our work.

The first year here I oscillated between the joy of being good at a skill which was of immediate use to people and the pain of becoming a physical laborer after thirty-eight years of being a dreamer and an intellectual. My new-found enthusiasm about being a body which was a skillful instrument often outran my ability. For the first time in my life I felt like fixing my own car, repairing plumbing and electricity, working in the garden, building things; but it was often too much. I sometimes found myself in pain and discouragement.

Things have settled into a rhythm now. Work comes easily.

A man came for his first session of Rolfing. His body was very twisted, his right shoulder was several inches wider than his left, and his trunk was shifted drastically to the right. As he gave an account of his past history (he was in his forties), he said he had had only a couple of minor accidents. He continued to describe the many specific miseries in his body. When I observed that he appeared to have undergone some serious mishap, he repeated that there had been none. We began working. Half-way through the session he remarked that he had had polio when he was eleven years old, "but it was completely cured." I asked what he meant by "completely cured." He replied, "I wasn't left in a wheelchair."

Something like this happens every day.

In class at Esalen one day Ida exclaimed, "People around here have been saying that Ida Rolf says that all there is is the body. Well, let it be known that Ida Rolf thinks there is more than the body, but the body is all we can get our hands on."

One of the striking experiences during my first series of Rolfings was the realization of the density of my body: that it was not a hollow pandora's box set upon wooden stilts, but that it was body all the way through. A very large man in his late forties who had been an athlete most of his life often expressed his fear during my work with him that I could easily puncture his rib cage since it seemed to him like a thin shell covered with a fine layer of skin. When observing another man rotating his pelvis underneath himself by tensing his belly muscles *(rectus abdominis)*, I asked him to move his pelvis from deep inside, relaxing his belly. He replied that the belly muscle is the only one we

have to move the pelvis. Another young man remarked that he had always thought and felt that muscles were the outer shell protecting the body inside.

Rolfing is my path. It isn't just a thing I do. I feel there is no limit within this path to what I can learn about the body and about myself and no limit to the changes I can effect.

Since I was a little kid I have felt alienated from those around me. Things seem different now. My life seems simple and straightforward. I am a craftsman like my father, his father, and his grandfather. I make my living in proportion to the amount of work I do. I feel at home with most everyone now; I no longer feel so apart. My father and the average American may think my work is weird, but that's their problem. It's clear to me at least that what I'm doing is directly related to what concerns them: making things easier, especially for those growing older, removing the tensions and conflicts which make our world so difficult to live in. And I do it in a way anyone with interest can understand. There is (almost) nothing obscure about Rolfing.

This new feeling is not unrelated to the Rolfing itself. I have observed countless times the transition in my clients from feelings of strangeness and apartness to feelings of wholeness and centeredness which emerge as the work progresses. As we begin to travel into our inner body, experiencing more clearly and constantly the center of our being, we begin to sense that we are interconnected with the whole.

75 76 77 78 10 9 8 7 6 5 4 3 2 1